THE BEDFORD SERIES IN HISTORY AND CULTURE

How the Other Half Lives: Studies Among the Tenements of New York

by Jacob A. Riis

Related Titles in
THE BEDFORD SERIES IN HISTORY AND CULTURE
Advisory Editors: Natalie Zemon Davis, Princeton University
Ernest R. May, Harvard University

Looking Backward: 2000–1887 by Edward Bellamy
Edited with an Introduction by Daniel H. Borus, *University of Rochester*

Muckraking: Three Landmark Articles
Edited with an Introduction by Ellen Fitzpatrick, *Harvard University*

A Traveler from Altruria by William Dean Howells
Edited with an Introduction by David W. Levy, *University of Oklahoma*

The Rebuilding of Old Commonwealths: Documents of Social Reform in the Progressive Era South
Edited with an Introduction by William A. Link, *University of North Carolina at Greensboro*

Plunkitt of Tammany Hall by William L. Riordon
Edited with an Introduction by Terrence J. McDonald, *University of Michigan*

The Principles of Scientific Management by Frederick Winslow Taylor (forthcoming)
Edited with an Introduction by Donald A. McQuade, *University of California, Berkeley*

Other People's Money and How the Bankers Use It by Louis D. Brandeis
Edited with an Introduction by Melvin I. Urofsky, *Virginia Commonwealth University*

THE BEDFORD SERIES IN HISTORY AND CULTURE

How the Other Half Lives: Studies Among the Tenements of New York

by Jacob A. Riis

Edited with an Introduction by

David Leviatin

BEDFORD BOOKS *of* ST. MARTIN'S PRESS

Boston   ♒   New York

For Bedford Books
President and Publisher: Charles H. Christensen
General Manager and Associate Publisher: Joan E. Feinberg
Associate Editor: Richard Keaveny
Managing Editor: Elizabeth M. Schaaf
Assistant Managing Editor: John Amburg
Production Assistant: Maureen Murray
Copyeditor: India Koopman
Indexer: Steve Csipke
Text Design: Claire Seng-Niemoeller
Cover Design: Richard Emery Design, Inc.
Cover Photograph: In the Home of an Italian Rag-Picker, Jersey Street. The Jacob A. Riis
Collection, Museum of the City of New York.

Library of Congress Catalog Card Number: 95–83514
Copyright © 1996 by BEDFORD BOOKS *of* St. Martin's Press

Manufactured in the United States of America.

0 9 8

f e d c

For information, write: St. Martin's Press, Inc., 175 Fifth Avenue, New York, NY 10010
Editorial Offices: Bedford Books *of* St. Martin's Press, 75 Arlington Street, Boston, MA 02116

ISBN: 0–312–11700–0 (paperback)
ISBN: 0–312–12809–6 (hardcover)

Foreword

The Bedford Series in History and Culture is designed so that readers can study the past as historians do.

The historian's first task is finding the evidence. Documents, letters, memoirs, interviews, pictures, movies, novels, or poems can provide facts and clues. Then the historian questions and compares the sources. There is more to do than in a courtroom, for hearsay evidence is welcome, and the historian is usually looking for answers beyond act and motive. Different views of an event may be as important as a single verdict. How a story is told may yield as much information as what it says.

Along the way the historian seeks help from other historians and perhaps from specialists in other disciplines. Finally, it is time to write, to decide on an interpretation and how to arrange the evidence for readers.

Each book in this series contains an important historical document or group of documents, each document a witness from the past and open to interpretation in different ways. The documents are combined with some element of historical narrative — an introduction or a biographical essay, for example — that provides students with an analysis of the primary source material and important background information about the world in which it was produced.

Each book in the series focuses on a specific topic within a specific historical period. Each provides a basis for lively thought and discussion about several aspects of the topic and the historian's role. Each is short enough (and inexpensive enough) to be a reasonable one-week assignment in a college course. Whether as classroom or personal reading, each book in the series provides firsthand experience of the challenge — and fun — of discovering, recreating, and interpreting the past.

Natalie Zemon Davis
Ernest R. May

Preface

Though published more than one hundred years ago, *How the Other Half Lives* is a sign of our times. The images of American society Jacob A. Riis managed to capture at the turn of the nineteenth century remain compelling at the end of the twentieth. The resonance of Riis's innovative documentary work is not surprising. The forces that shaped his classic photo-text continue to influence all aspects of contemporary American culture. Immigration, technological innovation, the transformation of industry, and the growth of the city still exert enormous impact on our lives. The difficulty of responding to the challenges posed by our nation's stunning examples of poverty, as well as its spectacular examples of progress, persist. In both its message and its method *How the Other Half Lives* reveals the progressive response and the traditional reaction to the excitement and the anxiety of historical change in the twentieth century. In its exploration of the nightmare and the dream of the modern American scene, *How the Other Half Lives* portrays the lives Americans once lived as well as the lives we continue to lead.

This volume benefits from the availability of a wealth of relatively new scholarship focusing on Riis's life and work. The most valuable part of this material is photographic. Recently the Museum of the City of New York, in association with Chicago Albumen Works, completed a reprinting of its vast collection of Riis's photographs. Hundreds of glass-plate negatives, lantern slides, and decaying prints were rephotographed and reprinted — without cropping — on printing-out paper. The printing-out process, popular at the turn of the nineteenth century, produces a photographic image when a negative and piece of paper (coated with gelatine chloride) are placed in contact and exposed to direct sunlight.

The significance of this project cannot be overemphasized. *How the Other Half Lives* is one of the first American photo-texts. Riis emphasized, often and openly, the decisive role played by his collection of pictures. He was well aware that his prose, when unaccompanied by the startling visual evidence of photography, failed to produce the powerful effect he sought. Unlike previous editions of *How the Other Half Lives*, the Bedford edition is the first to include the Museum's stunning new prints. These photographs will help clarify and redefine interpretations of Riis's classic work.

Consider the publication history of *How the Other Half Lives*. The first edition, released by Charles Scribner's Sons in 1890, combined prose and pictures, interspersing images throughout the text. Unfortunately, because the new process of halftone photoengraving was not yet perfected, the majority of Riis's collection of photographs were copied and reproduced as engravings. While the majority of these illustrations are competent and accurate renderings, several of them alter aspects of the photographs from which they were drawn. The children looking directly into the camera in the photograph "Gotham Court" are looking away in the illustration that appeared in the 1890 edition, and the two young boys in the lower right of the frame were replaced by two young girls, one of whom is holding an infant. Similarly, the building that rises above the bridge in the photograph titled "Hunting River Thieves" was replaced in the 1890 edition with a background cluttered with the masts of tall ships. The two figures in the doorway of the photograph titled "A Flat in the Pauper Barracks, West Thirty-Eighth Street, With All Its Furniture" do not appear in the illustration reproduced in the 1890 edition.

Even Kenyon Cox, considered the most talented and well respected of the several artists commissioned to draw illustrations from Riis's collection of photographs, took some liberties. In his rendition of the photograph titled "In the Home of an Italian Rag-Picker, Jersey Street," Cox has removed the stove in the bottom right corner, the hat hanging above the seated woman, and the brush and dustpan in the bottom left corner. These three objects have both narrative and compositional value; they help design and convey the picture's view and vision of "home." Without them, the powerful triangle framing the central subject is lost. In his drawing of the photograph titled "In a Chinese Joint," Cox has reversed the prone subject, elongated the picture's foreground, and revealed the facial features hidden beneath the subject's hat. While the Cox drawing is more sound stylistically, it fails to reveal the chaos captured in Riis's disorganized view. Overall, the illustrations drawn from photographs prove far less powerful when compared with the uncropped pictures in Riis's collection.

The next edition of *How the Other Half Lives,* published in 1957 by Hill and Wang as part of their American Century Series, was edited and introduced by Donald N. Bigelow. Curiously, this edition contains no photographs at all. While it is true that Riis's negatives were unavailable until they were rediscovered in 1945 and 1946, it is surprising that a decade later in 1957 the editors of the Hill and Wang edition were either unaware or disinterested in their existence. Perhaps the publisher's request for prints from the Museum of the City of New York, the institution responsible for the Riis collection soon after its reappearance, was denied. Whatever the explanation for the absence of the photographs, the visually bare Hill and Wang edition presents only half of Riis's story.

In 1970, the Belknap imprint of Harvard University Press published an edition of *How the Other Half Lives* that was edited and introduced by Sam Bass Warner, Jr. While an improvement over the Hill and Wang edition — due, among other things, to the editor's decision to reproduce all visual images that appeared in the 1890 edition as halftones — the Harvard edition, by placing all of the photographs *after* the text in their own separate gallery, fails to appreciate the brilliance of Riis's innovative combination of photo and text.

Perhaps Riis would have been most satisfied by the edition published by Dover in 1971. Introduced by Charles A. Madison, the oversized volume contains one hundred photographs, including all of the images that appeared in the 1890 edition as well as a selection of numerous other photographs and engravings drawn from photographs. Apparently aware that Riis originally planned for his book to contain one hundred photographs and, perhaps more importantly, aware of his commitment to combining pictures and prose, Dover created an edition that successfully integrates photo and text, producing an energetic display of powerful imagery. The Dover edition, while perhaps sensitive to Riis's plans, is a bold departure from the look of the original text. Its inclusion of numerous additional photographs, ones that did not appear in the original edition of *How the Other Half Lives,* as either halftones or engravings, presents problems for those readers interested in studying an edition that closely resembles the artifact Riis produced rather than a perceptive and sympathetic interpretation of his work.

To complicate matters more, both the Harvard and Dover editions relied on photographs that were cropped by printers. While some of these editorial decisions were minor (for example, cropping out the broken or fogged edges of a glass plate), others proved significant enough to change a picture's meaning. For example, in the Dover edition's rendering of the photograph titled " 'Knee-Pants' at Forty-Five Cents a Dozen—A Ludlow Street Sweater's Shop," the terrier lying beneath the chair has been cropped from the lower left corner. Also in the Dover edition, the photograph titled "Sewing and Starving in an Elizabeth Street Attic" has been cropped to remove the cat lying beneath the furnace in the lower right corner. (For another example of the effect cropping can have, compare the photograph titled "In the Home of an Italian Rag-Picker, Jersey Street" that appears on the cover of this edition with the one reproduced in the text on page 94. The cover shot crops out the bottom points of the triangle discussed above.)

Finally, in 1972 Corner House Publishers released an unedited facsimile of the original 1890 edition. While serving as a useful check and balance when placed alongside the various reconstructions of *How the Other Half Lives,* the Corner House edition, by reproducing the original edition's flat and fuzzy images, fails to deliver the punch of Riis's work.

My goal was to produce a text that resembled, as closely as possible, the original 1890 edition. The only substantive change is the inclusion of the Museum of the City of New York's new uncropped prints. These replace the weak halftones and the illustrations drawn from photographs that were reproduced in the 1890 edition. While certainly a departure from the original, I thought it foolish to limit the genius of Riis's work by replicating the technological problems that frustrated both Riis and his publishers one hundred years ago. That said, I would still encourage readers to compare the uncropped photographs with the illustrations drawn from them. It is interesting to look at the changes that were made and ponder the reasoning behind them; it is also worth considering the effect, if any, these changes may have had on Riis's work.

The new generation of uncropped prints also sheds light on the nettlesome question of the authorship of the photographs used in *How the Other Half Lives.* Although in a note written to his editor at Scribner's Riis makes it very clear that he was not the photographer of all of the pictures used in his book, the new uncropped prints further suggest that Riis borrowed the work of other photographers. For example, I know of no evidence that Riis owned a camera capable of producing the stereograph titled "Gotham Court." On the other hand, he certainly could have borrowed one. The thumbtacks (cropped out of all of the previous editions of *How the Other Half Lives*) make the pair of photographs titled "Typical Toughs (From the Rogues' Gallery)" seem to be part of a collection of mug shots to which Riis had access rather than photos he made himself. The other photographs of photographs, ones like " 'The Official Organ of Chinatown' " and "A Black-and-Tan Dive in 'Africa,' " suggest that Riis needed a negative that he did not have in his possession. Without this negative Riis would not have been able to make the lantern slides he used in his illustrated lectures or to have prints reproduced for publication and exhibition. It is possible that Riis's original glass plate was broken, lost, or given away. It is also possible that the negative Riis needed was unavailable to him because it belonged to the photographer whose photograph he was copying. This photographer may have refused to give Riis the negative; Riis may have also been unable to ask him or her for it, or he may have neglected to do so. (Many of the photographs Riis appears to have borrowed are most likely the work of Richard Hoe Lawrence. Lawrence's photographs are part of the collection of the New York Historical Society.)

It is important to know that Riis may not have taken all, or even many, of the photographs used in *How the Other Half Lives*. If, however, we consider Riis and his work in terms of film direction, the issue of authorship becomes less troubling. The comparison is hardly far-fetched. In fact, Riis's method of work and the type of work he produced, in many ways, anticipated the advent of moving pictures. (This applies to both the style and the scope of his work. For example, the book *How the Other Half Lives* was only one part of Riis's large, multifaceted production. In addition to his print work — which included newspaper reports, magazine articles, and books — Riis organized and delivered countless illustrated lectures in theaters throughout the country. These displays were in many ways precursors to the motion picture experience.) As well as writing his own script and photographing some of his story's pictures, Riis also directed the work of other photographers and made use of pictures that he did not take himself. (Thirty years earlier, the photographer Matthew Brady engaged in a similar practice using pictures of the Civil War taken by Alexander Gardner and Timothy O'Sullivan.) Riis was less concerned with being remembered as the photographer of the pictures used in *How the Other Half Lives* than he was with creating the most powerful document he could.

I hope this volume will help readers see Jacob Riis as one of the pioneers of photojournalism and progressive reform and see his classic text, *How the Other Half Lives,* as one of the earliest examples of modern documentary expression. Describing himself as "a man ahead of his time," Riis not only uncovered the value of looking at poverty, his work also helped construct the framework through which we look at the modern American scene.

ACKNOWLEDGMENTS

While working on this volume I had the good fortune of being assisted by a number of talented people. I would like to thank Lou Masur for hooking me up with Bedford Books. Eric Rothschild, Dan Borus, Alan Brinkley, David Scobey, Lauri Umansky, and Leo Marx read my introduction and offered valuable comments. The staff of the Prints and Photography Division at the Museum of the City of New York was extremely helpful. Librarians at the Library of Congress, Widener Library, the Rare Books and Manuscripts Division of the New York Public Library, the New York Historical Society, and the Princeton University Library were both gracious and invaluable. The staff at Chicago Albumen Works deserves credit for the impressive prints reproduced in this book. Students at Portland State University helped to inspire and focus my research and writing. At Bedford Books, Chuck Christensen, Joan Feinberg, Elizabeth Schaaf, Niels Aaboe, Richard Keaveny, Maureen Murray, and especially John Amburg did a fine job of preparing the manuscript for publication. Once again my parents, Victor and Rosalind, worked with me from the beginning: reading the manuscript, editing the proofs, debating ideas, providing encouragement and support. They are truly remarkable; their efforts essential. Lisa, my better half, tolerated my obsession with Riis's other half. Thank you all.

Contents

PART ONE

Framing the Poor:
The Irresistibility of
How the Other Half Lives

"For there is no quality in this world that is not what it is merely by contrast. Nothing exists in itself." — Herman Melville, *Moby-Dick*

THE FLASH: JACOB RIIS DISCOVERS LIGHT

The Tenants Bolted through the Windows.

Early one morning in the spring of 1887, Jacob A. Riis, an energetic and ambitious New York City police reporter, made an important discovery. Leafing through the newspaper before setting out for work, Riis put the paper down, he later recalled: "with an outcry that startled my wife. . . . There it was, the thing I had been looking for all those years. . . . A way had been discovered . . . to take pictures by flashlight. The darkest corner might be photographed that way." For ten years, while writing countless newspaper articles about the slums on Manhattan's Lower East Side, Riis had sought a more graphic way of capturing the disturbing presence of urban poverty. Finally, in a moment of serendipity characteristic of his life, Riis found the weapon he needed in his "battle with the slum" — *Blitzlichtpulver*. Riis's innovative and opportune use of the new German chemical substance, known in English as flashlight powder, was unprecedented. The explosive form of magnesium, providing the harsh brilliance of man-made light, enabled Riis to transform the American view of poverty and, in doing so, helped him define the modern vision of progress and prosperity.[1]

Less than two weeks after learning of the availability of *Blitzlichtpulver*, Riis organized what he referred to as a "raiding party." Enlisting the services of three amateur photographers — Richard Hoe Lawrence, a "gentleman banker," Dr. Henry G. Piffard, a surgeon at New York City

Hospital, and Dr. John T. Nagle, chief of the City Health Department's Bureau of Vital Statistics — Riis led his "invasion" team, occasionally accompanied by a police officer, into the dark tenements of lower Manhattan. Bursting into the apartments of their surprised subjects, "armed with big pistols" from which they shot flashpowder "recklessly," Riis's party, he admitted, "carried terror wherever it went." On one shoot, they set fire to the walls of an apartment inhabited by several blind tenants; on another, Riis's clumsy use of the cumbersome flash apparatus nearly blinded him.[2]

Impressed by the pictures the camera and flashlight produced, Riis looked forward to making them the focus of a series of illustrated lectures and magazine articles. His associates, more interested in experimenting with flashlight powder than in spending sleepless nights uncovering the squalid lives of the city's poor, soon abandoned him. "I found myself alone just when I needed help most. I had made out by the flashlight possibilities my companions little dreamed of." Determined to realize his dream of documenting the lives of the "Other Half," Riis hired a professional photographer. Complaining of the late hours, refusing to take certain pictures, and selling others, Riis's photographer quickly proved himself to be unreliable. After firing him, then briefly hiring an employee of the *Evening Sun* who also failed to satisfy his needs, Riis decided to teach himself photography.[3]

In January 1888, Riis bought a 4" × 5" detective camera and a dozen extraquick instantaneous glass plates, and went off to the frozen, snow-covered burial ground of Potter's Field — the final resting place of the city's poor — to make what he termed his "first observations." Although he returned from the island of the dead with only a single overexposed plate of one of the open graves, Riis had learned just enough to make his own photographs.[4]

Riis spent the rest of January gathering images (taking some of his own pictures as well as securing those of other photographers), writing, and making lantern slides. By the end of the month, he had organized an illustrated lecture that he was eager to deliver to church congregations. Unable to interest churches in his "lay sermon," Riis arranged to present his material to the members of the New York Society of Amateur Photographers.[5]

On the evening of 25 January 1888, working with a projection device known as a magic lantern, or stereopticon (a machine powered by the combination of oxygen, hydrogen gases, and burning lime that "made wonderfully sharp and luminous images, big enough for a whole auditorium of people to see"), Riis offered his viewers a cinematic experience, effectively combining his own words and pictures into a beguiling narrative he titled "The Other Half: How It Lives and Dies in New York."[6] According to newspaper reviews that appeared the following day, Riis's debut was a success. The *Tribune* noted: "Jacob Riis, a police reporter, who for some years served the *Tribune* in that capacity, showed nearly a hundred views from photographs taken by himself with the aid of members of the society, illustrating the scenes with which his work brought him in contact. Mr. Riis was so ingenious in describing the scenes and brought to his task such a vein of humor that after two hours every one wished that there was more of the exhibition, sad as much of it was." The *Herald*'s reviewer wrote, "A series of interesting and novel photographic views was exhibited last evening by Mr. Jacob A. Riis. More than a hundred pictures were exhibited and when the exhibition was over it was unanimously agreed by the large and appreciative audience that the entertainment provided for them had proved most excellent." Referring to Riis as "Rus," the *News* commented that with his camera the "police reporter catches queer pictures of the nether side of city life."[7]

Encouraged by the response, Riis sought a wider audience. To generate interest in his material, he oversaw the publication of two newspaper pieces, both of which appeared on 12 February 1888. One of these, an illustrated article titled "Flashes from the Slums: Pictures Taken in Dark Places by the Lightning Process," was published in the *New York Sun* and included twelve crude line drawings copied from Riis's collection of photographs. The other piece, offering an interview with Riis detailing his raiding-party adventures, was printed in the *New York Morning Journal* and titled "Visible Darkness: New York's Under Side Flashed on the Camera."[8]

The publicity was effective. Riis was engaged by the City Mission Society to deliver a series of lectures in several New York City churches. These lectures, the first of which took place on 28 February 1888 at the Broadway Tabernacle, were well publicized and attended. The *New York Evening Post* of 28 February 1888, advertising Riis's lecture at the Broadway Tabernacle, noted, "Mr. Jacob A. Riis, an experienced police reporter has made extensive use of the detective camera both by night and by day and taken many instantaneous photographs of scenes of New York life such as great numbers of citizens never witnessed or even imagined. These photographs will be shown by the stereopticon this evening." The Broadway Tabernacle lecture was a success, bringing in $143.50, almost all of which went to the City Mission Society.[9]

Riis so impressed the society's chairman, A. T. Schauffler, that Schauffler provided Riis with a valuable letter of introduction: "It gives me great pleasure to state to any who are interested in the welfare of their fellowmen, that Mr. Jacob Riis has a most remarkable set of stereopticon slides, illustrating the manner of life of many thousands of our fellow creatures in this city. With these pictures, are concerned stories of actual life, stranger than fiction, as instructive as well as fascinating. This lecture is an object lesson of the strongest kind. I may add that nothing is thrown upon the canvas that could shock the taste of any in the audience." On 1 March 1888, the *Brooklyn Times* reported that tickets for Riis's lecture on 7 March at Jamaica Town Hall were "selling with astonishing rapidity. Persons desirous of hearing Mr. Riis and witnessing his stirring views of life among the high and low of New York City should not fail to secure seats at once."[10]

Riis was less successful at interesting magazine editors in his tale of "The Other Half." An editor at *Harper's* offered to buy the photographs "and 'find a man who could write' to tell the story." Riis turned the offer down, hoping to find a magazine that would print the pictures along with his prose. Despite the rejections of several more editors, Riis was determined to see his lecture in print. In fact, on 19 March 1888, with little hope of having even a magazine article published, Riis secured a copyright for the title page of the book he dreamed of writing: " 'THE OTHER HALF, HOW IT LIVES AND DIES IN NEW YORK. WITH ONE HUNDRED ILLUSTRATIONS, PHOTOGRAPHS FROM REAL LIFE, OF THE HAUNTS OF POVERTY AND VICE IN THE GREAT CITY.' BY JACOB A. RIIS."[11]

Armed with a legally protected title and sustained by his ideas for a book, Riis continued delivering his illustrated lecture, primarily in metropolitan area churches. After one of these lectures, a parishioner told Riis how moved he was by his material and asked if Riis had considered having it published. Remembering the moment in his autobiography, *The Making of an American* (1901), Riis noted: "The thing I had sought vainly so long came in the end by another road than I planned. One of the editors of *Scribner's Magazine* saw my pictures and heard their story in his church, and came to talk the matter over with me. As a result of that talk I wrote an article that appeared in the Christmas *Scribner's*, 1889, under the title 'How the Other Half Lives.' . . . That was the beginning of better days."[12]

Riis began writing the *Scribner's* article, for which he was paid $150, in February 1889. The completed piece (a print version of his popular illustrated lecture) was composed on twenty double-column pages, integrating Riis's text and twenty-one illustrations — the majority of which were reproduced as engravings drawn from Riis's collection of photographs. The article was an instant success. During the first week it appeared, Riis received the following note: "Dear Sir: If you have not already made arrangements for publishing a book on 'How the Other Half Lives,' Messrs. Cassell & Co. 104–106 Fourth Avenue would be pleased to see you on this subject." On the note itself, part of the Riis Collection at the Library of Congress, Riis scribbled, "the beginning of 'How the Other Half Lives' and therefore it all." In his autobiography, Riis recalled, "My chance had come. I was at last to have my say."[13]

In January 1890, Riis began work on the book. Ten months later, often working through the night, Riis completed the handwritten manuscript. *How the Other Half Lives* was published on 15 November 1890, with the subtitle "Studies among the Tenements of New York" and the note "With Illustrations Chiefly from Photographs Taken by the Author." (The wording of the note is of some importance because its history helps clarify the debate concerning the authorship of Riis's photographs. The original copy for the note read "With Illustrations from Photographs Taken by the Author." In a letter to his editor, Riis wrote, "My dear Mr. Brownell: Wouldn't you say 'with illustrations from photographs taken chiefly (or mainly) by the author.' Some of them were not taken by me, and at least five, are copies of drawings. Fix it anyway you like it, but I would prefer that the statement should be qualified in some such way as to be within the lines of strict truth.")[14]

In less than a year, Riis had succeeded in expanding his illustrated essay into a 304-page book. In addition to offering more prose than the *Scribner's* article, *How the Other Half Lives* displayed more pictures: forty-three illustrations, seventeen of which were reproduced by the relatively new method of halftone photoengraving. Priced at $2.50, the two thousand copies Scribner's printed sold well — 1,656 in the first six months. Anticipating greater demand, Scribner's released two thousand copies of a "new edition," a bit smaller in size and priced at $1.25, on 28 March 1891. This edition sold briskly, encouraging Scribner's to run several more printings over the next four years.[15]

Reaction to the first two editions was enthusiastic. Hundreds of newspapers and magazines responded to Riis's call:

"A book like this, altho it may be disheartening to read, is extremely profitable reading. It is well for us to know exactly how we are situated." (*New York Evening Sun,* 18 November 1890)

"His facts are startling." (*Christian Inquirer,* 4 December 1890)

"The seamy side of tenement life in New York is presented in the most graphic way." (*San Francisco Chronicle,* 7 December 1890)

" 'How the Other Half Lives' is a book of immense shuddering interest. It is a gallery of pictures, each one reeking with the horror of its own kind." (*Chicago Times*, 20 December 1890)

"This is one of the sociological studies which characterize this age and time. It could not have been written a hundred years ago." (*Indianapolis News*, 24 December 1890)

"Books like this that lift the curtains, and expose to public gaze the great evils of the system will hasten the day of reform." (*Christian Intelligencer*, 24 December 1890)

"It is difficult to put this thrilling book aside. It is a self-denial to stop writing about it. It ought to circulate as freely as *Uncle Tom's Cabin*." (*Photography Magazine*, 21 February 1891)

" 'How the Other Half Lives' . . . is one of the strongest arraignments of our so-called civilization in the new world, which has yet appeared." (*New England Magazine*, June 1891)

Dr. A. T. Schauffler, influential religious leader and original Riis sponsor, found *How the Other Half Lives* to be "enormously more interesting than any novel that ever was written or that ever will be written. Dens, dives, hovels, sickness, death, sorrow, drink, and murder, all these exist in our midst in appalling magnitude. No book that has ever appeared in this land pours such light as Mr. Riis's book on 'The Other Half.' " Elbridge Gerry, the president of the New York Society for the Prevention of Cruelty to Children, commented, "I regard [*How the Other Half Lives*] as one of the most valuable contributions to the history of child-saving work in this great city." The poet James Russell Lowell wrote to Riis, "I cannot conceive how such a book should fail of doing great good, if it moves other people as it has moved me."[16]

An aspiring young politician named Theodore Roosevelt, a member of the nation's Civil Service Commission when *How the Other Half Lives* was published, remarked later in his autobiography: " 'How the Other Half Lives' had been to me both an enlightenment and an inspiration for which I felt I could never be too grateful. Soon after it was written I had called at [Riis's] office to tell him how deeply impressed I was by the book, and that I wished to help him in any practical way to try to make things a little better."[17]

There were few critical reviews. One, appearing in the *Critic* of December 1890, stated Riis's "book is literally a photograph, and as such has its value and lesson, but also its serious limitations. There is a lack of broad and penetrative vision, a singularly warped sense of justice at times, and a roughness amounting almost to brutality. The 'heathen Chinee,' and the Russian Jew fleeing from persecution in his own land, finds no mercy in Mr. Riis's creed."[18]

For the most part, however, Riis's view of the Other Half was celebrated. In fact, even the book's look and feel were lauded. The reviewer for the *Twentieth Century* noted, "I have not yet had time to read it, but it tells such an interesting story to him who handles it for five minutes that I do not hesitate to give it a preliminary notice, without waiting to read it. It is very handsomely bound in linen, and nothing is to be desired in its general typographical appearance."[19]

The popularity of *How the Other Half Lives* changed Riis's life. No longer an obscure police reporter with a peculiar obsession for slumming, Riis was suddenly a well-connected nationally known author and lecturer. Until his death in May 1914, Riis attempted to meet the "demand for more copy" by lecturing extensively throughout the country, writing numerous articles and several books, almost all of which dealt with the lives of the Other Half. None of this work, with the possible exception of his autobiography, received the attention of *How the Other Half Lives.*[20]

Although pleased with the public's reception of his first book, Riis claimed to be surprised by its spectacular success. Writing in his autobiography, he admitted, "For myself I have never been able to satisfactorily explain the great run 'How the Other Half Lives' had. It is a curiously popular book even to-day. Perhaps it was that I had it in me so long that it burst out at last with a rush that caught on. The title had a deal to do with it. Mr. Howells asked me once where I got it. I did not get it. It came of itself. Like Topsy, it growed. It had run in my mind ever since I thought of the things I tried to describe. Then there was the piece of real good luck that Booth's 'In Darkest England' [a work in which General Booth, leader of the Salvation Army, explored poverty in London] was published just then. People naturally asked, 'How about New York?'"[21]

Though correct in identifying the resonance of his book's title as well as the work's timely date of publication, these explanations only flirt with the essence of the initial popularity and enduring interest of *How the Other Half Lives.*

At first glance, one might think that the many illustrations, especially those reproduced as photographs, accounted for the book's stunning impact. Riis himself was aware that "written reports" "did not make much of an impression . . . until my negatives, still dripping from the darkroom, came to reinforce them. From them there was no appeal." In notes, he remarked of his collection of photographs, "The pictures were irresistible."[22]

While Riis's pictures did prove compelling, they were only part of what made *How the Other Half Lives* electrifying. Sowing the seeds of sensationalism, muckraking, photojournalism, documentary realism, vicarious slumming, and progressive social reform, *How the Other Half Lives* offered its readers a spellbinding glimpse of America's future. By skillfully combining word and picture, Riis managed to capture a view of poverty that revealed modern America's vision of progress. Riis's ability to cleverly and presciently illustrate the relationship between urban poverty and the nation's ideal of progress is what made *How the Other Half Lives* irresistible.

By igniting, and just barely controlling, spectacular and potentially lethal bursts of artificial light, Jacob Riis — the sentimental and stern Victorian, the realistic and pragmatic modern, the immigrant and the American — exposed and framed the Other Half while straddling a society in the throes of transition. The resulting view — a work of tradition and innovation that accurately reflected the anxieties and desires of a nascent middle class and helped forge the ideology of an emerging national culture — was a product of the opportune mingling of Riis's personal experience and the nation's historical destiny.

THE AMERICAN SCENE: THE SEARCH FOR ORDER

Hell. Flashlight in a Low Basement Dive.

Between 1870 and 1920 the United States was transformed. In fifty years of reconstruction and reform the nation moved from fractured rural confederacy to urban industrial union. Technological innovation, industrial expansion, population migration, and urban growth — the forces responsible for severe economic depressions and violent class conflict — were, when finally harnessed, the sources of profit and order. By 1920, a national economy and society had been organized. The middle class emerged as the nation's dominant class; the culture it produced guided the nation's way of life. New methods of manufacturing goods, consuming products, and communicating ideas were in place. According to social critic Alan Trachtenberg, America was "incorporated."[23]

During the same period, Jacob Riis underwent a similar process of conversion. Arriving in New York City in 1870, a twenty-one-year-old Danish immigrant, Riis, like millions of other unknown and eager young newcomers, sought a place for himself in the Promised Land. When he died in 1914, his close friend Theodore Roosevelt remarked, Riis was "a man nearest to being the ideal American citizen."[24]

Moving from poverty-stricken immigrant to middle-class American, Jacob Riis's transformation mirrored the nation's. In his autobiography,

The Making of an American, Riis emphasized, perhaps even exaggerated, this parallel. In his mind, national organization and individual assimilation were linked; the making of modern America was tied inextricably to the making of modern Americans. Neither process went smoothly, especially during the 1880s — the decade during which Riis produced *How the Other Half Lives.* Change was dramatic, development was uneven. Uncertainty and fear accompanied the shock of converting old structures and ways into new ones. From this relationship, in which the turbulent and unpredictable process of modernization was intertwined with Riis's own unsettling personal experience of Americanization, *How the Other Half Lives,* a product of the nation's "search for order," "burst out . . . with a rush."[25]

The Making of an American:
The Story of Jacob Riis

Born in Denmark in 1849, Jacob Riis was raised in the small, rural town of Ribe. The third of fourteen children, Riis recalled being a stubborn and impatient youth weaned on the works of Charles Dickens and James Fenimore Cooper and touched by a spirit of reform and adventure. While still a youngster, Riis devoted his energy to cleaning up Ribe's rat-infested sewer system and assisting (with his Christmas money) a poor family that lived in the town's only tenement. Instead of pursuing the literary career his father (the local schoolmaster) desired for him, Riis went off to Copenhagen to learn the carpenter's trade. He returned to Ribe four years later, a member of the guild, seeking to settle down and marry his childhood sweetheart, Elisabeth. Her father (the prosperous owner of the town's cotton mill) considered a common carpenter unworthy of his daughter's hand and rejected Riis. Young Jacob, eager to prove himself, left for America sustained by the "strong belief that in a free country, free from the dominion of custom, of caste, as well as of men, things would somehow come right in the end, and a man get shaken into the corner where he belonged if he took a hand in the game."[26]

Landing at New York's Castle Garden on Whitsunday, 5 June 1870, with little more than "a pair of strong hands" and "stubbornness enough to do for two," Riis spent seven difficult years being "shaken" while roaming throughout New York, New Jersey, Pennsylvania, and Illinois. In his first year, the work he found was temporary and usually menial; Riis labored in an iron works, coal mine, clay bank, and brick yard, and he was forced on several occasions to pawn his only valuables — a pair of boots and a revolver. After failing to get work on a railroad gang and in a hair factory, Riis found himself in New York City, a member of "the great army of tramps, wandering about the streets in the daytime with the one aim of somehow stilling the hunger that gnawed at my vitals, and fighting at night with vagrant curs or outcasts as miserable as myself for the protection of some sheltering ash-bin or doorway."[27]

Homeless, penniless, and suicidal, Riis tramped down into the slums on New York's Lower East Side. For wandering indigents such as Riis, the city offered shelter at the police station lodging-house. "Never was parody upon Christian charity more corrupting to human mind and soul than the frightful abomination of the police lodging-house, sole provision made by the municipality for its homeless wanderers." After being robbed by a fellow wanderer and witnessing a dog he had befriended being beaten to death by the "doorman" of the lodging-house, Riis "shook the dust of New York from [his] feet, vowing . . . never [to] return."[28]

Before he did return in the fall of 1873, Riis spent another trying period working and wandering in and around Philadelphia, Buffalo, Pittsburgh, and Chicago. He made cradles, chopped wood, harvested ice, and worked as a farmhand, hunter, and trapper. He worked in a lumberyard, planing mill, and shipyard, and was a traveling salesman, peddling mirrors, extension tables (to sell these, Riis used what he called a "mighty album" containing pictures of the tables), campaign books (for the Greeley and Grant presidential race), and clothes irons. During this flight from New York, Riis gave his first lectures (on astronomy and geology to the members of a Scandinavian workingmen's society), began writing magazine articles (on "the maltreatment of Denmark by Prussia"), and decided that someday he would be a reporter. While selling the clothes irons earned Riis his best income, his modest success was thwarted by his business naïveté and the dishonesty of those with whom he worked. Hopeless and broke, Riis set out on foot from northern Pennsylvania and walked to New York, peddling his irons along the way. Back in the city, he scraped together $20 and enrolled briefly in a business college to learn telegraphy, "with a dim idea of being sent into the farthest wilds as an operator." To support himself, Riis continued to dip into his dwindling stock of irons.[29]

Riis landed his first newspaper job after responding to the advertisement of a Long Island City weekly that was seeking a city editor. Unpaid after two weeks of work, Riis quit. Desperate for food and cash, he thought selling illustrated editions of Dickens might support him, at least temporarily. He was wrong. Stuck peddling an unpopular edition of *Hard Times*, Riis wondered: "How long was this to last? Was it any use to keep up a struggle so hopeless? . . . I drummed moodily upon my book. Wasted!

. . . My life was wasted, utterly wasted." At this grim moment, Riis claims he was spotted by the principal of the business school in which he had briefly studied telegraphy. Moved by Riis's story, the principal arranged a job for him with the New York News Association.[30]

In May 1874, having acquired some basic journalistic skills, Riis left the News Association to work as a reporter for the *South Brooklyn News*. In two weeks he was the paper's editor; in seven months, its owner, putting down $75 toward the asking price of $650. Riis described the *News* as "a big four-page sheet" for which he wrote every word. "I was my own editor, reporter, publisher, and advertising agent. . . . In the early morning hours I shouldered the edition . . . and carried it from Spruce Street down to Fulton Ferry, and then home on a Fifth Avenue car. . . . When I got home, I slept on the counter with the edition for my pillow, in order to be up with the first gleam of daylight to skirmish for newsboys."[31]

Convinced by a Methodist preacher named Ichabod Simmons that the world needed "consecrated pens," Riis devoted his to a "campaign for reform that made the town stare." He first exposed the corruption of the Democratic Party's local machine. After completing that charge, he directed his pen against the "beats" — shoppers with unpaid grocery bills. Publishing a list of their names along with how much they owed and for how long, Riis warned the "beats" "to pay or move out of the ward."[32]

Riis suggests that his "zeal for reform" encompassed the whole range of [his] little world." Not exactly. While still pining for his lost love, Elisabeth, Riis received a letter from his father. Elisabeth's fiancé (she became engaged soon after Riis left for the United States) had died. After a brief correspondence with his Danish sweetheart, Riis sold his newspaper for five times more than it cost him (having paid off the remaining debt in June 1875) and, in December 1875, sailed to Denmark to marry.[33]

When the newlyweds returned to New York in the summer of 1876, Riis went back to the *South Brooklyn News,* this time as its editor only. Although he continued his reform work, now railing against the evils of boarding-houses — "'ours,' I cried, weekly 'to fulfill its destiny, must be a nation of homes. Down with the boarding-house!'" — he realized that the paper's ownership, which was politically influenced, would soon attempt to direct the focus of his exposés. Rather than becoming the tool of local politicians, Riis began trying to get "a foothold on one of the metropolitan newspapers, but always without success."[34]

At about the same time, he purchased a magic lantern. When Riis bought the contraption, he claims not to have had any "definite idea of what to do with it. I suppose it ought to be set down as foolishness and a waste of money. And yet it was to play an important part in the real life-work that was waiting for me."[35]

After mastering the magic lantern, a task neither simple nor safe because of its reliance on burning lime pellets, Riis left his job at the *News* and turned to the lantern as his main source of income. "The notion of using it as a means of advertising had long allured me. There was a large population out on Long Island that traded in Brooklyn stores and could be reached in that way. . . . I made money that fall travelling through the towns and villages and giving open-air exhibitions in which the 'ads' of Brooklyn merchants were cunningly interlarded with very beautiful colored views, of which I had a fine collection. When the season was too far advanced to allow of this, I established myself in a window at Myrtle Avenue and Fulton Street and appealed to the city crowds with my pictures. . . . I liked my advertising scheme. I advertised nothing I would not have sold the people myself, and I gave it to them in a way that was distinctly pleasing and good for them; for my pictures were real work[s] of art, not the cheap trash you see nowadays on street screens."[36]

Inspired by his success as an adman, Riis planned a larger campaign with his friend Ed Wells, a drugstore clerk. The two decided to publish a business directory of the upstate city of Elmira, using nightly lantern slide exhibitions to generate interest in their "scheme of country advertising." Soon after Riis and Wells arrived in Elmira, the nationwide rail strike — spreading since it began on 17 July 1877 — erupted in the city. The two hustlers were advised to take their sixteen-foot curtain, gases, magic lantern, and advertising business elsewhere.[37]

Having barely avoided the violence of the strike in Elmira, Riis and Wells were caught in the middle of an uprising in Scranton, Pennsylvania, when obstacles on the track forced them off their train and curiosity led them into the tense city. "For want of something better to do, we went out to take a look at the town. At the head of the main street was a big crowd. Untaught by experience, we bored our way through it to where a line of men with guns, some in dusters, were blocking advance to the coal company's stores. The crowd hung sullenly back, leaving a narrow space clear in front of the line. Within it a man — I learned afterward that he was the Mayor of the town — was haranguing the people, counselling them to go back to their homes quietly. Suddenly a brick was thrown from behind me and struck him on the head. I heard a word of brief command, the rattle of a score of guns falling into as many extended hands, and a volley was fired into the crowd point blank. A man beside me weltered in his blood. There was an instant's dead silence, then the rushing of a thousand feet and wild cries of terror as the mob broke and fled. . . . In all my life I never ran so fast."[38]

Returning to New York, Riis abandoned the lantern slide business in the fall of 1877 when he was offered a position on the *New York Tribune*. After six months of poorly paid, entry-level work he considered "a waste of time," Riis decided to resign and "seek [his] fortune elsewhere." Instead, an accidental meeting with the city editor led Riis to discover his life's work. The *Tribune*'s police reporter, stationed in an office on Mulberry Street across from police headquarters, had left the paper, and the editor asked Riis to replace him. "I knew it by reputation as the hardest place on the paper, and it was in no spirit of exultation that I looked out upon the stirring life of the block." Riis was to cover "the Police Department, the Health Department, the Fire Department, the Coroner's office, and the Excise Bureau." "The police reporter on a newspaper . . . is the one who gathers and handles all the news that means trouble to some one: the murders, fires, suicides, robberies, and all that sort, before it gets to court." "If the truth be told, I think I was, if anything, a bit afraid." "So I dived in. But before I did it I telegraphed to my wife: 'Got staff appointment. Police Headquarters. $25.00 a week. Hurrah!' "[39]

After seven years of desperate, but ultimately successful, wandering, Jacob Riis, finally "shaken into the corner where he belonged," was set to experience a decisive decade in the nation's economic and cultural incorporation. During the 1880s — years in which the Chinese Exclusion Act was passed, the American Federation of Labor was founded, the Brooklyn Bridge was completed, the Statue of Liberty was unveiled, the practice of photography was popularized, Hull House was opened, the Haymarket anarchists were hanged, the machine gun was perfected, and the electric chair was first used — the combined force of industrialization, immigration, and urbanization was magnified. The unchecked power and potential of this force accelerated the nation's "search for order," hastening its modernization and Riis's own Americanization.[40]

The 1880s: A Decisive Decade

NEW PEOPLE, NEW PLACES

In 1881, the familiar pattern of immigration changed. Until that year, the majority of immigrants (with the exception of the Irish immigrants of the 1840s and 1850s) were Protestants of northern and western European background, arriving in the United States as families and settling on farms in the rural countryside. In 1881, the number of young single males, primarily unskilled Catholic and Jewish immigrants from southern and eastern Europe, increased dramatically. These so-called new immigrants, pushed from their countries by poverty and persecution and pulled to the Promised Land by the lure of jobs and freedom, settled almost exclusively in the nation's largest cities.[41]

The municipal services of Boston, Philadelphia, Milwaukee, Detroit, Chicago, and especially New York were strained by what was termed a "wave," a "flood," and an "invasion." The sudden and steady influx of millions of people to cities unprepared to accommodate their needs resulted in the rapid growth of a new world: the overcrowded urban slum — "teeming" with "aliens" of "queer" origin — plagued by unemployment, poverty, disease, and crime. And marked by the ominous growth of the tenement.[42]

Beginning in the middle 1830s, the division of one-family homes into dwellings designed to house several families and the construction of large tenement apartment buildings were both considered reasonable methods of offering affordable housing to poor and working-class urban migrants. The explosion of immigration in the 1880s, combined with the greed of landlords and builders — greed abetted by the ineffectiveness of the tenement-housing law enacted in 1867 (and amended in 1879 and 1887) — turned what once appeared to be the logical solutions to an increased demand for cheap housing into the causes of crisis.[43]

During the 1880s, many of the 5,256,613 immigrants arriving in the United States remained in New York City, increasing its population by 25 percent and making the tenement problem acute. By the end of the decade, Riis referred to the disturbing structure as "the Frankenstein of our city civilization." In 1890 (the year *How the Other Half Lives* was published), 35,000 of the city's 81,000 dwellings were defined as tenements. Of the city's population, 83 percent lived in dwellings of ten people or more (compared with only 14 percent of the U.S. population) and 67 percent lived in dwellings of twenty-one or more. The total population below 14th Street — the area including "the tenement house district" of Wards 4, 6, 7, 10, 11, 13, 14, and 17 — was 547,697; of this population, 83 percent lived in dwellings of twenty-one people or more. Forty-three percent of the city's total population of 1,515,301 was foreign born and 1,219,218 were of foreign parentage. Ten percent of those over ten years of age could not speak English. In *How the Other Half Lives,* Riis lamented, "The one thing you shall vainly ask for in the chief city of America is a distinctly American community. There is none; certainly not among the tenements." "In their place has come this queer conglomerate mass of heterogeneous elements."[44]

In his new job as police reporter, Riis witnessed the growth of the modern metropolis, the urban slum, and the tenement poor. The sights he saw seared his mind's eye. "My work in Mulberry Street was at night." "I went poking about among the foul alleys and fouler tenements of the Bend when they slept in their filth."

> My route from the office lay through the Fourth and the Sixth wards, the worst in the city, and for years I walked every morning between two and four o'clock the whole length of Mulberry Street, through the Bend and across the Five Points down to Fulton Ferry. There were cars on the Bowery, but I liked to walk, for so I saw the slum when off its guard. The instinct to pose is as strong there as it is on Fifth Avenue. It is a human impulse, I suppose. We all like to be thought well of by our fellows. But at 3 A.M. the veneering is off and you see the true grain of a thing. I got a picture of the Bend on my mind which so soon as I should be able to transfer it to that of the community would help settle that pigsty according to its desserts. It was not fit for Christian men and women let alone innocent children, to live in, and therefore it had to go.[45]

TRENDS IN SOCIAL THEORY AND RIIS'S POINT OF VIEW

In his autobiography, Riis notes that at the turn of the decade he was simply "absorbing impressions." When he switched from working nights to days, he claims a new life began for him. Assigned to cover the proceedings of a number of state-appointed commissions and locally organized conferences, Riis learned the details of the city's economic, social, and political problems. At the same time, he was introduced to the dynamic world of urban social reform. Meeting a number of Manhattan's leading activists, Riis was exposed to the many plans and theories designed to address the ills of modern city life. From this swirl of energy and impressions, personalities and ideas, Riis fashioned a unique view of urban reform.[46]

The factor most influential in shaping Riis's point of view was the agitation for tenement reform that began in 1879. Especially intriguing was the work of Alfred T. White, a builder who led the crusade for the construction of model tenements. White argued that decent homes would help solve the problems of urban poverty. Inspired by White's work, Riis began to seriously consider the relationship between tenement housing and urban poverty. Dr. Roger S. Tracy, a sanitary inspector and statistician in the city's health department, with whom Riis began to work in 1881, made the connection between ramshackle housing and urban decay clear by providing Riis with a wealth of revealing statistical data.

Riis's commitment to the ideal of tenement reform was heightened by two events he covered for the *Tribune* in 1884. The first, a series of lectures on the evils of tenement housing delivered by Felix Adler (the founder of the ethical culture movement), was followed by the proceedings of the Drexel Commission, a state committee organized to look into the problems raised by Adler's lectures.[47]

Riis's attraction to tenement reform, while sparked by his exposure to the problem of housing in New York City, was influenced by a larger, nationwide debate that focused on urban poverty, immigration, and ethnicity. This debate, drawn here in broad strokes, was divided between two groups of people: those who believed the new immigrant poor were genetically inferior and those who believed them to be materially disadvantaged.[48]

The first group, composed largely of social Darwinists and immigrant restrictionists, argued that heredity determined the character of individuals and groups. The advocates of this view, moved by the political diatribes of nativism and the pseudoscience of eugenics, believed that social reform and cultural assimilation were futile — ethnicity was destiny, natural selection determined those fit to survive.[49]

The second group, made up primarily of social reformers and Anglo-conformists (the proponents of Americanization) argued that material conditions determined the character of individuals and groups. The advocates of this view, moved by the social engineering of the settlement house movement and the enlightened paternalism of organized charity, believed social reform and cultural assimilation were crucial — environment was destiny, social conditions determined those fit to succeed.[50]

Though Riis can sometimes sound like a social Darwinist and a restrictionist, especially when he is discussing the Chinese, his experience as a poverty-stricken immigrant and his faith in the professed virtues of American civilization led him to embrace aspects of the emerging ideology of progressive reform rather than the reactionary theories of biological essentialism. The factors of environment, not the genes of heredity, are the key aspects of Riis's point of view.[51]

The tenets of the Social Gospel, a religious movement popular at the turn of the century, confirmed Riis's belief in the efficacy of social reform and convinced him of the necessity of practicing an active form of Christian charity. Devoted to uplifting and converting those considered deprived and alien, the mostly native-born, middle-class members of the charity societies, missions, and settlement houses (organizations that flourished throughout the 1880s) were engaged in a religious experience termed "muscular Christianity." As followers of the Social

Gospel, the members of these organizations were committed to bringing about change in this world rather than waiting passively for the Day of Judgment. Riis's dream of constructing a temporal Christian Commonwealth, one "founded upon justice and built of human hearts," informed his progressive view of reform and inspired his crusade. Of the city's tramps, Riis remarked, "That was what we had made of them with our infernal machinery of rum-shop, tenement, dive. . . . With Christian charity instead, what might they not have been?"[52]

There is little question that Riis's point of view was affected deeply by the specter of revolution. He knew of the chaos of New York's Draft Riots (1863) and of the horrors of the Paris Commune (1870–71). Having suffered hardship as a workingman and a tramp during what until then had been the nation's most severe economic depression (beginning in 1873 and lingering on throughout the decade), and having witnessed the tragic consequences of labor violence during the nation's bloodiest strike (the rail strike of 1877), Riis had developed a palpable fear of the mob and the revolution it might bring, a fear intensified by numerous novels and nonfiction accounts published throughout the 1880s.

These works depicted, in disturbing and graphic detail, a nightmarish vision of the uprising of the nation's downtrodden masses. Riis was familiar with Charles Loring Brace's *The Dangerous Classes* (1872, with a third edition published in 1880) and Josiah Strong's reactionary screed *Our Country* (1885). Riis may have read Edward Bellamy's best-selling utopian novel, *Looking Backward* (1888), and known of Ignatius Donnelly's description of revolutionary chaos, *Caesar's Column* (1889). It is also likely that he was aware of Karl Marx's work, if not *Capital* (1883), which was published in the United States in 1889 and considered one of the year's "better-sellers," then almost certainly with some of Marx's earlier works or with some of their many interpretations. (In fact, Riis seems to have agreed with the inevitability that guides Marx's logic of proletarian revolution. As a prophet of the ideal bourgeois society, however, Riis devoted his energies to figuring out a way of defusing the revolutionary potential of the "Nemesis" "the tenements had bred.")[53]

An account of Riis's view of urban reform would be incomplete if it did not acknowledge the importance of his memories of growing up in Denmark. Born and raised in a small rural town, a member of a large, closely knit family (overseen by a strong father figure), Riis saw the urban environment — especially that of New York City in the 1880s — as unwholesome and potentially dehumanizing. In his autobiography, Riis notes that his hatred for the slum was in large part a result of his "love" for "the open, the woods, the freedom of my Danish fields." "In my memory ... it is always summer there."[54]

Riis's idealization of rural life helped establish the contrast between rural heaven and urban hell that fired his view of urban reform. For Riis, the wholesome world of Mother Nature — as he remembered it to be in Denmark — was best suited for the work of nurturing character and civilization. The city, lacking forests and fields, fresh air and water, crowded with poor people living in poor homes, was the ideal environment for the breeding of beasts and barbarism. "Over against the tenement that we fight in our cities ever rises in my mind the fields, the woods, God's open sky, as accuser and witness that His temple is being so defiled, man so dwarfed in body and soul."[55]

Other influences on Riis's point of view were his decisions to become an American citizen in 1885 and to move (growing family in tow) from Brooklyn to the suburb of Richmond Hill in 1886. While furthering his faith in the ideals of upward mobility and cultural assimilation, these two events at the same time sharpened his fear of the Other Half and revolution. Now an aspiring member of the middle class, situated in the secure environs of the suburbs, Riis had a stake in defending his new homeland.[56]

This eclectic mix of material was the stuff with which Riis fashioned his idiosyncratic view of urban reform. Impatient with critical thinking, Riis simply picked those aspects of an entire system of thought he found personally affecting and then stitched the pieces together. The product of a decade of profound change, Riis's point of view was infused with an energy and passion that often overshadowed its many jarring intellectual inconsistencies. When seen as a reflection of the instability and uncertainty of the process of modernization and the experience of Americanization, however, Riis's view becomes more understandable. For example, when one considers the historical context within which he developed his point of view, it is hardly surprising to learn that he believed "a proletariat ready and able to avenge the wrongs of their crowds" could be tamed with Christian charity. Dramatic change inspired creative response.[57]

THE INFLUENCE OF REALISM

Throughout the decade, surveying the underside of the urban scene was a popular pastime. Fascination with the Other Half was satisfied by the sensationalism of police reporting, the emotion of sentimental melodrama, the adventure of true-crime fiction, the science of the sociological study, the inspiration of the rags-to-riches tale, the passion of the Social

Gospel sermon, and the outrage of the muckraker's exposé. Riis's work, affected by aspects of all of these forms of expression, was shaped most by the emerging style of realism. While championed and practiced throughout the decade by the editor and novelist William Dean Howells, the painters Thomas Eakins and Winslow Homer, and the photographer P. H. Emerson, the realism Riis absorbed was less the result of highbrow agitation than of a groundswell of popular interest in a wide variety of forms of inquiry designated to be scientific. Some of these, like phrenology (the reading of skull structure) and physiognomy (the reading of facial features), while taken seriously by some, were dismissed by most as pseudosciences. Other so-called sciences, like eugenics and social Darwinism, were more highly regarded. The biological and social sciences flourished during this period. Photography's great appeal was related in large part to its association with science, specifically chemistry and optics. Interest in the substance (the theory and practice) and the trappings (the mechanical devices) of scientific inquiry was widespread. Americans were fascinated by the objective quest for truth, eager to record all aspects of their social reality.[58]

The attraction to science and the allure of the realistic style science helped popularize were phenomena related to the upheaval and uncertainty unleashed by the forces of change. For a society shaken by immigration, industrialization, and urbanization, a society dominated increasingly by labor-saving machinery, trained technicians, and bureaucratic institutions, the passion for scientific study and realistic images seems appropriate. Accuracy and objectivity were the articles of a new faith, a faith based on the perceived virtues of mechanical reproduction and scientific management. Realism, like science, was seen as a means of isolating and controlling a host of powerful new forces considered alien, wild, and dangerous. As part of the larger social science of progressive reform, realism was designed to manage the course of revolutionary change.[59]

Riis quickly became an apostle of the new realistic style. Throughout his lectures, books, and correspondence he rarely failed to champion the efficacy of facts and the light of truth. "The power of fact is the mightiest lever of this or of any day." "Some one had to tell the facts; that is one reason why I became a reporter." "I had no stomach for abstract discussions of social wrongs; I wanted to tear down the Mulberry Bend and let in the light." Riis believed that a realistic image of the slum, one frozen by the harsh glare of the flashlight, would reveal the dangerous anarchy inherent in urban poverty. When accompanied by statistics and data, charts and maps (as in *How the Other Half Lives*), the photographic exposure became part of a larger body of evidence designed to provide progressive reformers with the subject matter essential to their program of social scientific analysis and control. Accuracy, order, control, progress. It was the allure of this progression that drew Riis to realism.[60]

Though the realistic style was becoming a more central force in American life in the last quarter of the nineteenth century, a romantic, picturesque view of poverty still proved popular. In prose, poetry, and the visual arts, poverty was prettified. The poor were rarely seen as threatening, potentially destructive agents of chaos; their simple lives were made to appear precious rather than vicious. While influenced by the romantic conventions of his day, especially aspects of sentimental melodrama, Riis gave his view of poverty a realistic spin, revealing in vivid detail the sordid lives of the Other Half. Riis's style is perhaps best defined as "living dramatic reality," a phrase Harriet Beecher Stowe used to describe her novel *Uncle Tom's Cabin, or Life among the Lowly* (1852), a work in many ways similar to *How the Other Half Lives*. In short, both Stowe and Riis sought to reveal uncomfortable truths in an accurate yet entertaining manner.[61]

In *How the Other Half Lives,* Riis claimed, "I have aimed to tell the truth as I saw it." Riis's blend of the sensationalism of police reporting, the emotion of sentimental melodrama, the facts of documentary realism, and the data of social science (a combination he used to entertain and to educate his audience) gave the "truth" he recorded its currency and its edge.[62]

Though he had found his subject matter, fashioned a point of view, and discovered a style, Riis remained frustrated, still lacking the technical means of rendering his image of the Other Half. "We used to go in the small hours of the morning into the worst tenements to count noses and see if the law against overcrowding was violated, and the sights I saw there gripped my heart until I felt that I must tell of them, or burst, or turn anarchist, or something." "I wrote, but it seemed to make no impression." "A drawing might have done it, but I cannot draw, never could." "But, anyway, a drawing would not have been evidence of the kind I wanted."[63]

ADVANCES IN PHOTOGRAPHY

During the 1880s, a series of technological advances gave Riis the tools he needed to record his view of poverty and to help realize his vision of progress and prosperity. While Riis's discovery of flashlight powder provided the critical spark, other factors — such as the manufacture of the detective camera, improvements in lens design, and the mass production of the gelatin dry plate — made it possible for him to finally capture the disturbing presence of urban poverty.[64]

The detective camera Riis used allowed him to work without a tripod, enabling him to capture unconventional-looking, candid snapshots as well as more traditional, posed portraits. The camera's small size and portability, when compared with its more cumbersome ancestors, also let Riis conceal the simple wooden box beneath his coat if he chose to take pictures undetected. The gelatin dry plates Riis exposed, more sensitive to light than the collodion or wet plates they would soon replace, reduced exposure time significantly, allowing Riis to freeze action instead of recording moderate movement as an indecipherable blur. Additionally, unlike wet plates, the dry plate did not have to be prepared by the photographer in the field or developed immediately after it was exposed; sensitized by the manufacturer, it could be stored either exposed or unexposed for months. This helped eliminate one of the major burdens of location work.[65]

Riis's effective use of the latest technology made him one of the first action or news photographers: a reporter (known today as a photojournalist) able to secure a visual token of order while standing amidst a scene of chaos. Only twenty-five years earlier, technology had limited the picture of battle recorded by the famed Civil War photographer Matthew Brady and his less well-known assistants. While producing haunting images, captured before and after the battle, the Civil War photographers were unable to record the clash of action owing to the primitive nature of what was then the most advanced technology: bulky, heavy, tripod-supported cameras, with in most cases no lens shutters, and slow, wet plates.[66]

A generation later, Riis succeeded in capturing the look of action in his battle with the slum. Describing himself as "a kind of war correspondent" engaged in "campaigns," "raids," "battles," "invasions," and "wars" on several "fronts," Riis took advantage of several new "weapons" to shoot and capture what he believed to be American civilization's enemy. The combination of flashlight powder, detective camera, and gelatin dry plate provided Riis with the tools he needed to uncover and record a dangerous world rarely seen, in a manner never imagined. "You must use the tools that come to hand, and be glad for them, if you want to get things done." "I had at last an ally in the fight with the Bend." "I laid in a stock of dry plates and buckled to."[67]

THE NEW VISUAL CULTURE

The invention and rapid improvement of halftone photoengraving, the transformation of the urban daily newspaper, the astonishing success of

George Eastman's line of Kodak products, the growth of advertising, the popularity of the mail-order catalog, and the rise of the national illustrated magazine all helped to create an exciting new visual culture saturated with graphic images. These new realistic images, the majority of which were either photographs or photographic in style, were designed to entice the eye — to make viewers stop, look, and buy. *How the Other Half Lives* was precisely the type of photographic catalog that consumers of the emerging culture of realism were trained to understand and admire. The halftone revolutionized the reproduction of reality. Refined in the 1880s, halftone photoengraving made it possible to print photographic images in newspapers, magazines, books, and catalogs rather than having them redrawn first and then reproduced as line drawings, woodcuts, or lithographs. The photograph, no longer limited to an engraver's translation, appeared instead as a frame taken directly from life. The partnership of photograph and halftone gave the world — including the one recorded by Riis in *How the Other Half Lives* — the mesmerizing look of reality. While the halftone provided viewers with a seemingly accurate reproduction of real life, it was the use of this process by big city newspapers, mail-order catalogs, and illustrated magazines that accelerated the emergence of a new visual culture built largely on photographic signs and symbols.[68]

Experimenting with new technologies and journalistic techniques, newspaper editors encouraged their reporters to seek news that would prove shocking — crimes, scandals, disasters — and to write their stories as vividly as possible. Riis himself notes that he "got into Mulberry Street at what might be called the heroic age of police reporting." In addition to printing sensational stories in their effort to attract readers, newspaper editors throughout the 1880s ran bold headlines, made use of color, included supplements, and made liberal use of the halftone.[69]

As early as 4 March 1880 the New York *Daily Graphic* published what is considered to be the "first newspaper halftone." An editor of the *Graphic* commented, "We have dealt heretofore with pictures made from drawings or engravings. Here we have one direct from nature. Our photographers made the plate from which this picture has been obtained in the immediate presence of the shanties which are shown in it. There has been no redrawing of the picture." Aware of the growing power of visual images, especially photographs, newspaper editors peppered their editions with them.[70]

The appeal of the photographic image was related to the fantastic reception of George Eastman's line of camera, film, and paper products. Only twenty-five years after Oliver Wendell Holmes predicted that "the mirror with a memory" (his phrase for the photograph) would change all aspects of society, his prescience — a bit of wise forecasting many of his contemporaries thought outlandish in 1859 — proved accurate.[71]

During the mid-1880s, photography was practiced widely. "Amateur photography gained rapidly in popularity during the last decades of the century. Photography courses were taught at local YMCAs, and the best hotels advertised darkrooms for the pleasure of their visitors." Photographs became common signs, familiar letters in the alphabet of a new visual language. People throughout the country were eager to look at photographs, primed to be affected by these new tokens of reality. The growth of advertising helped direct and define the culture's interest in photographic representation.[72]

During the 1880s, the relatively new profession of advertising relied heavily on visual images to promote consumer products. Manufacturers of national brands such as Kodak, the owners of department stores such as Filene's, Macy's, Marshall Fields, and Wanamaker's, and mail-order businesses such as Montgomery Ward and Sears were eager to show their customers, in appealing and accurate detail, the products they offered for sale. Consequently, the marketplace was flooded with images: huge ones painted on buildings, smaller ones reproduced in newspapers, mail-order catalogs, and illustrated magazines. Retailers and wholesalers sought to distinguish their products, to give them a unique look. The advertisers they hired soon realized that in an environment saturated with visual stimuli the best lure was photographic.[73]

Photography's "infinite adaptability as a tool for selling anything whatsoever was recognized, and called on, at every turn. In the 1880s, a Philadelphian photographer, Robert Newell, issued a special advertisement, an offer to make photographs of any product a company might want to market. 'If you produce an article of merit, get it photographed and distributed. The entire country is your market, this is the age of progress, keep up with the times and make money.'" Designed to present potential customers with the most realistic display of the latest item, the look of news and advertising became difficult to distinguish; in fact, both were treated and seen as commodities.[74]

The illustrated magazines, their number and influence growing during the 1880s and exploding in the 1890s, succeeded in refining the trend of cataloging the nation's emerging consumer culture. Developing a slick visual style — based heavily on the halftone image — illustrated magazines such as *Harper's,* the *Atlantic, Scribner's, Century,* and *Ladies' Home Journal* displayed knowledge and product as commodities to be consumed. Edward Bok, the editor of *Ladies' Home Journal,* one of the most influential illustrated magazines of the period, erased the line between articles of consumption by devising a form of magazine layout termed "running over into the back." By breaking up a story so it did not run from start to finish on consecutive pages, Bok was able to "make his advertisements more valuable by putting them next to the most expensive material [the stories and articles] in the magazine."[75]

In their effort to attract viewers to their display of articles, the illustrated magazines, like the city dailies, were eager to publish sensational stories. Rather than offering the crude shock of crime, scandal, and disaster, the illustrated magazines proffered what their editors considered a more refined form of entertainment: the anthropological and sociological study. In addition to presenting studies of the Other Half, these magazines became the exhibitors, as early as 1881, of a new type of investigative reporting — the exciting "literature of exposure" that Theodore Roosevelt would later label derisively, "muckraking." The illustrated magazine, by offering a combination of attractively packaged articles, cultivated Americans' taste for the graphic display of other worlds considered to be alien and corrupt.[76]

Riis took advantage of the public's hunger for realistic illustrated narratives and of its interest in the underside of society. He also capitalized on the increasingly widespread belief—encouraged by the burgeoning consumer culture — that control of an item or an idea could be purchased. The shocking images Riis was in the process of accumulating and organizing would result in a stunning and seductive catalog of the Other Half.

Two additional factors made Riis's work more than a mere reflection of current trends — the backdrop against which he displayed his images and the audience to which he offered them.

THE RELOCATION OF THE FRONTIER

Only five months after the publication of *How the Other Half Lives,* a bulletin published by the U.S. Census Bureau announced the closing of the western frontier. "Up to and including 1880 the country had a frontier of settlement, but at present the unsettled area has been so broken into by isolated bodies of settlement that there can hardly be said to be a frontier line. In the discussion of its extent, its westward movement, etc., it cannot, therefore, any longer have a place in the census reports."[77]

As the familiar line separating civilization from savagery was erased, Jacob Riis was busy invading the tenements of the Lower East Side, exploring and charting a new line of distinction.

With the western wilderness and the Indian conquered, American culture needed new symbols of "otherness" against which to define itself. While not alone in his discovery of the source of the Progressive order, Riis was one of the earliest explorers to see the value of exposing the urban slum and the unassimilated poor. Unlike those who depicted the slum and its inhabitants as picturesque, Riis, for the most part, saw the slum environment as hellish and the unassimilated poor as potential agents of the devil. According to Riis, "in the tenements all influences make for evil."[78]

By relocating the frontier line, refashioning the wild Indian as urban alien, and then invading and mapping the slum with the latest tools, Riis produced a catalog of images of the poor uncivilized Other designed to reveal their opposite: the prosperous civilized American. Riis's view of filth, stench, vice, drunkenness, crime, grub-worship, savagery, and the chaos of tenement life conjured up an opposing vision of cleanliness, sobriety, industriousness, godliness, civilization, and order. (Not surprisingly, given Riis's virulent anti-Chinese racism, "John Chinaman" looms as the absolute symbol of urban savagery. His religion, his language, his clothes, his cool, and his taste for drugs and white women all disturb Riis.)[79]

Those who cherished the myth of American progress and prosperity, who strove for the status and security represented by homes on the suburban fringe, found Riis's black-and-white view of urban poverty nothing less than a call to arms — a crusade to conquer new territory and convert the newest heathen. After reading *How the Other Half Lives,* James Russell Lowell wrote Riis, "I have read your book with deep and painful interest. I felt as Dante must when he looked over the edge of the Abyss at the bottom of which Gergon lay in ambush. . . . I found it hard to get asleep the night after I had been reading it."[80]

THE NEW MIDDLE CLASS

Between 1870 and 1920 the same forces that produced the Other Half and the slum created their antitheses, the new urban middle class and the suburbs. The development of this new class and its home was especially rapid between 1870 and 1900, specifically during the 1880s, when the transformation of the economy and the restructuring of business created a wide range of new white-collar jobs in the service sector. With help from the trolley and electric streetcar, the fluid "walking city" became the modern metropolis. In New York City in 1890, with the process of residential and business segregation under way (a process that all of the nation's major cities experienced), the poor could be found downtown crowded into tenements, the rich uptown in luxury apartment buildings, and members of the middle class along the developing suburban fringe, living in modest apartment buildings and single-family homes.[81]

Riis's work spoke to the members of an emerging middle class living in an urban space being reshaped by the effects of physical and demographic change. His view of poverty was disturbing both to those familiar with the heterogeneity of the "walking city" (in which different classes and ethnic groups lived in relative proximity) and to those who sought to separate themselves from the Other Half by moving into the newer suburban communities.

As the nation and its urban hubs were stretched and redefined, the new urban middle class grew in spectacular numbers, from 756,000 in 1870 to 5,609,000 in 1910. The economy and culture the new class helped to produce, administer, and promote made Jacob Riis's work and the reception of *How the Other Half Lives* possible. It was the members of the new urban middle class — the managers of the economy, the devotees of urban social reform, the arbiters of national culture, the conspicuous consumers, the hustling climbers — who were compelled, by curiosity and fear, to look at the lives of the Other Half. They were drawn to the Other for a number of reasons.[82]

First, there was an interest in acquiring information about foreigners living in strange places. Curious middle-class observers, influenced by the literature of tourism, the rage of social science, the spread of Chautauqua self-education organizations, and the popularity of illustrated magazines and of lectures, welcomed the opportunity to survey realistic studies of "queer" people living in their "odd" habitats. Second, the desire for entertainment that combined serious subject matter with the appealing narrative flow characteristic of sentimental melodrama attracted people; interest in tales of the Other Half came from much the same source as did interest in Harriet Beecher Stowe's *Uncle Tom's Cabin*. Third, there was the appeal of vicarious adventure. Riis admitted of his own work, "The beauty of looking into these places without actually being present there is that the excursionist is spared the vulgar sounds and odious scents and repulsive exhibition attendant upon such a personal examination." There was, however, something more than the curiosity of the tourist, the desire for meaningful and moving entertainment, and the thrill of slumming vicariously that drew one half to the Other. To define itself as a class, the new urban middle class needed to look at the new urban poor.[83]

Looking at the world of poverty and vice, in relative comfort and from a safe distance, established a sense of difference, of class distinction. Gazing upon misery — being able to purchase and thumb through a copy of the slum in the privacy and security of one's home — served to remind members of the new urban middle class of their difference from the Other Half they viewed. Images of urban squalor, overcrowded tenements, dark saloons, and broken families called to mind the opposing images of suburban bliss, spacious homes, bright churches, and tightly knit families. This vision of middle-class progress and prosperity was critical; it was the assurance and promise anxious members of an emerging class needed. The economic and social upheavals of the 1880s made the fear of falling from grace, of slipping into the yawning abyss of poverty, a nagging part of middle-class existence. Looking at the misfortune of others — even the picturesque and romantic images of the 1870s and 1880s that preceded and competed with Riis's more realistic view — helped the members of the new urban middle class to distinguish and define themselves.[84]

Throughout the middle and late 1880s, Riis himself was concerned about the tenuous nature of his class position. Aspects of his own experience were perhaps typical. Having overcome the trials of uprooting, migration, and poverty, Riis had by the early 1880s succeeded in making himself a part of the nascent urban professional class. When Riis decided to move from Brooklyn to what was then the suburb of Richmond Hill, Long Island, in 1886, he was forced to borrow money from friends and coworkers and to get additional work translating Danish insurance policies. If he were to assure his position in the middle class, Riis realized he would need to generate more income than his salary as a police reporter afforded him. After discovering flashlight powder in 1887, Riis dusted off the magic lantern he had used in his brief advertising career, convinced that images of urban poverty would sell.[85]

His campaign, while moved by sympathy for his less fortunate subjects (the result of his own experience as a poverty stricken immigrant) was also driven by his desire to secure a place for himself in the middle class. Riis's personal quest, however, helped fuel a larger collective mission: the organization and the empowerment of the new urban middle class. Riis's view of poverty inspired a sense of middle-class consciousness and solidarity. By drawing on a series of disturbing images, like the one quoted on the following page, Riis's work clarified the purpose and the identity of the middle class.[86]

"A man stood at the corner of Fifth Avenue and Fourteenth Street the other day, looking gloomily at the carriages that rolled by, carrying the wealth and fashion of the avenues to and from the big stores downtown. He was poor, and hungry, and ragged. This thought was in his mind: 'They behind their well-fed teams have no thought for the morrow; they know hunger only by name, and ride down to spend in an hour's shopping what would keep me and my little ones from want a whole year.' There rose up before him the picture of those little ones crying for bread around the cold and cheerless hearth — then he sprang into the throng and slashed about him with a knife, blindly seeking to kill, to revenge."[87]

Riis called on the middle class to control the conflict between rich and poor, to distinguish itself from the two extremes and oversee the smooth operation of American society. By assuming the functions of manager and engineer, the middle class would safeguard the nation's vision of progress and, in doing so, firmly establish its position as modern America's dominant class.

HOW THE OTHER HALF LOOKS:
INTERPRETING RIIS'S VIEW OF POVERTY

In Sweat Shop — Twelve-Year-Old Boy at Work.

In the final chapter of his autobiography, titled "The American Made," Riis writes of himself, "Nature, I think, intended me for a cobbler, or a patch-tailor. I love to mend and make crooked things straight. When I was a carpenter I preferred to make an old house over to building a new."[88]

Riis's description of himself is worth keeping in mind while reading *How the Other Half Lives*. For it is between the lines of this anecdotal aside that Riis reveals the spirit of reform that inspired his work as an author and an activist.

Some Sources of Confusion

How the Other Half Lives was produced during the less predictable stages of the nation's drive to organize a national economy and culture by an immigrant in the process of making himself an American. As a product of neither the Old World nor the new, Riis's text is a patch-work that combines the material of each. Consequently, *How the Other Half Lives* appears to be a discordant and inchoate work, groping awkwardly toward a vision of order that drifts in and out of focus. Because of this, many readers find it difficult to discern the manifest and latent levels of Riis's work — the popular stereotypes and styles that he used to realize a more progressive vision. Either outraged by his blatant prejudices or confused by his disturbing contradictions, readers rarely appreciate Riis's deft salesmanship. While speaking to his audience on one level as an American and a conservative Victorian, Riis whispered to them on another as an immigrant and a progressive modern.

For example, though Riis tends to corner and abuse his subjects — presenting the hostile front of an anxious and prejudiced middle-class missionary — this cold tone of bigotry is accompanied by poignant notes of compassion. In his prose, Riis treats children tenderly and northern and western European immigrants with respect. While these moments of empathy appear understandable given Riis's ethnic biases and society's general acceptance of the innocence of children, even when examining the lives of African Americans, Jews, and Italians (groups that fall somewhere in the middle of Riis's invidious ethnic hierarchy), he never fails to remind his audience that "to a certain extent, we are all the creatures of the conditions that surround us, physically and morally," and that "all life eventually accommodates itself to its environment, and human life is no exception."[89]

Flashes of sympathy can also be seen in Riis's collection of photographs. Because many of these images emphasize the impact of environment rather than heredity, they tend to portray the Other Half as the unfortunate victims of greed rather than of genetic inferiority.[90]

Riis's blend of sensationalism, melodrama, and realism also tends to confuse readers, forcing them to ask themselves, once again, if they are to pity the plight of the poor or fear their spread. (In fact, Riis wanted his readers to do both.) In his prose, Riis sighs and moans, addresses the reader directly, and makes liberal use of the second person — all devices characteristic of sentimental melodrama. These romantic touches, designed to tug on the chords of his readers' emotions, are counterbalanced by vivid photographic description, dry statistical data, and objective reportage, all of which Riis uses to alert and alarm his readers. Riis replicates the jarring combination of mawkish sentiment and scientific observation in his choice of illustrations. For example, the realistic edge of his photographs is softened by a number of picturesque drawings.[91]

It is also important to remember that the book *How the Other Half Lives* was only one part of Riis's thirty-five-year-long multimedia campaign against the slum. Though the magazine article and book stimulated widespread interest in his subject matter, Riis's illustrated lectures were perhaps closer to his ideal form of presentation. These live performances made far more effective use of Riis's photographs than any of his books or articles. Using his magic lantern, Riis could show many more pictures — usually between sixty and one hundred — and he could project them onto a large screen, allowing himself to fade from one image to another. There is also evidence that Riis hand-colored a few of his lantern slides — "Bandits' Roost," for instance — and delivered some of his lectures accompanied by music. Published versions of Riis's view of the Other Half must pale in comparison with the colorful immediacy of his cinematic performances.[92]

Despite the confusion caused by its manifest and latent levels of meaning, its blend of sensationalism, melodrama, and realism, the subtle but significant differences that were a result of the work's form of presentation (and those that were a result of the work's evolution from entertainment to entertaining reform), Riis's message and method of delivery remain clear.

The Message and the Method

Writing of his work in his autobiography Riis noted, "with tongue or pen, the argument shaped itself finally into the fundamental one for the rescue of the home imperilled by the slum. There all roads met. Good citizenship hung upon that issue. Say what you will, a man cannot live like a pig and vote like a man. . . . With no home to cherish, how long before love of country would be an empty sound? Life, liberty, pursuit of happiness? Wind! says the slum, and the slum is right if we let it be."[93]

In his lectures and print work, Riis delivered his message as if it were a sermon, specifically, a jeremiad. Seeking to stir the members of his middle-class audience to action, Riis persuaded them that they were the nation's "chosen" people destined to save America from the conflagration of class conflict. To make the significance of his message as clear as possible, Riis sought to root the religious rhetoric of his crusade in the social conditions of everyday life familiar to the big-city police reporter. As he writes in his autobiography, "The reporter who is behind the scenes sees the tumult of passions, and not rarely a human heroism that redeems all the rest. It is his task so to portray it that we can all see its meaning, or at all events catch the human drift of it, not merely the foulness and the reek of human blood. If he can do that, he has performed a signal service, and his murder story may easily come to speak more eloquently to the minds of thousands than the sermon preached to a hundred in the church on Sunday."[94]

To make sure the members of his audience saw the "meaning behind the scenes," Riis, described as "one of the brightest and most interesting talkers in the profession to which he belongs," made the revelation of his gospel a visual experience. In the margins of "the only stenographic report" of his lecture, "The Other Half and How They Live" (delivered in Washington, D.C., on 9 November 1891 at the Sixth Convention of Christian Workers in the United States and Canada), Riis scribbled, "As I speak without notes, from memory and to the pictures, the result is according to how I feel."[95]

A fine example of Riis's improvisational and conversational method of phototextual discourse can be seen in the book in his discussion of the picture "'Knee-Pants' at Forty-Five Cents a Dozen — A Ludlow Street Sweater's Shop." Riis works with the picture, providing rich detail beyond the photographic frame. We learn from his prose that the labor is taking place on Sunday; that the tenement building in which the sweatshop is located "smells of cabbage, of onions, of frying fish"; that inside the sweatshop the Jewish workers are speaking in "the Ludlow Street dialect"; that in a corner of the room, beyond the view of Riis's lens, a "bare-legged baby with pinched face" sleeps on a couch amidst piles of clothing. The combination of descriptive prose and graphic illustration results in a powerfully revealing visual image. As the subtitle to his Washington, D.C., lecture indicates, Riis's lay sermon was very much a "Story in Pictures."[96]

Riis further enhanced his sermon's feeling of virtual reality by conducting it as if it were a guided tour. "The time allotted to me to-night is so brief and the subject is so very big that we begin right away, all of us going together down into the slums of New York City to see what has got to be done down there and learn how by the blessing of God to help in the work."[97]

Having skillfully transported the members of his audience to the slums of New York City, Riis asked them: "Have [you] the courage to follow me into the heart of one of these tenement blocks and see the sights that are seen there?"[98]

With his group following him closely, Riis stops in front of one of the tenements and offers a photographic description: "Of the handsome cornice barely a trace is left. Dirt and desolation reign in the wide hallway, and danger lurks on the rickety stairs. . . . The old garden gate long since went to decay and fell from its hinges. The arched gateway is there still, but it leads no longer to a garden. In its place has come a dark and nameless alley, shut in by high brick walls, cheerless as the lives of those they shelter."[99]

Riis moves his audience along, beckoning, "Let me take you . . ."; "Let me show you . . ."; "Let us take a look at . . ."; "Let us go into . . ."[100]

Once inside the tenement — the proverbial belly of the beast — Riis excites all of the senses. Blending sensational police reporting, sentimental melodrama, and realistic detail, Riis advises,

> Be a little careful please! The hall is dark. . . . You can feel your way, if you cannot see it. Close? Yes! What would you have? All the fresh air that ever enters these stairs comes from the hall-door that is forever slamming, and from the windows of dark bedrooms that in turn receive from the stairs their sole supply of the elements God meant to be free, but man deals out with such niggardly hand. That was a woman filling her pail by the hydrant you just bumped against. The sinks are in the hallway, that all the tenants may have access — and all be poisoned alike by their summer stenches. Hear the pump squeak! It is the lullaby of the tenement-house babies. In summer, when a thousand thirsty throats pant for a cooling drink in this block, it is worked in vain. But the saloon, whose open door you passed in the hall, is always there. The smell of it has followed you up. Here is a door. Listen! That short hacking cough, that tiny, helpless wail — what do they mean? They mean that the soiled bow of white you saw on the door downstairs will have another story to tell — Oh! a sadly familiar story — before the day is at an end. The child is dying with measles. With half a chance it might have lived; but it had none. That dark bedroom killed it.[101]

After overwhelming his audience with the tragic scene's filth, stench, and noise — made vivid by Riis's eye for realistic detail and affecting by his ear for sensationalism and melodrama — Riis stokes their fears by using animal imagery to describe the slum and its denizens. Ripping through the slum's human surface, Riis reveals a far more terrifying "wild life" of "inhuman dens, lairs, hovels, holes, perches, pig-sties, webs, hives, and nests," inhabited by "inhuman bands, swarms, hordes and herds" of "brutes, beasts, pests, spiders, cats, curs, foxes, weasels, rats, rabbits, fleet footed mountain goats, blood-thirsty tigers, and wolves that hunt with the pack."

This liberal use of animal imagery (anticipating the work of naturalists Hamlin Garland, Frank Norris, and Stephen Crane — whose *Maggie: A*

Girl of the Streets [1893] may have been inspired by Crane's familiarity with Riis's work), was designed to illustrate the deleterious influence of the slum environment. Riis presented the squalor and the chaos of tenement life as uncivilized forces capable of turning human beings into vicious beasts.[102]

To further excite the fears and entertain the interests of his audience, Riis drew on a stock of crude racial and ethnic stereotypes. These simplistic character studies, a sort of vulgar sociological shorthand, magnified the wild, alien Otherness of the urban poor. Jews are cheap, "money is their God"; Italians are dumb and "learn slowly if at all"; Chinese are inscrutable, "stealth and secretiveness are as much a part of the Chinaman in New York as the cat-like tread of his felt shoes"; African Americans are infantile — they "look at the sunny side of life and enjoy it." Though less hostile to children and northern and western Europeans, Riis generally portrayed the poor unassimilated Other, of whatever background, as a threatening heathen, sprung from an evil environment. "They are shiftless, destructive, and stupid; in a word, they are what the tenements have made them."[103]

As mentioned earlier, Riis's work was a "story in pictures." Because his view of poverty relied so heavily on his clever use of photographs, it is necessary to discuss them in detail. Offering interiors, exteriors, group shots, portraits, mug shots, scapes, details, posed and candid shots, natural and artificial light, verticals and horizontals, tight and wide angles, Riis's total coverage moved his viewers in and out, up and down, around and throughout the world of the Other Half.

These visual images can be divided into two large categories — posed and candid — and then divided further within these two categories, since there are extreme versions of both posed and candid shots. For example, in the posed category, there are a number of set pieces that Riis appears to have staged ("Street Arabs in Sleeping Quarters") and one photograph (that of "The Tramp") for which he paid the subject to pose. As for the more candid shots, there are images that — because of the darkness and rapid movement when the exposure was made — cause one to wonder if Riis, while making the photograph, had any of idea of how the resulting image would look.

In many of the posed shots, Riis seems to identify with those struggling against tremendous hardship. We see portraits of families and individuals trying to make themselves, as well as their living and working quarters (often the same), presentable. The message appears clear: despite brutal conditions, people are driven by such human instincts as work, family, and order. These images, indicting the slum environment and those responsible for its creation and maintenance — rather than those trapped in its hovels — generate a sense of pity and guilt.

The second category of images, those that appear to be more spontaneous, succeed in generating terror as well as sympathy. These images — because of their grainy, fuzzy, scratched, over- and underexposed atonal composition; their lines, forms, and figures cropped and scrambled senselessly across the frame (their quite accidental modernism) — emphasize the disturbing spin of chaos. The gritty, amateurish disarray of these crude snapshots reflects a candid, or real, view of squalor — a view Riis wanted his audience to feel they had literally stumbled into.

Although the distinction between posed and spontaneous is useful to make when viewing Riis's images, it would be a mistake to think that all of them fall neatly into these two categories. A number combine elements of both. It is also important to remember that a photograph's meaning may differ in some ways when reproduced as an engraving or viewed as a lantern slide; when reproduced as a halftone, printing and cropping can determine the message of an image. Captions can also alter a picture's meaning. (Apparently aware that several of his photographs recorded an ambiguous view of poverty, Riis attempted to shape the message of some of these troublesome pictures by using captions. Perhaps the best example of this is the photograph titled "Sewing and Starving in an Elizabeth Street Attic" [p. 217]. Without the caption the reader simply sees two women sewing, possibly in the cozy confines of their own home. The picture itself says little about poverty; the scene is clean, orderly, even celebratory in its depiction of diligent work. The caption, however, informs the reader that the women are starving and that in all probability they live and labor in the cramped quarters of a tenement attic. Suddenly, the picture tells another story; a story of poverty more consistent with Riis's view of the slum environment. This photograph, one of the seventeen halftones in *How the Other Half Lives*, first appeared as a line drawing in the 1888 article "Flashes from the Slums" above the caption "White Slaves."[104])

Let's take a look at three pictures: the first posed, the third candid, the second something in between.[105]

"In Poverty Gap, West Twenty-Eighth Street. An English Coal-Heaver's Home" (p. 170), which was reproduced in the 1890 edition as an engraving from a photo, Riis presents a family of four sitting in their "home" — what appears to be a one-room flat. Despite the cramped quarters, the peeling plaster, the worn and cracked floorboards, the hole in the wall, the unappealing bedding, there is a sense of tidiness and order. The few household objects are placed neatly on the table, there is a broom leaning against the wall, an empty basket in the foreground. The family seems to possess qualities of patience, strength, and dignity. The children are well-behaved; the mother stolid. The father, seated with his young daughter on his lap, is presented as both gentle and determined. He makes eye contact with Riis as if he were the photographer's equal. Having shot the scene from a low angle, almost looking up at his subjects, Riis emphasized his compassion for this family and his outrage that fellow human beings should be forced to live in such conditions. In this image, while Riis celebrates the strength of the nuclear family and the importance of discipline and order, he also condemns those forces that threaten these traditional values. The respect Riis shows the family and the order he has made of their scene also reveal his own bias in favor of Anglo-Saxon immigrants.[106]

Now consider the photograph titled "'Knee-Pants' at Forty-Five Cents a Dozen — A Ludlow Street Sweater's Shop" (p. 143). The picture, depicting a small room crowded with seven people, one dog, and piles of fabric, hums with frantic activity. Having thrust the door open, Riis places the viewer in the middle of the ragged scene. The eye searches for a point of focus, a spot from which to begin the process of reading, but there is no such spot. Riis fails to direct the eye to any specific part of the frame; the viewer is forced to search for a focal point amidst several areas competing for attention. Where to begin? The bearded man in white shirt sitting, striped pants, polka-dot kerchief, his scissor flashing through the blanket of fabric covering his legs; below his black boot, a pair of clasped hands belonging to a mysterious figure cropped from view; the youth in the right corner, framed by the abstract designs of the flash-soaked window and its panes, who catches us looking at him; the lamp hovering in the right corner above the ripped and dangling sash; the Hebrew words hanging above the baby picture, both images falling left; the burst of daylight; the figure standing, his back toward us, his left arm moving so rapidly his hand disappears in a blur into the shoulder of a woman, her head bowed; the young girl smiling, looking at the camera, one of the scissor blades in her mouth, the other resting on her lip; the blur of a head shaking; the pile of material on the chair; the dog below, staring out; the scraps, the threads, the furniture, the fabric, the bodies. The chaotic whir of piece work is distressing. Unlike the English family Riis depicts in "Coal Heaver's Home" or the orderly work scene he shows in "Bohemian Cigarmakers at Work in Their Tenement," here Riis records the wild industry of Jews.[107]

In the photograph titled "An All-Night Two-Cent Restaurant, in 'The Bend,' " (p. 109), Riis takes his viewer into the subterranean world of despair. Much like his depiction of the chaos of Jewish tenement work, but to a greater degree, Riis's image of night life is without clear focus. Shot from table height, as if Riis himself were lifting his groggy head for a drunken glimpse of the disheveled scene, the picture's central figure is collapsed on an adjacent table, apparently overcome by fatigue and "stale beer." To the figure's left, occupying the same table, is a blur of body parts; the rest of the picture, sunk in darkness, suggests both the mysterious depths of misery and the foul, murky realm, through which beasts prowl and danger springs. Here, where there is not even a trace of ethnicity with which Riis might order his picture, total drunken anonymity plunges the disorganized and barely discernible scene into the bowels of hell.[108]

While clearly a "Victorian illustrator," Riis, perhaps unintentionally, anticipated the look of modern photography. His visual images of urban poverty, like his prose, reveal the tastes and the prejudices of his day. At the same time, image and text anticipate a more progressive vision.[109] Riis captured the uncertainty of the contemporary American scene using two lights — the receding glow of sentimental melodrama and the rising glare of documentary realism.

Discreet and entertaining, Riis's work is also raw and haunting. Offering a decorous performance deemed appropriate and appealing (in addition to Riis's attractive mix of sensationalism, melodrama, and realism and to his effective blend of illustration and text, consider his decision to gloss over prostitution and make use of ethnic "humor"), Riis also presented the Other Half with ugly and frightening immediacy. Seeking to persuade his audience to enlist in the "battle with the slum," Riis wove a cord of terrifying reality throughout his alluring web of entertainment.[110]

With his view of urban poverty looming before their eyes, Riis asked the members of his audience bluntly: "What are you going to do about it?"[111]

Riis's drama was not designed or offered to illustrate the futility of change. While Riis felt that "unfavorable" inherited characteristics were significant factors in determining an individual's material success and capacity for American citizenship, he believed that an individual's future was shaped ultimately by environmental factors. The slum — specifically the dark, overcrowded tenement — hindered the process of social evolution and American progress, resulting in a process Riis termed "survival of the unfittest." Because he believed this process was determined by environmental factors, the threat it posed to the individual, the family, the group, the community, and the nation could be controlled. Poverty could be managed; Americans could be made.[112]

The secret to preventing human and American *de*volution lay, in Riis's mind, in the hands of the middle class. The work of urban social reform, specifically, the renovation of the slum and the Americanization of its inhabitants, was its business. Riis reminded his audience that "the security of one no less than of the other half demands, on sanitary, moral, and economic grounds, that . . . [the] tremendous, ever swelling crowd of wage earners . . . be housed decently." If the harmonious American social order Riis envisioned was to be realized, the middle class would have to get busy, devising and overseeing a thorough program of social reform. By accepting its mission, the middle class could determine its fate — and the nation's. Riis warned his audience with biblical authority, "Whatsoever a man soweth, that shall he also reap."[113]

Arguing that progress and prosperity were the result of physical cleanliness, cultural conformity, and spiritual light, Riis presented the filth, the disorder, and the darkness of urban poverty as malevolent forces responsible for America's decay; if unchallenged, these forces of evil would lead to the nation's collapse. Riis's obsession with cleanliness and light, images he frequently employed in metaphorical terms, is clear throughout his work. "I hate darkness and dirt anywhere, and naturally want to let in the light. I will have no dark corners in my own cellar; it must be whitewashed clean." The flash and its blinding light, its ability to freeze movement and whitewash darkness, are the weapons (literal and symbolic) of Riis's reform crusade; the members of the middle class, the crusade's missionaries and soldiers, are the agents of American civilization.[114]

By managing the disparity between rich and poor and reconciling the distinction between alien and citizen — by cleaning up what was considered to be a mess — Riis believed the middle class could save American society from ruin and in the process establish itself as the nation's conscience and bulwark. America could only realize the promise of its mythology if the middle class disarmed and retrained the nation's class of gravediggers. "We know now that there is no way out; that the 'system' that was the evil offspring of public neglect and private greed has come to stay, a storm-centre forever of our civilization. Nothing is left but to make the best of a bad bargain." If the middle class failed to accept its role, "to make the best of a bad bargain,"

American civilization would be swept aside, destroyed by "the sea of a mighty population, held in galling fetters [that] heaves uneasily in the tenements."[115]

The Legacy

Riis's apocalyptic and entertaining view of poverty was one of the first signs of the budding progressive effort to secure the American dream of progress and prosperity. Composed of traditional and innovative images, conservative and progressive ideas, Riis's view proved successful, sparking a crusade of middle-class reform work that helped to more firmly establish the middle class and its culture. As for urban poverty, significant improvements in tenement housing and sanitation were a result of the flurry of middle-class reform activity. While these material changes were important in advancing America's war on poverty, it is worth considering some of the other affects of Riis's crusade.

For example, some may wonder whether housing projects, a conservative vision of the good life, and a perverse form of slumming are worth the image of urban poverty and ethnicity Riis bequeathed to future Americans; others, seeing Riis's legacy in a less cynical light, may see his work as the most practical means of advancing the interests of the poor and the middle class. In fact, Riis's brilliance may lie in his ability to deliver, in an entertaining manner, what was an unpopular message (environment, not heredity, determined character) to a middle-class audience leery of his progressive outlook. Playing on the fears and tastes of his audience, and drawing on his own ethnic immigrant sympathies and American middle-class concerns, Riis had his audience sweating with terror, sighing with pity, squirming with guilt, and laughing with relief, all in an effort to make the opportunity of progress for the poor a reality, a reality designed to safeguard the middle-class vision of prosperity. Others still, seeing less of a strategy behind Riis's theatrical lay sermon, may simply agree with his frank pragmatism: "It is a dreary old truth that those who would fight for the poor must fight the poor to do it."[116]

Concerned with the physical signs rather than the underlying causes of poverty, Riis's work focused on cleaning up its visible symptoms rather than pulling up its systemic roots. In his effort to renovate the slum and assimilate the poor immigrant, Riis constructed a view of urban poverty that, while significant in style, scope, and energy, lacked the depth and clarity of critical insight.

Designed specifically to improve the immediate material conditions of the poor while advancing the long-term interests of the middle class,

Riis's view of poverty and his vision of progress and prosperity persist to this day. Perhaps the pull of *How the Other Half Lives* — its continued currency and relevance — rests in its peculiar ability to speak to the middle class over time. An example of the early influence of progressive reform, scientific management, and mass consumption — which made effective use of the new look of documentary realism, sensationalism, and advertising — *How the Other Half Lives*, ideologically and technologically, heralded the emergence of modern American society and culture.

Members of today's middle class are influenced by many of the same fears, stereotypes, sources of entertainment, and remedies of reform that seduced and structured the lives of their turn-of-the-century peers. The slum, the poor, the immigrant, the Other are framed by the insecurities and desires of contemporary middle-class popular culture. Today, instead of New York's Lower East Side and "John the Chinaman," the middle class demonizes the inner city and the young black male, the border with Mexico and the illegal alien. The cycle of chaos and control continues to draw its crowd.

***

In 1890, after twenty years of working and wandering, Jacob A. Riis, police reporter and guide, salesman and preacher, explorer and crusader — a pioneer ahead of his time — released his catalog of studies. Engaging the blunt force of tradition and some of the sharper tools of modernity, Riis battled the forces of industrialization, immigration, and urbanization. *How the Other Half Lives*, a product of the nation's search for order, accurately reflects the historical circumstances responsible for its production and reception. Pieced together from the stuff of waning and emerging worlds by an immigrant and an American who proudly made his way from rags to respectability, Riis's classic text, offering the new urban middle class the familiar bathos of sensational melodrama along with the unnerving detail of documentary realism, represents the struggle to reconcile the nightmares and the dreams of American culture. Aiming to tell the truth as he saw it, Jacob Riis constructed an image of urban poverty designed to secure the myth of America. His view of the Other Half was, and continues to be, irresistible.

"Leaving the Elevated Railroad where it dives under the Brooklyn Bridge at Franklin Square, scarce a dozen steps will take us where we wish to go. With its rush and roar yet echoing in our ears, we have turned the corner from prosperity to poverty. We stand upon the domain of the tenement." "Suppose we look into one?"[117]

NOTES

[1] Jacob Riis, *The Making of an American* (New York: Macmillan, 1901, 1906), 267; Beaumont Newhall, *The History of Photography: From 1839 to the Present* (Boston: Little, Brown and Co.), 133; Peter Hales, *Silver Cities: The Photography of American Urbanization, 1839–1915* (Philadelphia: Temple University Press, 1984), 8, 163–64, 213–17; Maren Stange, *Symbols of Ideal Life: Social Documentary Photography in America, 1890–1950* (New York: Cambridge University Press, 1989), 2, 24–25.

[2] Stange, *Symbols of Ideal Life,* 6; Riis, *The Making of an American,* 267, 268; Jacob Riis, *How the Other Half Lives: Studies among the Tenements of New York* (New York: Scribner's, 1890), 80–81; Riis, *The Making of an American,* 271.

[3] Riis, *The Making of an American,* 269–70. The professional photographer is thought to have been A. D. Fisk; see Alexander Alland, Sr., *Jacob Riis: Photographer and Citizen* (New York: Aperture, 1973, 1993), 27.

[4] Alland, *Jacob Riis,* 27; Riis, *The Making of an American,* 270–71.

[5] There has been a great deal of discussion concerning the authorship of Riis's photographs. According to John Szarkowski, "In the late 1880s Jacob Riis (or Richard Hoe Lawrence, or Henry G. Piffard, or all three) made an extended series of photographs that described the appalling living and working conditions endured by the new immigrant poor in the New York slums. The authorship of the individual pictures of the series will probably never be settled beyond dispute." See Szarkowski, *Photography until Now* (New York: Museum of Modern Art, 1993), 189; also see Hales, *Silver Cities;* Stange, *Symbols of Ideal Life;* Hales, "The Hidden Hand: Jacob Riis and the Rhetoric of Reform," *Exposure,* 20, no. 3, 1982, 52–58; Bonnie Yochelson, "What Are the Photographs of Jacob Riis?" *culturefront,* Fall 1994, 28–38.

[6] Szarkowski, *Photography until Now,* 189; Riis Papers, Library of Congress.

[7] *New York Tribune,* 26 January 1888; *New York Herald,* 26 January 1888; *New York News,* 27 January 1888.

[8] Riis Papers, Library of Congress. According to Hales, *Silver Cities,* 302, "All twelve photographs reproduced by line drawing in 'Flashes' . . . are incorrectly attributed to Riis." Maren Stange (see *Symbols of Ideal Life,* 6–10) agrees that these early "Riis" photographs were probably made by Lawrence and/or Piffard.

[9] Riis Papers, Library of Congress; Riis, *The Making of an American,* 298–99.

[10] Riis Papers, Library of Congress.

[11] Riis, *The Making of an American,* 297. Although Riis suggests that magazines were initially uninterested in his story, this is not entirely accurate. Soon after hosting Riis's lecture in his Plymouth Church on 12 April 1888, Lyman Abbott, also editor of the *Christian Union,* wrote to Riis on 10 May 1888 regarding his lecture. "Don't you want to give us in *The Christian Union* two articles on 'The Other Half'?" The articles, which included five illustrations, appeared a year later, on 9 May and 16 May 1889, after Riis had already secured the *Scribner's Magazine* contract. The first article (p. 590) opens with the sentence, "Over on the East Side, in the shadow of a thousand tall tenements, lives New York's Other Half." Riis Papers, Library of Congress.

[12] Riis, *The Making of an American,* 300.

[13] According to Hales, *Silver Cities,* 178, the artists who copied Riis's collection of photographs for the *Scribner's* article, among them the well-known painter Kenyon Cox, "did an excellent job. . . . Even as line drawings . . . the illustrations suggested a profoundly photographic quality." Scribner's Papers, Princeton University; Riis Papers, Library of Congress; Riis, *The Making of an American,* 303.

[14] The hand-written manuscript is part of the Riis Collection of New York Public Library; Scribner's Papers, Princeton University.

[15] According to Alland, *Jacob A. Riis,* 30–31, *How the Other Half Lives* was "apparently the first book to use a large number of pictures reproduced by the new halftone process."

Scribner's Papers, Princeton University. Scribner's kept *How the Other Half Lives* in print until 1947. After being out of print for ten years, *How the Other Half Lives* was published in an edition without photographs by Hill and Wang in 1957. Harvard University Press published an edition in 1970, Dover in 1971, and Corner House published a copy of the 1890 edition in 1972.

[16] Riis Papers, Library of Congress; *The Making of an American,* 308.

[17] *Theodore Roosevelt: An Autobiography* (New York: Macmillan, 1914), 174; Roosevelt's reading of *How the Other Half Lives* began a close and important friendship between Riis and the future president.

[18] Riis Papers, Library of Congress.

[19] Ibid. Riis claims not to have paid much attention to the reviews. "I don't believe I have read fifteen reviews of any of my books. Life is too short." *The Making of an American,* 68.

[20] Riis, *The Making of an American,* 309. In addition to numerous newspaper and magazine articles, Riis published fourteen books after *How the Other Half Lives*; see Lewis Fried and John Fierst, eds., *Jacob A. Riis: A Reference Guide* (Boston: G. K. Hall, 1977).

[21] While surprised by the book's popularity, Riis did all he could to see that it would be successful. In a letter to Charles Scribner dated 14 August 1890, Riis wrote, "If I can be of any service whatever in helping the business end of the book along, and you will indicate from your experience how, I shall be very glad indeed." Riis Papers, Princeton University. Riis, *The Making of an American,* 309. The phrase "how the other half lives" is thought to have been used first by Rabelais. It also appears in a work published in 1845 by John H. Griscom titled *The Sanitary Condition of the Laboring Population of New York;* in 1872, the phrase was part of the title of a series of illustrated essays devoted to "Our Homeless Poor" that appeared in *Frank Leslie's Illustrated Newspaper;* in 1884, the phrase was part of the caption of an illustration that was printed on the cover of the *Daily Graphic* on 20 June. See Sally Stein, "Making Connections with the Camera: Photography and Social Mobility in the Career of Jacob Riis," *Afterimage* 10, no. 10: (May 1983).

[22] Riis, *The Making of an American,* 273; Riis Papers, Library of Congress.

[23] Alfred Chandler, *The Visible Hand: The Managerial Revolution in American Business* (Cambridge: Belknap Press, 1977); Herbert Gutman, *Work, Culture, and Society in Industrializing America* (New York: Vintage, 1977); Samuel P. Hays, *The Response to Industrialism, 1885–1914* (Chicago: University of Chicago Press, 1957); Morton Keller, *Affairs of State: Public Life in Late Nineteenth Century America* (Cambridge: Belknap Press, 1977); Stephen Kern, *The Culture of Time and Space, 1880–1918* (Cambridge: Harvard University Press, 1983); Gabriel Kolko, *The Triumph of Conservatism: A Reinterpretation of American History, 1900–1916* (New York: Free Press, 1963, 1967); Jackson Lears, *No Place of Grace: Anti-modernism and the Transformation of American Culture, 1800–1920* (New York: Pantheon, 1981); Douglass C. North, *Growth and Welfare in the American Past* (Englewood Cliffs: Prentice Hall, 1966); Nell Irvin Painter, *Standing at Armageddon: The United States, 1877–1919* (New York: Norton, 1987); Thomas J. Schlereth, *Victorian America: Transformations in Everyday Life, 1876–1915* (New York: Harper Collins, 1991); Alan Trachtenberg, *The Incorporation of America: Culture and Society in the Gilded Age* (New York: Hill and Wang, 1982); Robert H. Wiebe, *The Search for Order, 1877–1920* (New York: Hill and Wang, 1967).

[24] Riis Papers, Library of Congress. Roosevelt also said of Riis, "I am tempted to call [him] the best American I ever knew." *Theodore Roosevelt: An Autobiography,* 64.

[25] The bulk of *The Making of an American* was first published serially in Lyman Abbott's *Outlook* magazine between 2 March and 5 October 1901. Additional chapters appeared in the *Churchman* and the *Century Magazine.* Riis's immigrant autobiography, published as a book by Macmillan in 1901, is perhaps the first example of what would become a genre. Similar works by the immigrants Mary Antin, S. S. McClure, Edward

Steiner, and Edward Bok were designed to celebrate America's virtues (specifically, those of self-reliance, equality, justice, economic and social mobility) and prove that "aliens" could become citizens. (Although not the work of an immigrant, Booker T. Washington's autobiography, *Up from Slavery,* which was also serialized in the *Outlook,* is similar to the autobiographies of the immigrants cited above.) As pleas for inclusion, the authors of these works reveal themselves in a manner that conforms to American ideals. While not untrue, the lives these works present are edited to prove a point. Consequently, readers of these autobiographies must realize that facts are being selected and shaped to suit the author's larger purpose. For example, in his autobiography, Riis suggests that his "battle with the slum" was set in motion by the brutal murder of a dog he befriended while he was still an impoverished immigrant. This tale is striking in its similarities to an episode narrated by Harriet Beecher Stowe in volume 1, chapter 3, of *Uncle Tom's Cabin.* For biographies of Riis, see Alland, *Jacob A. Riis: Photographer and Citizen;* James B. Lane, *Jacob A. Riis and the American City* (Port Washington: Kennikat Press, 1974); Edith Meyer, *"Not Charity but Justice": The Story of Jacob A. Riis* (New York: Vanguard, 1974); Louise Ware, *Jacob A. Riis: Police Reporter, Reformer, Useful Citizen* (New York: Appleton-Century, 1938); Wiebe, *The Search for Order.*

[26] Riis, *The Making of an American,* 35–36. According to Riis biographer, James B. Lane, losing Elisabeth was not the only reason Riis left Denmark. Because of a depressed Danish economy, Riis was unable to find steady work. Only after being denied both woman and work did Riis decide to leave for America (*Jacob A. Riis and the American City* [Port Washington: Kennikat Press, 1974, 12–13]).

[27] Ibid., 35. Riis did have letters of introduction to family friends, but, feeling too proud to use these, he claims to have destroyed them. *The Making of an American,* 69. Riis also claims to have abandoned carpentry because "I was tired of hammer and saw. They were indissolubly bound up with my dreams of Elisabeth that were now gone to smash. Therefore I hated them." *The Making of an American,* 36, 66.

[28] Ibid., 232, 74.

[29] Ibid., 102, 90. At one point, Riis was doing so well with the irons that his mother, in a letter to Riis dated 26 March 1873, wrote, "Everything is very big in America, my boy. You talk about dollars and we about pennies. Perhaps you would be able once to help your mother. (You know from the old days I have always money-trouble at the end of the month.)" Riis Papers, New York Public Library; Riis, *The Making of an American,* 116.

[30] Riis, *The Making of an American,* 120–22.

[31] Ibid., 132–33.

[32] Ibid., 135, 139–40.

[33] Ibid., 139; Riis Papers, Library of Congress; *The Making of an American,* 148–51, 166–74.

[34] Ibid., 178, 192.

[35] Ibid., 180–81.

[36] Ibid., 183–84.

[37] Ibid., 186–88.

[38] Ibid., 189–90.

[39] Ibid., 194–95, 198, 200, 203, 198, 199.

[40] Trachtenberg, *The Incorporation of America;* Wiebe, *The Search for Order.*

[41] John Higham, *Strangers in the Land: Patterns of American Nativism, 1860–1925* (Atheneum: New York, 1977); John Higham, *Send These to Me: Immigrants in Urban America* (Baltimore: Johns Hopkins University Press, 1975, 1984); Maldwyn Allen Jones, *American Immigration* (Chicago: University of Chicago Press, 1960, 1992); Stephen Thernstrom et al., *The Harvard Encyclopedia of American Ethnic Groups* (Cambridge: Belknap Press, 1980).

[42] Roy Lubove, *The Progressives and the Slum: Tenement House Reform in New York City, 1890–1917* (Pittsburgh: University of Pittsburgh Press, 1962); Moses Rischin, *The*

Promised City: New York's Jews, 1870–1914 (Cambridge: Harvard University Press, 1962, 1970); David Ward, *Cities and Immigrants: A Geography of Change in Nineteenth-Century America* (New York: Oxford University Press, 1971).

[43] Lubove, *The Progressives and the Slums.*

[44] Riis, "How the Other Half Lives," *Scribner's Magazine,* December 1889, 643; U.S. Census, 1890; Riis, *How the Other Half Lives,* 73.

[45] Riis, *The Making of an American,* 234–35.

[46] Ibid., 242.

[47] Ibid., 246–47.

[48] Robert Bremner, *The Discovery of Poverty in the United States* (New York: New York University Press, 1956, 1992), 16–30, 31–85, 123–39.

[49] Richard Hofstadter, *Social Darwinism in American Thought* (Boston: Beacon Press, 1944, 1955); Higham, *Strangers in the Land;* Milton Gordon, *Assimilation in American Life: The Role of Race, Religion, and National Origins* (New York: Oxford University Press, 1964).

[50] Bremner, *The Discovery of Poverty in the United States;* Gordon, *Assimilation in American Life.*

[51] Riis, *How the Other Half Lives,* 120–28.

[52] Bremner, *The Discovery of Poverty in the United States,* 44–66; Hofstadter, *Social Darwinism in American Thought,* 105–10; Riis, *How the Other Half Lives,* 254; Riis, *The Making of an American,* 262.

[53] Frank Luther Mott, *Golden Multitudes* (New York: Macmillan, 1947), 310, 323; Riis, *How the Other Half Lives,* 69.

[54] Riis, *The Making of an American,* 423, 1.

[55] Ibid., 8.

[56] Stein, "Making Connections with the Camera."

[57] Riis, *How the Other Half Lives,* 69–70; Riis, *The Making of an American,* 262.

[58] Luc Sante, *Low Life: Lures and Snares of Old New York* (New York: Vintage, 1991); Marcus Klein, *Easterns, Westerns, and Private Eyes: American Matters, 1870–1900* (Madison: University of Wisconsin Press); Hales, *Silver Cities;* see *Harper's* from January 1886 to March 1892 for the editorials in which Howells wages his battle for realism.

[59] Amy Kaplan, *The Social Construction of American Realism* (Chicago: University of Chicago Press, 1988), 1–14; Trachtenberg, *The Incorporation of America,* 182–207.

[60] Riis, *The Making of an American,* 99, 68, 370.

[61] Bremner, *The Discovery of Poverty in the United States,* 86–120; Hales, *Silver Cities,* 185–92; Harriet Beecher Stowe, *Uncle Tom's Cabin, or, Life among the Lowly* (New York: Norton, 1994), 383. Riis's style also resembles the one adopted by Charles Dickens in his *American Notes for General Circulation* (New York: Penguin, 1842, 1985); see especially chapter 6 on New York, 127–44.

[62] Riis, *How the Other Half Lives,* 254.

[63] Riis, *The Making of an American,* 266–67.

[64] Reese V. Jenkins, *Images and Enterprise: Technology and the American Photographic Industry, 1839–1925* (Baltimore: Johns Hopkins University Press, 1975); Robert Taft, *Photography and the American Scene: A Social History, 1839–1889* (New York: Dover, 1938, 1964); Hales, *Silver Cities;* Stange, *Symbols of Ideal Life.*

[65] Taft, *Photography and the American Scene,* 361–83.

[66] Newhall, *The History of Photography,* 85–94; Trachtenberg, *Reading American Photographs: Images as History, Matthew Brady to Walker Evans* (New York: Hill and Wang, 1989), 71–118.

[67] Riis, *The Making of an American,* 310, 273, 274.

[68] Taft, *Photography and the American Scene,* 430–50.

[69] Riis, *The Making of an American,* 217.

[70] Taft, *Photography and the American Scene,* 437–38.

[71] Oliver Wendell Holmes, "The Stereoscope and the Stereograph," *Atlantic Monthly,* June 1859.

[72] Ferenc M. Szasz and Ralph F. Bogardus, "The Camera and the American Social Conscience: The Documentary Photography of Jacob A. Riis," *New York History,* October 1974, 412.

[73] Trachtenberg, *The Incorporation of America,* 130–39.

[74] Heinz K. Henisch and Bridget A. Henisch, *The Photographic Experience, 1839–1914: Images and Attitudes* (University Park: Pennsylvania State University Press, 1994), 235.

[75] Frank Luther Mott, *A History of American Magazines* (Cambridge: Harvard University Press, 1957), 43–70; Edward Bok, *The Americanization of Edward Bok: The Autobiography of a Dutch Boy Fifty Years After* (New York: Scribner's, 1923), 234.

[76] In 1881, Howells, then editor of the *Atlantic Monthly,* published Henry Demarest Lloyd's essay "The Story of a Great Monopoly"; Theodore Roosevelt, "The Man with the Muck-Rake," *Outlook,* 21 April 1906, 883; also see Bunyan's *Pilgrim's Progress* for perhaps the first use of this term; Riis "trained" the most famous muckraker of them all, Lincoln Steffens, who was the *Evening Post's* police reporter beginning in 1892.

[77] *Extra Census Bulletin* (Washington), no. 2, 20 April 1891. It was on this quotation that Frederick Jackson Turner built his "Frontier Thesis." See Turner, *The Frontier in American History* (Huntington: Krieger, 1920, 1976).

[78] Hales, *Silver Cities,* 163–64, 179–83; Szasz and Bogardus, "The Camera and the American Social Conscience," 413–18; Bremner, *The Discovery of Poverty in the United States,* 69; Riis, *How the Other Half Lives,* 60. It is worth quoting Riis's initial encounter with the urban frontier. Soon after he arrived in New York, Riis purchased "a navy revolver of the largest size" and "strapped the weapon on the outside of [his] coat and strode up Broadway," believing that he "was following the fashion of the country." Riis's image of America, drawn from his reading of Fenimore Cooper, led him to think that there would be "buffaloes and red Indians charging up and down Broadway." *The Making of an American,* 38.

[79] Benedict Anderson, *Imagined Communities: Reflections on the Origin and Spread of Nationalism* (London: Verso, 1983, 1985); Stange, *Symbols of Ideal Life,* xiii–xvii, 1–2.

[80] Stange, *Symbols of Ideal Life,* 17–18; Riis, *The Making of an American,* 308.

[81] Stuart Blumin, *The Emergence of the Middle-Class: Social Experience in the American City, 1760–1900* (Cambridge: Cambridge University Press, 1989); Hays, *The Response to Industrialism;* Kenneth T. Jackson, *Crabgrass Frontier: The Suburbanization of the United States* (New York: Oxford, 1985); Stephan Thernstrom, *Poverty and Progress: Social Mobility in a Nineteenth-Century City* (Cambridge: Harvard University Press, 1964); Stephan Thernstrom and Richard Sennett, eds., *Nineteenth-Century Cities: Essays in the New Urban History* (New Haven: Yale University Press, 1969); David Ward, *Cities and Immigrants;* David Ward and Oliver Zunz, *The Landscape of Modernity: Essays on New York City, 1900–1940* (New York: Russell Sage Foundation, 1992); Sam Bass Warner, Jr., *Streetcar Suburbs: The Process of Growth in Boston* (Cambridge: Harvard University Press, 1962).

[82] Hays, *The Response to Industrialization,* 73.

[83] *New York Morning Journal,* 12 February 1888.

[84] John Berger, "Why Look at Animals?" in *About Looking* (New York: Pantheon, 1980), 1–26; Thorstein Veblen, *The Theory of the Leisure Class* (New York: Mentor, 1899, 1953); Stange, *Symbols of Ideal Life.*

[85] Riis, *The Making of an American,* 286; Stein, "Making Connections with the Camera," 12. Throughout his career, Riis was concerned about having enough money and maintaining his place in the middle class. On 20 July 1895, Riis wrote to his editor at Charles Scribner's, "I have received the check of Charles Scribner's Sons for $58 and odd cents royalty payments on my three books. I often think, when people from one end of the country to the other foil me or the author of 'The Other Half,' on what a slender

financial base an author's popularity rests. Don't you?" Ten years later, on 24 November 1905, Riis wrote to his friend Mary Butler, "I cannot come to you before January, because every hour I have is given to the effort to raise the money necessary to pay the mortgage on our houses. I am sorry I have to refuse so near a neighbor, but you see how I am fixed. However, there is a good time coming, when I shall get where I want to, not where I have to." Scribner's Papers, Princeton University.

[86] Riis, *How the Other Half Lives,* 254.

[87] Ibid., 233.

[88] Riis, *The Making of an American,* 424.

[89] Riis, *How the Other Half Lives,* 234, 166. Perhaps of interest to those studying the early history of the social construction of the white race is Riis's assertion, based on data compiled by the *Real Estate Record* of 1889, that "the negroes proved cleaner, better, and steadier tenants" than "the tenants of a 'low European' type who had been turned out on account of filthy habits and poor pay." According to "one of the largest real estate firms in the city: we would rather have negro tenants in our poorest class of tenements than the lower groups of foreign white people. We find the former cleaner than the latter and they do not destroy the property so much. We also get higher prices." *How the Other Half Lives,* 157–59.

[90] For example, consider "In the Home of an Italian Rag-Picker, Jersey Street," 94; "In Poverty Gap, West Twenty-Eighth Street. An English Coal-Heaver's Home," 170; "Sewing and Starving in an Elizabeth Street Attic," 217; and even the more ambiguous pictures "The Tramp," 112, and "The Official Organ of Chinatown," 126. There are a number of ways of explaining these sympathetic images of the Other Half. First, perhaps Riis included these images to temper the hostility of his prose. Second, perhaps these photographs were not taken by Riis. Third, perhaps Riis's self-proclaimed incompetence as a photographer ("I am downright sorry to confess here that I am no good at all as a photographer, for I would like to be"; see *The Making of an American,* 265) prevented him from capturing on film what he was able to convey in words. Stange, *Symbols of Ideal Life,* 24; Luc Sante, *Low Life,* 35.

[91] Riis, *How the Other Half Lives,* see "At the Cradle of the Tenement," 79; "A Market Scene in the Jewish Quarter," 133; "The Old Clo'e's Man," 137; "Coffee at One Cent," 226.

[92] Yochelson, "What Are the Photographs of Jacob Riis?"; Stange, *Symbols of Ideal Life,* 12–13; Hales, *Silver Cities,* 193–94.

[93] Riis, *The Making of an American,* 319–20.

[94] Sacvan Bercovitch, *The American Jeremiad* (Madison: University of Wisconsin Press, 1978); Riis, *The Making of an American,* 204.

[95] Stenographic Report of lecture titled "The Other Half and How They Live," delivered on 9 November 1891 in Washington, D.C., as part of the Proceedings of the Sixth Convention of Christian Workers in the United States and Canada," Riis Papers, Library of Congress.

[96] Riis, *How the Other Half Lives,* 141–42. Stenographic Report of "The Other Half and How They Live."

[97] Hales, *Silver Cities,* 201–2; Stange, *Symbols of Ideal Life,* 16–18, 23; Riis, Stenographic Report of "The Other Half and How They Live."

[98] Riis, "The Tenement-House Question," *Christian Union,* 9 May 1889, 590.

[99] Riis, "How the Other Half Lives," *Scribner's Magazine,* December 1889, 644. Compare the description quoted in *Scribner's* with the version published in *How the Other Half Lives,* 78. This is an example of the sort of change that was made when "How the Other Half Lives" was expanded from a magazine article into a book.

[100] Stenographic Report of "The Other Half and How They Live"; Riis's "you are there" style was clearly influenced by Dickens's *American Notes;* see 127–44.

[101] Riis, *How the Other Half Lives,* 88.

[102] Thomas A. Gullason, ed., *Maggie: A Girl of the Streets, Stephen Crane* (New York:

Norton, 1979); see the essay by Gullason, "A Minister, a Social Reformer, and Maggie," 103–8.

[103] Riis, *How the Other Half Lives,* 130, 92, 121, 159. It is important to remember that Riis's bigotry was not limited to ethnic groups. He despised greedy landlords, directing some of his most vicious comments toward them, 239.

[104] Recently, the Museum of the City of New York completed a reprinting of the Riis photographs held in its collection. These uncropped prints (used in this volume), when compared with previous ones cropped by Riis and subsequent printers, provide valuable information regarding Riis's photographic vision. See Yochelson, "What Are the Photographs of Jacob Riis?"; Riis, *How the Other Half Lives,* 217; Riis, "Flashes from the Slums."

[105] While it is problematic to look at Riis's photographs as if he took them all (even though the authorship of some is uncertain and others have been proven not to have been taken by him), Peter Hales, in his article "The Hidden Hand," makes a strong argument for considering Riis the "director" of his collection of photographs.

[106] Riis, *How the Other Half Lives,* 170.

[107] Ibid., 143, 170, 153.

[108] Ibid., 109.

[109] Yochelson, "What Are the Photographs of Jacob Riis?" 31; Hales, *Silver Cities* 8, 213–17; Stange, *Symbols of Ideal Life,* 1–29; Stein, "Making Connections with the Camera," 9–16.

[110] The following excerpt from the Stenographic Report of Riis's 9 November 1891 lecture gives some idea of Riis's "humor." Describing a scene in Chinatown, Riis is recorded as saying, "We heard cries and shouts and went with a policeman across the street and in the cellar we found a Chinaman beating the white girl he called his wife with a broom handle. While the policeman spoke to her I tried to reason with the Chinaman. I said, 'John, what are you doing? You must not beat your wife.' 'She bad,' he sputtered. 'Well, if she is bad you must not beat her.' He said, 'Suppose your wife bad, you no lickee her?' I said, 'Certainly not.' He eyed me a while in stupid silence, poked the linen in his tub and made up his mind: 'Then, I guess she lickee you,' he said. [Laughter and applause]," 308. In *The Making of an American,* 432, Riis notes, "The longer I live the more I think of humor as in truth the saving sense. A civil-service examination to hit home might well be one to make sure the man could appreciate a good story."

[111] Riis, *How the Other Half Lives,* 61.

[112] Riis, *The Battle with the Slum* (New York: Macmillan, 1902), 33.

[113] Riis, *How the Other Half Lives,* 245, 254.

[114] Riis, *The Making of an American,* 423–24.

[115] Riis, *How the Other Half Lives,* 60, 254.

[116] Ibid., 239.

[117] Ibid., 78, 88.

PART TWO

The Document

Gotham Court.

How the Other Half Lives
Studies Among the Tenements
of New York
By Jacob A. Riis
With Illustrations Chiefly from Photographs Taken by the Author

Preface

The belief that every man's experience ought to be worth something to the community from which he drew it, no matter what that experience may be, so long as it was gleaned along the line of some decent, honest work, made me begin this book. With the result before him, the reader can judge for himself now whether or not I was right. Right or wrong, the many and exacting duties of a newspaper man's life would hardly have allowed me to bring it to an end but for frequent friendly lifts given me by willing hands. To the President of the Board of Health, Mr. Charles G. Wilson, and to Chief Inspector Byrnes of the Police Force I am indebted for much kindness. The patient friendship of Dr. Roger S. Tracy, the Registrar of Vital Statistics, has done for me what I never could have done for myself; for I know nothing of tables, statistics and percentages, while there is nothing about them that he does not know. Most of all I owe in this, as in all things else, to the womanly sympathy and the loving companionship of my dear wife, ever my chief helper, my wisest counsellor, and my gentlest critic.

J. A. R.

Contents

List of Illustrations

   * An asterisk indicates that the illustration was reproduced as a halftone in the 1890 Scribner's edition. All of the other illustrations, with a few exceptions, were "drawn from" or "after" photographs in Riis's collection by several artists (including Otto Bacher, Kenyon Cox, and Clifton Johnson) and were reproduced in the 1890 edition as engravings.

   † This photograph differs slightly from the halftone, which was unobtainable, that appeared in the 1890 Scribner's edition. This suggests that Riis had at least two pictures of this scene in his collection.

   ‡ Given the similarity of this illustration to several others in the 1890 edition, "A Tramp's Nest in Ludlow Street" was most likely copied from a photograph which was unobtainable. It appears here as an illustration.

"With gates of silver and bars of gold
Ye have fenced my sheep from their father's fold
I have heard the dropping of their tears
In heaven these eighteen hundred years."

"O Lord and Master, not ours the guilt,
We build but as our fathers built;
Behold thine images, how they stand,
Sovereign and sole, through all our land."

Then Christ sought out an artisan,
A low-browed, stunted, haggard man,
And a motherless girl, whose fingers thin
Pushed from her faintly want and sin.

These set he in the midst of them,
And as they drew back their garment-hem,
For fear of defilement, "Lo, here," said he,
"The *images* ye have made of me!"

      — James Russell Lowell*

*James Russell Lowell (1819 –1891), American poet. The lines are from the poem "A Parable" (1848).

How the Other Half Lives

Introduction

Long ago it was said that "one half of the world does not know how the other half lives."[1] That was true then. It did not know because it did not care. The half that was on top cared little for the struggles, and less for the fate of those who were underneath, so long as it was able to hold them there and keep its own seat. There came a time when the discomfort and crowding below were so great, and the consequent upheavals so violent, that it was no longer an easy thing to do, and then the upper half fell to inquiring what was the matter. Information on the subject has been accumulating rapidly since, and the whole world has had its hands full answering for its old ignorance.

In New York, the youngest of the world's great cities, that time came later than elsewhere, because the crowding had not been so great. There were those who believed that it would never come; but their hopes were vain. Greed and reckless selfishness wrought like results here as in the cities of older lands. "When the great riot occurred in 1863,"[2] so reads the testimony of the Secretary of the Prison Association of New York before a legislative committee appointed to investigate causes of the increase of crime in the State twenty-five years ago, "every hiding-place and nursery of crime discovered itself by immediate and active participation in the operations of the mob. Those very places and domiciles, and all that are like them, are to-day nurseries of crime, and of the vices and disorderly courses which lead to crime.

---

[1] See note 21 of Editor's Introduction. — ED.

[2] Riis is referring to the Draft Riots that erupted in New York City on July 13, 1863. The riots were sparked by the passage of a congressional law ordering the conscription of all males between the ages of twenty and forty-five into Union military service. The rioters, mainly poor and working-class Irish, were incensed by a provision of the law that enabled those who paid a fee of three hundred dollars to avoid conscription. The rioters directed their rage at New York's black community. — ED.

By far the largest part — eighty per cent. at least — of crimes against property and against the person are perpetrated by individuals who have either lost connection with home life, or never had any, or whose *homes had ceased to be sufficiently separate, decent, and desirable to afford what are regarded as ordinary wholesome influences of home and family.* . . . The younger criminals seem to come almost exclusively from the worst tenement house districts, that is, when traced back to the very places where they had their homes in the city here." Of one thing New York made sure at that early stage of the inquiry: the boundary line of the Other Half lies through the tenements.

It is ten years and over, now, since that line divided New York's population evenly. To-day three-fourths of its people live in the tenements, and the nineteenth century drift of the population to the cities is sending ever-increasing multitudes to crowd them. The fifteen thousand tenant-houses that were the despair of the sanitarian in the past generation have swelled into thirty-seven thousand, and more than twelve hundred thousand persons call them home. The one way out he saw — rapid transit to the suburbs — has brought no relief. We know now that there is no way out; that the "system" that was the evil offspring of public neglect and private greed has come to stay, a storm-centre forever of our civilization. Nothing is left but to make the best of a bad bargain.

What the tenements are and how they grew to what they are, we shall see hereafter. The story is dark enough, drawn from the plain public records, to send a chill to any heart. If it shall appear that the sufferings and the sins of the "other half," and the evil they breed, are but as a just punishment upon the community that gave it no other choice, it will be because that is the truth. The boundary line lies there because, while the forces for good on one side vastly outweigh the bad — it were not well otherwise — in the tenements all the influences make for evil; because they are the hot-beds of the epidemics that carry death to rich and poor alike; the nurseries of pauperism and crime that fill our jails and police courts; that throw off a scum of forty thousand human wrecks to the island asylums and workhouses year by year; that turned out in the last eight years a round half million beggars to prey upon our charities; that maintain a standing army of ten thousand tramps with all that that implies; because, above all, they touch the family life with deadly moral contagion. This is their worst crime, inseparable from the system. That we have to own it the child of our own wrong does not excuse it, even though it gives it claim upon our utmost patience and tenderest charity.

What are you going to do about it? is the question of to-day. It was asked once of our city in taunting defiance by a band of political cutthroats, the legitimate outgrowth of life on the tenement-house level.[3] Law and order found the answer then and prevailed. With our enormously swelling population held in this galling bondage, will that answer always be given? It will depend on how fully the situation that prompted the challenge is grasped. Forty per cent. of the distress among the poor, said a recent official report, is due to drunkenness. But the first legislative committee ever appointed to probe this sore went deeper down and uncovered its roots. The "conclusion forced itself upon it that certain conditions and associations of human life and habitation are the prolific parents of corresponding habits and morals," and it recommended "the prevention of drunkenness by providing for every man a clean and comfortable home." Years after, a sanitary inquiry brought to light the fact that "more than one-half of the tenements with two-thirds of their population were held by owners who made the keeping of them a business, *generally a speculation.* The owner was seeking a certain percentage on his outlay, and that percentage very rarely fell below fifteen per cent., and frequently exceeded thirty.[4] . . . The complaint was universal among the tenants that they were entirely uncared for, and that the only answer to their requests to have the place put in order by repairs and necessary improvements was that they must pay their rent or leave. The agent's instructions were simple but emphatic: 'Collect the rent in advance, or, failing, eject the occupants.' " Upon such a stock grew this upas-tree.[5] Small wonder the fruit is bitter. The remedy that shall be an effective answer to the coming appeal for justice must proceed from the public conscience. Neither legislation nor charity can cover the ground. The greed of capital that wrought the evil must itself undo it, as far as it can now be undone. Homes must be built for the working masses by those who employ their labor; but tenements must cease to be "good property" in the old, heartless sense. "Philanthropy and five per cent." is the penance exacted.

[3] The Tweed band of municipal robbers. (A group of New York City officials, Democratic party workers, and contractors [known as a "machine"] that, through the leadership of William Marcy "Boss" Tweed [1823 –1878], the leader of the influential, benevolent Association Tammany Hall, controlled municipal affairs. — ED.)

[4] Forty per cent. was declared by witnesses before a Senate Committee to be a fair average interest on tenement property. Instances were given of its being one hundred per cent. and over.

[5] A large, poisonous evergreen tree of southeast Asian origin thought capable of killing anything living in its vicinity. — ED.

Hell's Kitchen and Sebastopol.

If this is true from a purely economic point of view, what then of the outlook from the Christian standpoint? Not long ago a great meeting was held in this city, of all denominations of religious faith, to discuss the question how to lay hold of these teeming masses in the tenements with Christian influences, to which they are now too often strangers. Might not the conference have found in the warning of one Brooklyn builder,[6] who has invested his capital on this plan and made it pay more than a money interest, a hint worth heeding: "How shall the love of God be understood by those who have been nurtured in sight only of the greed of man?"

[6] Riis is probably referring to Alfred T. White, a Brooklyn builder responsible for the construction of numerous model tenements in the 1870s and 1880s. — ED.

Chapter I

Genesis of the Tenement

The first tenement New York knew bore the mark of Cain from its birth, though a generation passed before the writing was deciphered. It was the "rear house," infamous ever after in our city's history. There had been tenant-houses before, but they were not built for the purpose. Nothing would probably have shocked their original owners more than the idea of their harboring a promiscuous crowd; for they were the decorous homes of the old Knickerbockers, the proud aristocracy of Manhattan in the early days.

It was the stir and bustle of trade, together with the tremendous immigration that followed upon the war of 1812 that dislodged them. In thirty-five years the city of less than a hundred thousand came to harbor half a million souls, for whom homes had to be found. Within the memory of men not yet in their prime, Washington had moved from his house on Cherry Hill as too far out of town to be easily reached. Now the old residents followed his example; but they moved in a different direction and for a different reason. Their comfortable dwellings in the once fashionable streets along the East River front fell into the hands of real-estate agents and boarding-house keepers; and here, says the report to the Legislature of 1857, when the evils engendered had excited just alarm, "in its beginning, the tenant-house became a real blessing to that class of industrious poor whose small earnings limited their expenses, and whose employment in workshops, stores, or about the warehouses and thoroughfares, render a near residence of much importance." Not for long, however. As business increased, and the city grew with rapid strides, the necessities of the poor became the opportunity of their wealthier neighbors, and the stamp was set upon the old houses, suddenly become valuable, which the best thought and effort of a later age have vainly struggled to efface. Their "*large* rooms were partitioned into *several smaller ones,* without regard to light or ventilation, the rate of rent being lower in proportion to space or height from the street; and they soon became filled from cellar to garret with a class of tenantry living from hand to mouth, loose in morals, improvident in habits, degraded, and squalid as beggary itself." It was thus the dark bedroom, prolific of untold depravities, came into the world. It was destined to survive the old houses. In their new rôle, says the old report, eloquent in its indignant denunciation of "evils more destructive than wars," "they were not intended to last.

Rents were fixed high enough to cover damage and abuse from this class, from whom nothing was expected, and the most was made of them while they lasted. Neatness, order, cleanliness, were never dreamed of in connection with the tenant-house system, as it spread its localities from year to year; while reckless slovenliness, discontent, privation, and igno- rance were left to work out their invariable results, until the entire premises reached the level of tenant-house dilapidation, containing, but sheltering not, the miserable hordes that crowded beneath mouldering, water-rotted roofs or burrowed among the rats of clammy cellars." Yet so illogical is human greed that, at a later day, when called to account, "the proprietors frequently urged the filthy habits of the tenants as an excuse for the condition of their property, utterly losing sight of the fact that it was the tolerance of those habits which was the real evil, and that for this they themselves were alone responsible."

Still the pressure of the crowds did not abate, and in the old garden where the stolid Dutch burgher[7] grew his tulips or early cabbages a rear house was built, generally of wood, two stories high at first. Presently it was carried up another story, and another. Where two families had lived ten moved in. The front house followed suit, if the brick walls were strong enough. The question was not always asked, judging from complaints made by a contemporary witness, that the old buildings were "often carried up to a great height without regard to the strength of the foundation walls." It was rent the owner was after; nothing was said in the contract about either the safety or the com- fort of the tenants. The garden gate no longer swung on its rusty hinges. The shell-paved walk had become an alley; what the rear house had left of the garden, a "court." Plenty such are yet to be found in the Fourth Ward,[8] with here and there one of the original rear tene- ments.

Worse was to follow. It was "soon perceived by estate owners and agents of property that a greater percentage of profits could be realized by the conversion of houses and blocks into barracks, and dividing their space into smaller proportions capable of containing human life within four walls.... Blocks were rented of real estate owners, or 'purchased on time,' or taken in charge at a percentage, and held for under-letting." With the appearance of the middleman, wholly irresponsible, and utterly reck- less and unrestrained, began the era of tenement building which turned

---

[7] The prosperous middle-class Dutch inhabitant of a town or city. — ED.
[8] New York City was divided into several numbered wards for administrative and electoral purposes. — ED.

out such blocks as Gotham Court, where, in one cholera epidemic[9] that scarcely touched the clean wards, the tenants died at the rate of one hundred and ninety-five to the thousand of population; which forced the general mortality of the city up from 1 in 41.83 in 1815, to 1 in 27.33 in 1855, a year of unusual freedom from epidemic disease, and which wrung from the early organizers of the Health Department this wail: "There are numerous examples of tenement-houses in which are lodged several hundred people that have a *pro rata* allotment of ground area scarcely equal to two square yards upon the city lot, court-yards and all included." The tenement-house population had swelled to half a million souls by that time, and on the East Side, in what is still the most densely populated district in all the world, China not excluded, it was packed at the rate of 290,000 to the square mile, a state of affairs wholly unexampled. The utmost cupidity of other lands and other days had never contrived to herd much more than half that number within the same space. The greatest crowding of Old London was at the rate of 175,816. Swine roamed the streets and gutters as their principal scavengers.[10] The death of a child in a tenement was registered at the Bureau of Vital Statistics as "plainly due to suffocation in the foul air of an unventilated apartment," and the Senators, who had come down from Albany to find out what was the matter with New York, reported that "there are annually cut off from the population by disease and death enough human beings to people a city, and enough human labor to sustain it." And yet experts had testified that, as compared with uptown, rents were from twenty-five to thirty per cent. higher in the worst slums of the lower wards, with such accommodations as were enjoyed, for instance, by a "family with boarders" in Cedar Street, who fed hogs in the cellar that contained eight or ten loads of manure; or "one room 12 × 12 with five families living in it, comprising twenty persons of both sexes and all ages, with only two beds, without partition, screen, chair, or table." The rate of rent has been successfully maintained to the present day, though the hog at least has been eliminated.

Lest anybody flatter himself with the notion that these were evils of a day that is happily past and may safely be forgotten, let me mention here three very recent instances of tenement-house life that came under my

[9] Highly infectious and potentially fatal disease carried by a micro-organism that thrives in unsanitary conditions. Cholera epidemics swept through New York in 1832, 1849, 1854, and 1866. The disease remained a serious problem throughout the second half of the nineteenth century until the advent of municipal sewage systems, water purification systems, and more effective methods of street cleaning. — ED.

[10] It was not until the winter of 1867 that owners of swine were prohibited by ordinance from letting them run at large in the built-up portions of the city.

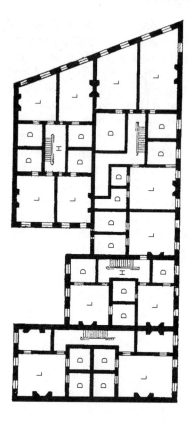

Tenement of 1863, for
Twelve Families on
Each Flat.[11]

D, dark. L, light. H, halls.

notice. One was the burning of a rear house in Mott Street, from appearances one of the original tenant-houses that made their owners rich. The fire made homeless ten families, who had paid an average of $5 a month for their mean little cubby-holes. The owner himself told me that it was *fully* insured for $800, though it brought him in $600 a year rent. He evidently considered himself especially entitled to be pitied for losing such valuable property. Another was the case of a hard-working family of man and wife, young people from the old country, who took poison together in a Crosby Street tenement because they were "tired." There

---

[11] This "unventilated and fever-breeding structure" the year after it was built was picked out by the Council of Hygiene, then just organized, and presented to the Citizens' Association of New York as a specimen "multiple domicile" in a desirable street, with the following comment: "Here are twelve living-rooms and twenty-one bedrooms, and only six of the latter have any provision or possibility for the admission of light and air, excepting through the family sitting- and living-room; being utterly dark, close, and unventilated. The living-rooms are but 10 × 12 feet; the bedrooms 6½ × 7 feet."

was no other explanation, and none was needed when I stood in the room in which they had lived. It was in the attic with sloping ceiling and a single window so far out on the roof that it seemed not to belong to the place at all. With scarcely room enough to turn around in they had been compelled to pay five dollars and a half a month in advance. There were four such rooms in that attic, and together they brought in as much as many a handsome little cottage in a pleasant part of Brooklyn. The third instance was that of a colored family of husband, wife, and baby in a wretched rear rookery in West Third Street. Their rent was eight dollars and a half for a single room on the top-story, so small that I was unable to get a photograph of it even by placing the camera outside the open door. Three short steps across either way would have measured its full extent.

There was just one excuse for the early tenement-house builders, and their successors may plead it with nearly as good right for what it is worth. "Such," says an official report, "is the lack of house-room in the city that any kind of tenement can be immediately crowded with lodgers, if there is space offered." Thousands were living in cellars. There were three hundred underground lodging-houses in the city when the Health Department was organized. Some fifteen years before that the old Baptist Church in Mulberry Street, just off Chatham Street, had been sold, and the rear half of the frame structure had been converted into tenements that with their swarming population became the scandal even of that reckless age. The wretched pile harbored no less than forty families, and the annual rate of deaths to the population was officially stated to be 75 in 1,000. These tenements were an extreme type of very many, for the big barracks had by this time spread east and west and far up the island into the sparsely settled wards. Whether or not the title was clear to the land upon which they were built was of less account than that the rents were collected. If there were damages to pay, the tenant had to foot them. Cases were "very frequent when property was in litigation, and two or three different parties were collecting rents." Of course under such circumstances "no repairs were ever made."

The climax had been reached. The situation was summed up by the Society for the Improvement of the Condition of the Poor in these words: "Crazy old buildings, crowded rear tenements in filthy yards, dark, damp basements, leaking garrets, shops, outhouses, and stables[12] converted into dwellings, though scarcely fit to shelter brutes, are habitations of thousands of our fellow-beings in this wealthy, Christian city." "The city," says its historian, Mrs. Martha Lamb, commenting on the era of aqueduct

---

[12] "A lot 50 × 60, contained twenty stables, rented for dwellings at $15 a year each; cost of the whole $600."

building between 1835 and 1845, "was a general asylum for vagrants." Young vagabonds, the natural offspring of such "home" conditions, over-ran the streets. Juvenile crime increased fearfully year by year. The Children's Aid Society[13] and kindred philanthropic organizations were yet unborn, but in the city directory was to be found the address of the "American Society for the Promotion of Education in Africa."

---

[13] Established by Charles Loring Brace in 1853, the Society's main purpose was to find foster homes in rural areas for New York's vagrant children. — ED.

Chapter II

The Awakening

The dread of advancing cholera, with the guilty knowledge of the harvest field that awaited the plague in New York's slums, pricked the conscience of the community into action soon after the close of the war.[14] A citizens' movement resulted in the organization of a Board of Health and the adoption of the "Tenement-House Act" of 1867, the first step toward remedial legislation. A thorough canvass of the tenements had been begun already in the previous year; but the cholera first, and next a scourge of small-pox,[15] delayed the work, while emphasizing the need of it, so that it was 1869 before it got fairly under way and began to tell. The dark bedroom fell under the ban first. In that year the Board ordered the cutting of more than forty-six thousand windows in interior rooms, chiefly for ventilation — for little or no light was to be had from the dark hallways. Air-shafts were unknown. The saw had a job all that summer; by early fall nearly all the orders had been carried out. Not without opposition; obstacles were thrown in the way of the officials on the one side by the owners of the tenements, who saw in every order to repair or clean up only an item of added expense to diminish their income from the rent; on the other side by the tenants themselves, who had sunk, after a generation of unavailing protest, to the level of their surroundings, and were at last content to remain there. The tenements had bred their Nemesis, a proletariat ready and able to avenge the wrongs of their crowds. Already it taxed the city heavily for the support of its jails and charities. The basis of opposition, curiously enough, was the same at both extremes; owner and tenant alike considered official interference an infringement of personal rights, and a hardship. It took long years of weary labor to make good the claim of the sunlight to such corners of the dens as it could reach at all. Not until five years after did the department succeed at last in ousting the "cave-dwellers" and closing some five hundred and fifty cellars south of Houston Street, many of them below tide-water, that had been used as living apartments. In many instances the police had to drag the tenants out by force.

The work went on; but the need of it only grew with the effort. The Sanitarians[16] were following up an evil that grew faster than they went;

---

[14] The U.S. Civil War (1861–1865). — ED.

[15] A highly contagious viral disease that, though more virulent in the colonial period, still continued to plague Americans living in nineteenth-century cities. — ED.

[16] Activists devoted to improving New York City's sanitary conditions. — ED.

like a fire, it could only be headed off, not chased, with success. Official reports, read in the churches in 1879, characterized the younger criminals as victims of low social conditions of life and unhealthy, overcrowded lodgings, brought up in "an atmosphere of actual darkness, moral and physical." This after the saw had been busy in the dark corners ten years! "If we could see the air breathed by these poor creatures in their tenements," said a well-known physician, "it would show itself to be fouler than the mud of the gutters." Little improvement was apparent despite all that had been done. "The new tenements, that have been recently built, have been usually as badly planned as the old, with dark and unhealthy rooms, often over wet cellars, where extreme overcrowding is permitted," was the verdict of one authority. These are the houses that to-day perpetuate the worst traditions of the past, and they are counted by thousands. The Five Points[17] had been cleansed, as far as the immediate neighborhood was concerned, but the Mulberry Street Bend[18] was fast outdoing it in foulness not a stone's throw away, and new centres of corruption were continually springing up and getting the upper hand whenever vigilance was relaxed for ever so short a time. It is one of the curses of the tenement-house system that the worst houses exercise a levelling influence upon all the rest, just as one bad boy in a schoolroom will spoil the whole class. It is one of the ways the evil that was "the result of forgetfulness of the poor," as the Council of Hygiene[19] mildly put it, has of avenging itself.

The determined effort to head it off by laying a strong hand upon the tenement builders that has been the chief business of the Health Board of recent years, dates from this period. The era of the air-shaft has not solved the problem of housing the poor, but it has made good use of limited opportunities. Over the new houses sanitary law exercises full control. But the old remain. They cannot be summarily torn down, though in extreme cases the authorities can order them cleared. The outrageous overcrowding, too, remains. It is characteristic of the tenements. Poverty, their badge and typical condition, invites — compels it. All efforts to abate it result only in temporary relief. As long as they exist it will exist with them. And the tenements will exist in New York forever.

To-day, what is a tenement? The law defines it as a house "occupied by three or more families, living independently and doing their cooking

---

[17] An area of New York's Lower East Side considered to be the nation's worst slum at the turn of the nineteenth century. — ED.

[18] A Lower East Side neighborhood that rivaled the squalor of the Five Points. — ED.

[19] Established by the Citizen's Association in 1864 to document, by means of extensive statistical data, the city's unsanitary living conditions. — ED.

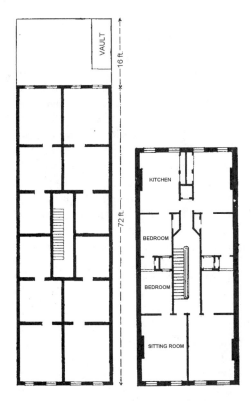

Tenement of the Old Style. Birth of the Air-Shaft.

on the premises; or by more than two families on a floor, so living and cooking and having a common right in the halls, stairways, yards, etc." That is the legal meaning, and includes flats and apartment-houses, with which we have nothing to do. In its narrower sense the typical tenement was thus described when last arraigned before the bar of public justice: "It is generally a brick building from four to six stories high on the street, frequently with a store on the first floor which, when used for the sale of liquor, has a side opening for the benefit of the inmates and to evade the Sunday law;[20] four families occupy each floor, and a set of rooms consists of one or two dark closets, used as bedrooms, with a living room twelve feet by ten. The staircase is too often a dark well in the centre of the house, and no direct through ventilation is possible, each family being separated from the other by partitions. Frequently the rear of the lot is occupied by

[20] Law prohibiting the sale of liquor on the Sabbath; also known as a "blue law." — ED.

another building of three stories high with two families on a floor." The picture is nearly as true to-day as ten years ago, and will be for a long time to come. The dim light admitted by the air-shaft shines upon greater crowds than ever. Tenements are still "good property," and the poverty of the poor man his destruction. A barrack down town where he *has to live* because he is poor brings in a third more rent than a decent flat house in Harlem. The statement once made a sensation that between seventy and eighty children had been found in one tenement. It no longer excites even passing attention, when the sanitary police report counting 101 adults and 91 children in a Crosby Street house, one of twins, built together. The children in the other, if I am not mistaken, numbered 89, a total of 180 for two tenements! Or when a midnight inspection in Mulberry Street unearths a hundred and fifty "lodgers" sleeping on filthy floors in two buildings. Spite of brown-stone trimmings, plate-glass and mosaic vestibule floors, the water does not rise in summer to the second story, while the beer flows unchecked to the all-night picnics on the roof. The saloon with the side-door and the landlord divide the prosperity of the place between them, and the tenant, in sullen submission, foots the bills.

Where are the tenements of to-day? Say rather: where are they not? In fifty years they have crept up from the Fourth Ward slums and the Five Points the whole length of the island, and have polluted the Annexed District to the Westchester line. Crowding all the lower wards, wherever business leaves a foot of ground unclaimed; strung along both rivers, like ball and chain tied to the foot of every street, and filling up Harlem with their restless, pent-up multitudes, they hold within their clutch the wealth and business of New York, hold them at their mercy in the day of mob-rule and wrath. The bullet-proof shutters, the stacks of hand-grenades, and the Gatling guns of the Sub-Treasury[21] are tacit admissions of the fact and of the quality of the mercy expected. The tenements to-day are New York, harboring three-fourths of its population. When another generation shall have doubled the census of our city, and to that vast army of workers, held captive by poverty, the very name of home shall be as a bitter mockery, what will the harvest be?

---

[21] Devised by President Van Buren in 1837 and established by Congress in 1840, the subtreasury or independent treasury system was designed to replace the services previously rendered by the collapsed Bank of the United States. Under the system, an independent treasury was based in Washington and subtreasuries were located in a number of the nation's cities. New York was the site of one of these subtreasuries. The Gatling guns Riis refers to were early examples of machine guns. — ED.

Chapter III
The Mixed Crowd

When once I asked the agent of a notorious Fourth Ward alley how many people might be living in it I was told: One hundred and forty families, one hundred Irish, thirty-eight Italian, and two that spoke the German tongue. Barring the agent herself, there was not a native-born individual in the court. The answer was characteristic of the cosmopolitan character of lower New York, very nearly so of the whole of it, wherever it runs to alleys and courts. One may find for the asking an Italian, a German, a French, African, Spanish, Bohemian, Russian, Scandinavian, Jewish, and Chinese colony. Even the Arab, who peddles "holy earth" from the Battery as a direct importation from Jerusalem, has his exclusive preserves at the lower end of Washington Street. The one thing you shall vainly ask for in the chief city of America is a distinctively American community. There is none; certainly not among the tenements. Where have they gone to, the old inhabitants? I put the question to one who might fairly be presumed to be of the number, since I had found him sighing for the "good old days" when the legend "no Irish need apply" was familiar in the advertising columns of the newspapers. He looked at me with a puzzled air. "I don't know," he said. "I wish I did. Some went to California in '49,[22] some to the war and never came back. The rest, I expect, have gone to heaven, or somewhere. I don't see them 'round here."

Whatever the merit of the good man's conjectures, his eyes did not deceive him. They are not here. In their place has come this queer conglomerate mass of heterogeneous elements, ever striving and working like whiskey and water in one glass, and with the like result: final union and a prevailing taint of whiskey. The once unwelcome Irishman has been followed in his turn by the Italian, the Russian Jew, and the Chinaman, and has himself taken a hand at opposition, quite as bitter and quite as ineffectual, against these later hordes. Wherever these have gone they have crowded him out, possessing the block, the street, the ward with their denser swarms. But the Irishman's revenge is complete. Victorious in defeat over his recent as over his more ancient foe, the one who opposed his coming no less than the one who drove him out, he dictates to both their politics, and, secure in possession of the offices, returns the native his greeting with interest, while collecting the rents of the Italian whose house he has bought with the profits of his saloon. As a landlord he is

---

[22] To reap the rewards of the California Gold Rush in 1849. — ED.

73

picturesquely autocratic. An amusing instance of his methods came under my notice while writing these lines. An inspector of the Health Department found an Italian family paying a man with a Celtic name twenty-five dollars a month for three small rooms in a ramshackle rear tenement — more than twice what they were worth — and expressed his astonishment to the tenant, an ignorant Sicilian laborer. He replied that he had once asked the landlord to reduce the rent, but he would not do it.

"Well! What did he say?" asked the inspector.

"'Damma, man!' he said; 'if you speaka thata way to me, I fira you and your things in the streeta.'" And the frightened Italian paid the rent.

In justice to the Irish landlord it must be said that like an apt pupil he was merely showing forth the result of the schooling he had received, re-enacting, in his own way, the scheme of the tenements. It is only his frankness that shocks. The Irishman does not naturally take kindly to tenement life, though with characteristic versatility he adapts himself to its conditions at once. It does violence, nevertheless, to the best that is in him, and for that very reason of all who come within its sphere soonest corrupts him. The result is a sediment, the product of more than a generation in the city's slums, that, as distinguished from the larger body of his class, justly ranks at the foot of tenement dwellers, the so-called "low Irish."

It is not to be assumed, of course, that the whole body of the population living in the tenements, of which New Yorkers are in the habit of speaking vaguely as "the poor," or even the larger part of it, is to be classed as vicious or as poor in the sense of verging on beggary.

New York's wage-earners have no other place to live, more is the pity. They are truly poor for having no better homes; waxing poorer in purse as the exorbitant rents to which they are tied, as ever was serf to soil, keep rising. The wonder is that they are not all corrupted, and speedily, by their surroundings. If, on the contrary, there be a steady working up, if not out of the slough, the fact is a powerful argument for the optimist's belief that the world is, after all, growing better, not worse, and would go far toward disarming apprehension, were it not for the steadier growth of the sediment of the slums and its constant menace. Such an impulse toward better things there certainly is. The German rag-picker of thirty years ago, quite as low in the scale as his Italian successor, is the thrifty tradesman or prosperous farmer of to-day.[23]

---

[23] The Sheriff Street Colony of rag-pickers, long since gone, is an instance in point. The thrifty Germans saved up money during years of hard work in squalor and apparently wretched poverty to buy a township in a Western State, and the whole colony moved out there in a body. There need be no doubt about their thriving there.

The Italian scavenger of our time is fast graduating into exclusive control of the corner fruit-stands, while his black-eyed boy monopolizes the boot-blacking industry in which a few years ago he was an intruder. The Irish hod-carrier[24] in the second generation has become a brick-layer, if not the Alderman of his ward, while the Chinese coolie[25] is in almost exclusive possession of the laundry business. The reason is obvious. The poorest immigrant comes here with the purpose and ambition to better himself and, given half a chance, might be reasonably expected to make the most of it. To the false plea that he prefers the squalid homes in which his kind are housed there could be no better answer. The truth is, his half chance has too long been wanting, and for the bad result he has been unjustly blamed.

As emigration from east to west follows the latitude, so does the foreign influx in New York distribute itself along certain well-defined lines that waver and break only under the stronger pressure of a more gregarious race or the encroachments of inexorable business. A feeling of dependence upon mutual effort, natural to strangers in a strange land, unacquainted with its language and customs, sufficiently accounts for this.

The Irishman is the true cosmopolitan immigrant. All-pervading, he shares his lodging with perfect impartiality with the Italian, the Greek, and the "Dutchman,"[26] yielding only to sheer force of numbers, and objects equally to them all. A map of the city, colored to designate nationalities, would show more stripes than on the skin of a zebra, and more colors than any rainbow. The city on such a map would fall into two great halves, green for the Irish prevailing in the West Side tenement districts, and blue for the Germans on the East Side. But intermingled with these ground colors would be an odd variety of tints that would give the whole the appearance of an extraordinary crazy-quilt. From down in the Sixth Ward, upon the site of the old Collect Pond that in the days of the fathers drained the hills which are no more, the red of the Italian would be seen forcing its way northward along the line of Mulberry Street to the quarter of the French purple on Bleecker Street and South Fifth Avenue, to lose itself and reappear, after a lapse of miles, in the "Little Italy" of Harlem, east of Second Avenue. Dashes of red, sharply defined, would be seen strung through the Annexed District, northward to the city

[24] Specifically a carrier of coal but more generally a term used to refer to the work done by unskilled laborers. — ED.

[25] Name Europeans gave to East Indians and Chinese engaged in hard labor. Used by Americans in a derogatory manner to refer to Chinese laborers who helped build the nation's rail system. — ED.

[26] Term used to refer to any of the several groups of Germanic peoples of Europe. — ED.

line. On the West Side the red would be seen overrunning the old Africa of Thompson Street, pushing the black of the negro rapidly uptown, against querulous but unavailing protests, occupying his home, his church, his trade and all, with merciless impartiality. There is a church in Mulberry Street that has stood for two generations as a sort of milestone of these migrations. Built originally for the worship of staid New Yorkers of the "old stock," it was engulfed by the colored tide, when the draft-riots drove the negroes out of reach of Cherry Street and the Five Points. Within the past decade the advance wave of the Italian onset reached it, and to-day the arms of United Italy adorn its front. The negroes have made a stand at several points along Seventh and Eighth Avenues; but their main body, still pursued by the Italian foe, is on the march yet, and the black mark will be found overshadowing to-day many blocks on the East Side, with One Hundredth Street as the centre, where colonies of them have settled recently.

Hardly less aggressive than the Italian, the Russian and Polish Jew, having overrun the district between Rivington and Division Streets, east of the Bowery, to the point of suffocation, is filling the tenements of the old Seventh Ward to the river front, and disputing with the Italian every foot of available space in the back alleys of Mulberry Street. The two races, differing hopelessly in much, have this in common: they carry their slums with them wherever they go, if allowed to do it. Little Italy already rivals its parent, the "Bend," in foulness. Other nationalities that begin at the bottom make a fresh start when crowded up the ladder. Happily both are manageable, the one by rabbinical, the other by the civil law. Between the dull gray of the Jew, his favorite color, and the Italian red, would be seen squeezed in on the map a sharp streak of yellow, marking the narrow boundaries of Chinatown. Dovetailed in with the German population, the poor but thrifty Bohemian might be picked out by the sombre hue of his life as of his philosophy, struggling against heavy odds in the big human bee-hives of the East Side. Colonies of his people extend northward, with long lapses of space, from below the Cooper Institute[27] more than three miles. The Bohemian is the only foreigner with any considerable representation in the city who counts no wealthy man of his race, none who has not to work hard for a living, or has got beyond the reach of the tenement.

Down near the Battery the West Side emerald would be soiled by a dirty stain, spreading rapidly like a splash of ink on a sheet of blotting paper, headquarters of the Arab tribe, that in a single year has swelled

---

[27] College located on Astor Place that was founded by Peter Cooper in 1859. Cooper Union offered tuition-free higher education to members of the working class. — ED.

from the original dozen to twelve hundred, intent, every mother's son, on trade and barter. Dots and dashes of color here and there would show where the Finnish sailors worship their djumala (God), the Greek pedlars the ancient name of their race, and the Swiss the goddess of thrift. And so on to the end of the long register, all toiling together in the galling fetters of the tenement. Were the question raised who makes the most of life thus mortgaged, who resists most stubbornly its levelling tendency — knows how to drag even the barracks upward a part of the way at least toward the ideal plane of the home — the palm must be unhesitatingly awarded the Teuton.[28] The Italian and the poor Jew rise only by compulsion. The Chinaman does not rise at all; here, as at home, he simply remains stationary. The Irishman's genius runs to public affairs rather than domestic life; wherever he is mustered in force the saloon is the gorgeous centre of political activity. The German struggles vainly to learn his trick; his Teutonic wit is too heavy, and the political ladder he raises from his saloon usually too short or too clumsy to reach the desired goal. The best part of his life is lived at home, and he makes himself a home independent of the surroundings, giving the lie to the saying, unhappily become a maxim of social truth, that pauperism and drunkenness naturally grow in the tenements. He makes the most of his tenement, and it should be added that whenever and as soon as he can save up money enough, he gets out and never crosses the threshold of one again.

Chapter IV

The Down Town Back-alleys

Down below Chatham Square, in the old Fourth Ward, where the cradle of the tenement stood, we shall find New York's Other Half at home, receiving such as care to call and are not afraid. Not all of it, to be sure, there is not room for that; but a fairly representative gathering, representative of its earliest and worst traditions. There is nothing to be afraid of. In this metropolis, let it be understood, there is no public street where the stranger may not go safely by day and by night, provided he knows how to mind his own business and is sober. His coming and going will excite little interest, unless he is suspected of being a truant officer, in

[28] Term used to refer to peoples of Germanic origin. — ED.

which case he will be impressed with the truth of the observation that the American stock is dying out for want of children. If he escapes this suspicion and the risk of trampling upon, or being himself run down by the bewildering swarms of youngsters that are everywhere or nowhere as the exigency and their quick scent of danger direct, he will see no reason for dissenting from that observation. Glimpses caught of the parents watching the youngsters play from windows or open doorways will soon convince him that the native stock is in no way involved.

Leaving the Elevated Railroad[29] where it dives under the Brooklyn Bridge at Franklin Square, scarce a dozen steps will take us where we wish to go. With its rush and roar echoing yet in our ears, we have turned the corner from prosperity to poverty. We stand upon the domain of the tenement. In the shadow of the great stone abutments the old Knicker-bocker houses linger like ghosts of a departed day. Down the winding slope of Cherry Street — proud and fashionable Cherry Hill that was — their broad steps, sloping roofs, and dormer windows are easily made out; all the more easily for the contrast with the ugly barracks that elbow them right and left. These never had other design than to shelter, at as little outlay as possible, the greatest crowds out of which rent could be wrung. They were the bad after-thought of a heedless day. The years have brought to the old houses unhonored age, a querulous second childhood that is out of tune with the time, their tenants, the neighbors, and cries out against them and against you in fretful protest in every step on their rotten floors or squeaky stairs. Good cause have they for their fretting. This one, with its shabby front and poorly patched roof, what glowing firesides, what happy children may it once have owned? Heavy feet, too often with unsteady step, for the pot-house is next door — where is it not next door in these slums? — have worn away the brown-stone steps since; the broken columns at the door have rotted away at the base. Of the handsome cornice barely a trace is left. Dirt and desolation reign in the wide hallway, and danger lurks on the stairs. Rough pine boards fence off the roomy fire-places — where coal is bought by the pail at the rate of twelve dollars a ton these have no place. The arched gateway leads no longer to a shady bower on the banks of the rushing stream, inviting to day-dreams with its gentle repose, but to a dark and nameless alley, shut in by high brick walls, cheerless as the lives of those they shelter. The wolf knocks loudly at the gate in the troubled dreams that come to this

---

[29] The elevated railroad followed the horse-drawn streetcar as the principal form of municipal mass transportation. The steam-powered trains, which traveled above city streets on elevated iron structures, preceded the electric streetcar and the subway. New York City's first elevated began operation in 1870. — ED.

At the Cradle of the Tenement. — Doorway of an Old-Fashioned Dwelling on Cherry Hill.

alley, echoes of the day's cares. A horde of dirty children play about the dripping hydrant, the only thing in the alley that thinks enough of its chance to make the most of it: it is the best it can do. These are the children of the tenements, the growing generation of the slums; this their home. From the great highway overhead, along which throbs the life-tide of two great cities, one might drop a pebble into half a dozen such alleys.

One yawns just across the street; not very broadly, but it is not to blame. The builder of the old gateway had no thought of its ever becoming a public thoroughfare. Once inside it widens, but only to make room for a big box-like building with the worn and greasy look of the slum tenement that is stamped alike on the houses and their tenants down here, even on the homeless cur that romps with the children in yonder building lot, with an air of expectant interest plainly betraying the forlorn hope that at some stage of the game a meat-bone may show up in the role of "It." Vain hope, truly! Nothing more appetizing than a bare-legged ragamuffin appears. Meat-bones, not long since picked clean, are as scarce in Blind Man's Alley as elbow-room in any Fourth Ward back-yard. The shouts of the children come hushed over the house-tops, as if apologizing for the intrusion. Few glad noises make this old alley ring. Morning and evening it echoes with the gentle, groping tap of the blind man's staff as he feels his way to the street. Blind Man's Alley bears its name for a reason. Until little more than a year ago its dark burrows harbored a colony of blind beggars, tenants of a blind landlord, old Daniel Murphy, whom every child in the ward knows, if he never heard of the President of the United States.[30] "Old Dan" made a big fortune — he told me once four hundred thousand dollars — out of his alley and the surrounding tenements, only to grow blind himself in extreme old age, sharing in the end the chief hardship of the wretched beings whose lot he had stubbornly refused to better that he might increase his wealth. Even when the Board of Health at last compelled him to repair and clean up the worst of the old buildings, under threat of driving out the tenants and locking the doors behind them, the work was accomplished against the old man's angry protests. He appeared in person before the Board to argue his case, and his argument was characteristic.

"I have made my will," he said. "My monument stands waiting for me in Calvary. I stand on the very brink of the grave, blind and helpless, and now (here the pathos of the appeal was swept under in a burst of angry indignation) do you want me to build and get skinned, skinned? These people are not fit to live in a nice house. Let them go where they can, and let my house stand."

In spite of the genuine anguish of the appeal, it was downright amusing to find that his anger was provoked less by the anticipated waste of luxury on his tenants than by distrust of his own kind, the builder. He knew intuitively what to expect. The result showed that Mr. Murphy had gauged his tenants correctly. The cleaning up process apparently destroyed the home-feeling of the alley; many of the blind people moved away and did not return. Some remained, however, and the name has clung to the place.

Some idea of what is meant by a sanitary "cleaning up" in these slums may be gained from the account of a mishap I met with once, in taking a flash-light picture of a group of blind beggars in one of the tenements down here. With unpractised hands I managed to set fire to the house. When the blinding effect of the flash had passed away and I could see

---

[30] Benjamin Harrison was president of the United States from 1889 to 1893. — ED.

once more, I discovered that a lot of paper and rags that hung on the wall were ablaze. There were six of us, five blind men and women who knew nothing of their danger, and myself, in an attic room with a dozen crooked, rickety stairs between us and the street, and as many households as helpless as the one whose guest I was all about us. The thought: how were they ever to be got out? made my blood run cold as I saw the flames creeping up the wall, and my first impulse was to bolt for the street and shout for help. The next was to smother the fire myself, and I did, with a vast deal of trouble. Afterward, when I came down to the street I told a friendly policeman of my trouble. For some reason he thought it rather a good joke, and laughed immoderately at my concern lest even then sparks should be burrowing in the rotten wall that might yet break out in flame and destroy the house with all that were in it. He told me why, when he found time to draw breath. "Why, don't you know," he said, "that house is the Dirty Spoon? It caught fire six times last winter, but it wouldn't burn. The dirt was so thick on the walls, it smothered the fire!" Which, if true, shows that water and dirt, not usually held to be harmonious elements, work together for the good of those who insure houses.

Sunless and joyless though it be, Blind Man's Alley has that which its compeers of the slums vainly yearn for. It has a pay-day. Once a year sunlight shines into the lives of its forlorn crew, past and present. In June, when the Superintendent of Out-door Poor[31] distributes the twenty thousand dollars annually allowed the poor blind by the city, in half-hearted recognition of its failure to otherwise provide for them, Blindman's Alley takes a day off and goes to "see" Mr. Blake. That night it is noisy with unwonted merriment. There is scraping of squeaky fiddles in the dark rooms, and cracked old voices sing long-forgotten songs. Even the blind landlord rejoices, for much of the money goes into his coffers.

From their perch up among the rafters Mrs. Gallagher's blind boarders might hear, did they listen, the tramp of the policeman always on duty in Gotham Court, half a stone's throw away. His beat, though it takes in but a small portion of a single block, is quite as lively as most larger patrol rounds. A double row of five-story tenements, back to back under a common roof, extending back from the street two hundred and thirty-four feet, with barred openings in the dividing wall, so that the tenants may see but cannot get at each other from the stairs, makes the "court." Alleys — one wider by a couple of feet than the other, whence the distinction

---

[31] The Out-door Poor was a program designed to aid those living in poverty in New York City. It was probably established by the County Medical Society which created the Out-door Lying-in Charity System in 1824 to provide destitute expectant mothers with free medical care. — ED.

Upstairs in Blindman's Alley.

Single and Double Alley — skirt the barracks on either side. Such, briefly, is the tenement that has challenged public attention more than any other in the whole city and tested the power of sanitary law and rule for forty years. The name of the pile is not down in the City Directory,[32] but in the public records it holds an unenviable place. It was here the

[32] A published volume listing names and addresses that preceded the telephone directory. — ED.

mortality rose during the last great cholera epidemic[33] to the unprecedented rate of 195 in 1,000 inhabitants. In its worst days a full thousand could not be packed into the court, though the number did probably not fall far short of it. Even now, under the management of men of conscience, and an agent, a King's Daughter,[34] whose practical energy, kindliness and good sense have done much to redeem its foul reputation, the swarms it shelters would make more than one fair-sized country village. The mixed character of the population, by this time about equally divided between the Celtic and the Italian stock, accounts for the iron bars and the policeman. It was an eminently Irish suggestion that the latter was to be credited to the presence of two German families in the court, who "made trouble all the time." A Chinaman whom I questioned as he hurried past the iron gate of the alley, put the matter in a different light. "Lem Ilish velly bad," he said. Gotham Court has been the entering wedge for the Italian hordes, which until recently had not attained a foothold in the Fourth Ward, but are now trailing across Chatham Street from their stronghold in "the Bend" in ever increasing numbers, seeking, according to their wont, the lowest level.

It is curious to find that this notorious block, whose name was so long synonymous with all that was desperately bad, was originally built (in 1851) by a benevolent Quaker for the express purpose of rescuing the poor people from the dreadful rookeries they were then living in. How long it continued a model tenement is not on record. It could not have been very long, for already in 1862, ten years after it was finished, a sanitary official counted 146 cases of sickness in the court, including "all kinds of infectious disease," from small-pox down, and reported that of 138 children born in it in less than three years 61 had died, mostly before they were one year old. Seven years later the inspector of the district reported to the Board of Health that "nearly ten per cent. of the population is sent to the public hospitals each year." When the alley was finally taken in hand by the authorities, and, as a first step toward its reclamation, the entire population was driven out by the police, experience dictated, as one of the first improvements to be made, the putting in of a kind of sewer-grating, so constructed, as the official report patiently puts it, "as to prevent the ingress of persons disposed to make a hiding-place" of the sewer and the cellars into which they opened. The fact was that the big

---

[33] Riis is actually referring to the epidemic of 1866, which claimed the lives of 1,137 people. The "last" cholera epidemic to hit New York was in 1892, killing 120. — ED.

[34] The King's Daughters were a group of churchwomen that established a nursery and school to help care for the children of indigent and working mothers. They also helped create a settlement house on Henry Street that was eventually named after Riis. — ED.

vaulted sewers had long been a runway for thieves — the Swamp Angels[35] — who through them easily escaped when chased by the police, as well as a storehouse for their plunder. The sewers are there to-day; in fact the two alleys are nothing but the roofs of these enormous tunnels in which a man may walk upright the full distance of the block and into the Cherry Street sewer — if he likes the fun and is not afraid of rats. Could their grimy walls speak, the big canals might tell many a startling tale. But they are silent enough, and so are most of those whose secrets they might betray. The flood-gates connecting with the Cherry Street main are closed now, except when the water is drained off. Then there were no gates, and it is on record that the sewers were chosen as a short cut habitually by residents of the court whose business lay on the line of them, near a manhole, perhaps, in Cherry Street, or at the river mouth of the big pipe when it was clear at low tide. "Me Jimmy," said one wrinkled old dame, who looked in while we were nosing about under Double Alley, "he used to go to his work along down Cherry Street that way every morning and come back at night." The associations must have been congenial. Probably "Jimmy" himself fitted into the landscape.

Half-way back from the street in this latter alley is a tenement, facing the main building, on the west side of the way, that was not originally part of the court proper. It stands there a curious monument to a Quaker's revenge, a living illustration of the power of hate to perpetuate its bitter fruit beyond the grave. The lot upon which it is built was the property of John Wood, brother of Silas, the builder of Gotham Court. He sold the Cherry Street front to a man who built upon it a tenement with entrance only from the street. Mr. Wood afterward quarrelled about the partition line with his neighbor, Alderman Mullins, who had put up a long tenement barrack on his lot after the style of the Court, and the Alderman knocked him down. Tradition records that the Quaker picked himself up with the quiet remark, "I will pay thee for that, friend Alderman," and went his way. His manner of paying was to put up the big building in the rear of 34 Cherry Street with an immense blank wall right in front of the windows of Alderman Mullins's tenements, shutting out effectually light and air from them. But as he had no access to the street from his building for many years it could not be let or used for anything, and remained vacant until it passed under the management of the Gotham Court property. Mullins's Court is there yet, and so is the Quaker's vengeful wall that has cursed the lives of thousands of innocent people since. At its farther end the alley between the two that begins inside the Cherry

[35] The name of one of the Lower East Side's many gangs. — ED.

Street tenement, six or seven feet wide, narrows down to less than two feet. It is barely possible to squeeze through; but few care to do it, for the rift leads to the jail of the Oak Street police station, and therefore is not popular with the growing youth of the district.

There is crape on the door of the Alderman's court as we pass out, and upstairs in one of the tenements preparations are making for a wake. A man lies dead in the hospital who was cut to pieces in a "can racket"[36] in the alley on Sunday. The sway of the excise law is not extended to these back alleys. It would matter little if it were. There are secret by-ways, and some it is not held worth while to keep secret, along which the "growler"[37] wanders at all hours and all seasons unmolested. It climbed the stairs so long and so often that day that murder resulted. It is nothing unusual on Cherry Street, nothing to "make a fuss" about. Not a week before, two or three blocks up the street, the police felt called upon to interfere in one of these can rackets at two o'clock in the morning, to secure peace for the neighborhood. The interference took the form of a general fusillade, during which one of the disturbers fell off the roof and was killed. There was the usual wake and nothing more was heard of it. What, indeed, was there to say?

The "Rock of Ages" is the name over the door of a low saloon that blocks the entrance to another alley, if possible more forlorn and dreary than the rest, as we pass out of the Alderman's court. It sounds like a jeer from the days, happily past, when the "wickedest man in New York" lived around the corner a little way and boasted of his title. One cannot take many steps in Cherry Street without encountering some relic of past or present prominence in the ways of crime, scarce one that does not turn up specimen bricks of the coming thief. The Cherry Street tough is all-pervading. Ask Superintendent Murray, who, as captain of the Oak Street squad, in seven months secured convictions for theft, robbery, and murder aggregating no less than five hundred and thirty years of penal servitude, and he will tell you his opinion that the Fourth Ward, even in the last twenty years, has turned out more criminals than all the rest of the city together.

But though the "Swamp Angels" have gone to their reward, their successors carry on business at the old stand as successfully, if not as boldly. There goes one who was once a shining light in thiefdom. He has reformed since, they say. The policeman on the corner, who is addicted to a professional unbelief in reform of any kind, will tell you that while on

[36] A noisy street fight in which cans are thrown about. — ED.

[37] A vessel in which beer is carried; also used to describe the carrier of such a vessel. — ED.

the Island[38] once he sailed away on a shutter, paddling along until he was picked up in Hell Gate[39] by a schooner's crew, whom he persuaded that he was a fanatic performing some sort of religious penance by his singular expedition. Over yonder, Tweed, the arch-thief, worked in a brush-shop and earned an honest living before he took to politics. As we stroll from one narrow street to another the odd contrast between the low, old-looking houses in front and the towering tenements in the back-yards grows even more striking, perhaps because we expect and are looking for it. Nobody who was not would suspect the presence of the rear houses, though they have been there long enough. Here is one seven stories high behind one with only three floors. Take a look into this Roosevelt Street alley; just about one step wide, with a five-story house on one side that gets its light and air — God help us for pitiful mockery! — from this slit between brick walls. There are no windows in the wall on the other side; it is perfectly blank. The fire-escapes of the long tenement fairly touch it; but the rays of the sun, rising, setting, or at high noon, never do. It never shone into the alley from the day the devil planned and man built it. There was once an English doctor who experimented with the sunlight in the soldiers' barracks, and found that on the side that was shut off altogether from the sun the mortality was one hundred per cent. greater than on the light side, where its rays had free access. But then soldiers are of some account, have a fixed value, if not a very high one. The people who live here have not. The horse that pulls the dirt-cart one of these laborers loads and unloads is of ever so much more account to the employer of his labor than he and all that belongs to him. Ask the owner; he will not attempt to deny it, if the horse is worth anything. The man too knows it. It is the one thought that occasionally troubles the owner of the horse in the enjoyment of his prosperity, built of and upon the successful assertion of the truth that all men are created equal.

With what a shock did the story of yonder Madison Street alley come home to New Yorkers one morning, eight or ten years ago, when a fire that broke out after the men had gone to their work swept up those narrow stairs and burned up women and children to the number of a full half score. There were fire-escapes, yes! but so placed that they could not be reached. The firemen had to look twice before they could find the opening that passes for a thoroughfare; a stout man would never venture in. Some

---

[38] Blackwell's Island. Located in the East River, the Island was the site of a hospital, asylum, workhouse, almshouse, and prison, all of which were designed to deal with the city's Other Half. — ED.

[39] A strait connecting the East River and the Long Island Sound, named for its treacherous waters. — ED.

wonderfully heroic rescues were made at that fire by people living in the adjoining tenements. Danger and trouble — of the imminent kind, not the everyday sort that excites neither interest nor commiseration — run even this common clay into heroic moulds on occasion; occasions that help us to remember that the gap that separates the man with the patched coat from his wealthy neighbor is, after all, perhaps but a tenement. Yet, what a gap! and of whose making? Here, as we stroll along Madison Street, workmen are busy putting the finishing touches to the brown-stone front of a tall new tenement. This one will probably be called an apartment house. They are carving satyrs' heads in the stone, with a crowd of gaping youngsters looking on in admiring wonder. Next door are two other tenements, likewise with brown-stone fronts, fair to look at. The youngest of the children in the group is not too young to remember how their army of tenants was turned out by the health officers because the houses had been condemned as unfit for human beings to live in. The owner was a wealthy builder who "stood high in the community." Is it only in our fancy that the sardonic leer on the stone faces seems to list that way? Or is it an introspective grin? We will not ask if the the new house belongs to the same builder. He too may have reformed.

We have crossed the boundary of the Seventh Ward. Penitentiary Row, suggestive name for a block of Cherry Street tenements, is behind us. Within recent days it has become peopled wholly with Hebrews, the overflow from Jewtown adjoining, pedlars and tailors, all of them. It is odd to read this legend from other days over the door: "No pedlars allowed in this house." These thrifty people are not only crowding into the tenements of this once exclusive district — they are buying them. The Jew runs to real estate as soon as he can save up enough for a deposit to clinch the bargain. As fast as the old houses are torn down, towering structures go up in their place, and Hebrews are found to be the builders. Here is a whole alley nicknamed after the intruder, Jews' Alley. But abuse and ridicule are not weapons to fight the Israelite with. He pockets them quietly with the rent and bides his time. He knows from experience, both sweet and bitter, that all things come to those who wait, including the houses and lands of their persecutors.

Here comes a pleasure party, as gay as any on the avenue, though the carry-all is an ash-cart. The father is the driver and he has taken his brown-legged boy for a ride. How proud and happy they both look up there on their perch! The queer old building they have halted in front of is "The Ship," famous for fifty years as a ramshackle tenement filled with the oddest crowd. No one knows why it is called "The Ship," though there is a tradition that once the river came clear up here to Hamilton Street, and boats were moored along-side it. More likely it is because it is as bewildering inside as a crazy old ship, with its ups and downs of ladders parading as stairs, and its unexpected pitfalls. But Hamilton Street, like Water Street, is not what it was. The missions drove from the latter the worst of its dives. A sailors' mission has lately made its appearance in Hamilton Street, but there are no dives there, nothing worse than the ubiquitous saloon and tough tenements.

Enough of them everywhere. Suppose we look into one? No. — Cherry Street. Be a little careful, please! The hall is dark and you might stumble over the children pitching pennies back there. Not that it would hurt them; kicks and cuffs are their daily diet. They have little else. Here where the hall turns and dives into utter darkness is a step, and another, another. A flight of stairs. You can feel your way, if you cannot see it. Close? Yes! What would you have? All the fresh air that ever enters these stairs comes from the hall-door that is forever slamming, and from the windows of dark bedrooms that in turn receive from the stairs their sole supply of the elements God meant to be free, but man deals out with such niggardly hand. That was a woman filling her pail by the hydrant you just bumped against. The sinks are in the hallway, that all the tenants may have access — and all be poisoned alike by their summer stenches. Hear the pump squeak! It is the lullaby of tenement-house babes. In summer, when a thousand thirsty throats pant for a cooling drink in this block, it is worked in vain. But the saloon, whose open door you passed in the hall, is always there. The smell of it has followed you up. Here is a door. Listen! That short hacking cough, that tiny, helpless wail — what do they mean? They mean that the soiled bow of white you saw on the door downstairs will have another story to tell — Oh! a sadly familiar story — before the day is at an end. The child is dying with measles. With half a chance it might have lived; but it had none. That dark bedroom killed it.

"It was took all of a suddint," says the mother, smoothing the throbbing little body with trembling hands. There is no unkindness in the rough voice of the man in the jumper, who sits by the window grimly smoking a clay pipe, with the little life ebbing out in his sight, bitter as his words sound: "Hush, Mary! If we cannot keep the baby, need we complain — such as we?"

Such as we! What if the words ring in your ears as we grope our way up the stairs and down from floor to floor, listening to the sounds behind the closed doors — some of quarrelling, some of coarse songs, more of profanity. They are true. When the summer heats come with their suffering they have meaning more terrible than words can tell. Come over here. Step carefully over this baby — it is a baby, spite of its rags and dirt

An Old Rear-Tenement in Roosevelt Street.

— under these iron bridges called fire-escapes, but loaded down, despite the incessant watchfulness of the firemen, with broken household goods, with wash-tubs and barrels, over which no man could climb from a fire. This gap between dingy brick-walls is the yard. That strip of smoke-colored sky up there is the heaven of these people. Do you wonder the name does not attract them to the churches? That baby's parents live in the rear tenement here. She is at least as clean as the steps we are now climbing.

There are plenty of houses with half a hundred such in. The tenement is much like the one in front we just left, only fouler, closer, darker — we will not say more cheerless. The word is a mockery. A hundred thousand people lived in rear tenements in New York last year. Here is a room neater than the rest. The woman, a stout matron with hard lines of care in her face, is at the wash-tub. "I try to keep the childer clean," she says, apologetically, but with a hopeless glance around. The spice of hot soapsuds is added to the air already tainted with the smell of boiling cabbage, of rags and uncleanliness all about. It makes an overpowering compound. It is Thursday, but patched linen is hung upon the pulley-line from the window. There is no Monday cleaning in the tenements. It is wash-day all the week round, for a change of clothing is scarce among the poor. They are poverty's honest badge, these perennial lines of rags hung out to dry, those that are not the washerwoman's professional shingle. The true line to be drawn between pauperism and honest poverty is the clothes-line. With it begins the effort to be clean that is the first and the best evidence of a desire to be honest.

What sort of an answer, think you, would come from these tenements to the question "Is life worth living?" were they heard at all in the discussion? It may be that this, cut from the last report but one of the Association for the Improvement of the Condition of the Poor,[40] a long name for a weary task, has a suggestion of it: "In the depth of winter the attention of the Association was called to a Protestant family living in a garret in a miserable tenement in Cherry Street. The family's condition was most deplorable. The man, his wife, and three small children shivering in one room through the roof of which the pitiless winds of winter whistled. The room was almost barren of furniture; the parents slept on the floor, the elder children in boxes, and the baby was swung in an old shawl attached to the rafters by cords by way of a hammock. The father, a seaman, had been obliged to give up that calling because he was in consumption, and was unable to provide either bread or fire for his little ones."

Perhaps this may be put down as an exceptional case, but one that came to my notice some months ago in a Seventh Ward tenement was typical enough to escape that reproach. There were nine in the family: husband, wife, an aged grandmother, and six children; honest, hard-working Germans, scrupulously neat, but poor. All nine lived in two rooms, one about ten feet square that served as parlor, bedroom, and

---

[40] Established by Robert M. Hartley in 1843, the Association was designed to improve the material conditions of the poor. — ED.

eating-room, the other a small hall-room made into a kitchen. The rent was seven dollars and a half a month, more than a week's wages for the husband and father, who was the only bread-winner in the family. That day the mother had thrown herself out of the window, and was carried up from the street dead. She was "discouraged," said some of the other women from the tenement, who had come in to look after the children while a messenger carried the news to the father at the shop. They went stolidly about their task, although they were evidently not without feeling for the dead woman. No doubt she was wrong in not taking life philosophically, as did the four families a city missionary found housekeeping in the four corners of one room. They got along well enough together until one of the families took a boarder and made trouble. Philosophy, according to my optimistic friend, naturally inhabits the tenements. The people who live there come to look upon death in a different way from the rest of us — do not take it as hard. He has never found time to explain how the fact fits into his general theory that life is not unbearable in the tenements. Unhappily for the philosophy of the slums, it is too apt to be of the kind that readily recognizes the saloon, always handy, as the refuge from every trouble, and shapes its practice according to the discovery.

Chapter V

The Italian in New York

Certainly a picturesque, if not very tidy, element has been added to the population in the "assisted"[41] Italian immigrant who claims so large a share of public attention, partly because he keeps coming at such a tremendous rate, but chiefly because he elects to stay in New York, or near enough for it to serve as his base of operations, and here promptly reproduces conditions of destitution and disorder which, set in the frame-work of Mediterranean exuberance, are the delight of the artist, but in a matter-of-fact American community become its danger and reproach. The reproduction is made easier in New York because he finds the material ready to hand in the worst of the slum tenements; but even where it is not he soon reduces what he does find to his own level, if allowed to

[41] An immigrant whose passage is paid for by a "sponsor," usually an employer, in return for the immigrant's labor after arrival in the United States. — ED.

follow his natural bent.[42] The Italian comes in at the bottom, and in the generation that came over the sea he stays there. In the slums he is welcomed as a tenant who "makes less trouble" than the contentious Irishman or the order-loving German, that is to say: is content to live in a pig-sty and submits to robbery at the hands of the rent-collector without murmur. Yet this very tractability makes of him in good hands, when firmly and intelligently managed, a really desirable tenant. But it is not his good fortune often to fall in with other hospitality upon his coming than that which brought him here for its own profit, and has no idea of letting go its grip upon him as long as there is a cent to be made out of him.

Recent Congressional inquiries[43] have shown the nature of the "assistance" he receives from greedy steamship agents and "bankers," who persuade him by false promises to mortgage his home, his few belongings, and his wages for months to come for a ticket to the land where plenty of work is to be had at princely wages. The padrone — the "banker" is nothing else — having made his ten per cent. out of him en route, receives him at the landing and turns him to double account as a wage-earner and a rent-payer. In each of these rôles he is made to yield a profit to his unscrupulous countryman, whom he trusts implicitly with the instinct of utter helplessness. The man is so ignorant that, as one of the sharpers who prey upon him put it once, it "would be downright sinful not to take him in." His ignorance and unconquerable suspicion of strangers dig the pit into which he falls. He not only knows no word of English, but he does not know enough to learn. Rarely only can he write his own language. Unlike the German, who begins learning English the day he lands as a matter of duty, or the Polish Jew, who takes it up as soon as he is able as an investment, the Italian learns slowly, if at all. Even his boy, born here, often speaks his native tongue indifferently. He is forced, therefore, to have constant recourse to the middle-man, who makes him pay handsomely at every turn. He hires him out to the railroad contractor, receiving a commission from the employer as well as from the laborer, and repeats the performance monthly, or as often as he can have him dismissed. In the city he contracts for his lodging, subletting to him space in the vilest tenements at extortionate rents, and sets an example that does not lack imitators. The "princely wages" have vanished with his coming,

---

[42] The process can be observed in the Italian tenements in Harlem (Little Italy), which, since their occupation by these people, have been gradually sinking to the slum level.

[43] Riis is probably referring to the Congressional inquiries conducted in 1889 on the illegal importation and use of immigrant labor. — ED.

and in their place hardships and a dollar a day, beheft with the padrone's merciless mortgage, confront him. Bred to even worse fare, he takes both as a matter of course, and, applying the maxim that it is not what one makes but what he saves that makes him rich, manages to turn the very dirt of the streets into a hoard of gold, with which he either returns to his Southern home, or brings over his family to join in his work and in his fortunes the next season.

The discovery was made by earlier explorers that there is money in New York's ash-barrel, but it was left to the genius of the padrone to develop the full resources of the mine that has become the exclusive preserve of the Italian immigrant. Only a few years ago, when rag-picking was carried on in a desultory and irresponsible sort of way, the city hired gangs of men to trim the ash-scows[44] before they were sent out to sea. The trimming consisted in levelling out the dirt as it was dumped from the carts, so that the scow might be evenly loaded. The men were paid a dollar and a half a day, kept what they found that was worth having, and allowed the swarms of Italians who hung about the dumps to do the heavy work for them, letting them have their pick of the loads for their trouble. To-day Italians contract for the work, paying large sums to be permitted to do it. The city received not less than $80,000 last year for the sale of this privilege to the contractors, who in addition have to pay gangs of their countrymen for sorting out the bones, rags, tin cans and other waste that are found in the ashes and form the staples of their trade and their sources of revenue. The effect has been vastly to increase the power of the padrone, or his ally, the contractor, by giving him exclusive control of the one industry in which the Italian was formerly an independent "dealer," and reducing him literally to the plane of the dump. Whenever the back of the sanitary police is turned, he will make his home in the filthy burrows where he works by day, sleeping and eating his meals under the dump, on the edge of slimy depths and amid surroundings full of unutterable horror. The city did not bargain to house, though it is content to board, him so long as he can make the ash-barrels yield the food to keep him alive, and a vigorous campaign is carried on at intervals against these unlicensed dump settlements; but the temptation of having to pay no rent is too strong, and they are driven from one dump only to find lodgement under another a few blocks farther up or down the river. The fiercest warfare is waged over the patronage of the dumps by rival factions represented by opposing contractors, and it has happened that the defeated party has endeavored to capture by strategy what he failed to carry

---

[44] Boats on which waste was stored and transported. — ED.

In the Home of an Italian Rag-Picker, Jersey Street.

by assault. It augurs unsuspected adaptability in the Italian to our system of self-government that these rivalries have more than once been suspected of being behind the sharpening of city ordinances, that were apparently made in good faith to prevent meddling with the refuse in the ash-barrels or in transit.

Did the Italian always adapt himself as readily to the operation of the civil law as to the manipulation of political "pull" on occasion, he would save himself a good deal of unnecessary trouble. Ordinarily he is easily enough governed by authority — always excepting Sunday, when he settles down to a game of cards and lets loose all his bad passions. Like the Chinese, the Italian is a born gambler. His soul is in the game from the moment the cards are on the table, and very frequently his knife is in it too before the game is ended. No Sunday has passed in New York since "the Bend" became a suburb of Naples without one or more of these murderous affrays coming to the notice of the police. As a rule that happens only when the man the game went against is either dead or so badly wounded as to require instant surgical help. As to the other, unless he be caught red-handed, the chances that the police will ever get him are slim indeed. The wounded man can seldom be persuaded to betray him. He wards off all inquiries with a wicked "I fix him myself," and there the matter rests until he either dies or recovers. If the latter, the community hears after a while of another Italian affray, a man stabbed in a quarrel, dead or dying, and the police know that "he" has been fixed, and the account squared.

With all his conspicuous faults, the swarthy Italian immigrant has his redeeming traits. He is as honest as he is hot-headed. There are no Italian burglars in the Rogues' Gallery;[45] the ex-brigand toils peacefully with pickaxe and shovel on American ground. His boy occasionally shows, as a pick-pocket, the results of his training with the toughs of the Sixth Ward slums. The only criminal business to which the father occasionally lends his hand, outside of murder, is a bunco game,[46] of which his confiding countrymen, returning with their hoard to their native land, are the victims. The women are faithful wives and devoted mothers. Their vivid and picturesque costumes lend a tinge of color to the otherwise dull monotony of the slums they inhabit. The Italian is gay, lighthearted and, if his fur is not stroked the wrong way, inoffensive as a child. His worst offence is that he keeps the stale-beer dives.[47] Where his headquarters is, in the Mulberry Street Bend, these vile dens flourish and gather about them all the wrecks, the utterly wretched, the hopelessly lost, on the lowest slope of depraved humanity. And out of their misery he makes a profit.

[45] Collection of photographs of criminals kept at police headquarters. See page 210. Riis took these two photographs from the Rogues' Gallery. — ED.

[46] A con-game. — ED.

[47] Saloon in which cheap beer was sold. — ED.

Chapter VI

The Bend

Where Mulberry Street crooks like an elbow within hail of the old depravity of the Five Points, is "the Bend," foul core of New York's slums. Long years ago the cows coming home from the pasture trod a path over this hill. Echoes of tinkling bells linger there still, but they do not call up memories of green meadows and summer fields; they proclaim the home-coming of the rag-picker's cart. In the memory of man the old cow-path has never been other than a vast human pig-sty. There is but one "Bend" in the world, and it is enough. The city authorities, moved by the angry protests of ten years of sanitary reform effort, have decided that it is too much and must come down. Another Paradise Park[48] will take its place and let in sunlight and air to work such transformation as at the Five Points, around the corner of the next block. Never was change more urgently needed. Around "the Bend" cluster the bulk of the tenements that are stamped as altogether bad, even by the optimists of the Health Department. Incessant raids cannot keep down the crowds that make them their home. In the scores of back alleys, of stable lanes and hidden byways, of which the rent collector alone can keep track, they share such shelter as the ramshackle structures afford with every kind of abomination rifled from the dumps and ash-barrels of the city. Here, too, shunning the light, skulks the unclean beast of dishonest idleness. "The Bend" is the home of the tramp as well as the rag-picker.

It is not much more than twenty years since a census of "the Bend" district returned only twenty-four of the six hundred and nine tenements as in decent condition. Three-fourths of the population of the "Bloody Sixth" Ward[49] were then Irish. The army of tramps that grew up after the disbandment of the armies in the field, and has kept up its muster-roll, together with the in-rush of the Italian tide, have ever since opposed a stubborn barrier to all efforts at permanent improvement. The more that has been done, the less it has seemed to accomplish in the way of real relief, until it has at last become clear that nothing short of entire demolition will ever prove of radical benefit. Corruption could not have chosen ground for its stand with better promise of success. The whole district is a maze of narrow, often unsuspected passageways — necessarily, for there is scarce a lot that has not two, three, or four tenements upon

---

[48] Park built in the run-down environs of Paradise Square. — ED.
[49] One of New York's most violent districts. — ED.

it, swarming with unwholesome crowds. What a birds-eye view of "the Bend" would be like is a matter of bewildering conjecture. Its everyday appearance, as seen from the corner of Bayard Street on a sunny day, is one of the sights of New York.

Bayard Street is the high road to Jewtown across the Bowery, picketed from end to end with the outposts of Israel. Hebrew faces, Hebrew signs, and incessant chatter in the queer lingo that passes for Hebrew on the East Side attend the curious wanderer to the very corner of Mulberry Street. But the moment he turns the corner the scene changes abruptly. Before him lies spread out what might better be the market-place in some town in Southern Italy than a street in New York — all but the houses; they are still the same old tenements of the unromantic type. But for once they do not make the foreground in a slum picture from the American metropolis. The interest centres not in them, but in the crowd they shelter only when the street is not preferable, and that with the Italian is only when it rains or he is sick. When the sun shines the entire population seeks the street, carrying on its household work, its bargaining, its love-making on street or sidewalk, or idling there when it has nothing better to do, with the reverse of the impulse that makes the Polish Jew coop himself up in his den with the thermometer at stewing heat. Along the curb women sit in rows, young and old alike with the odd head-covering, pad or turban, that is their badge of servitude — her's to bear the burden as long as she lives — haggling over baskets of frowsy weeds, some sort of salad probably, stale tomatoes, and oranges not above suspicion. Ash-barrels serve them as counters, and not infrequently does the arrival of the official cart en route for the dump cause a temporary suspension of trade until the barrels have been emptied and restored. Hucksters and pedlars' carts make two rows of booths in the street itself, and along the houses is still another — a perpetual market doing a very lively trade in its own queer staples, found nowhere on American ground save in "the Bend." Two old hags, camping on the pavement, are dispensing stale bread, baked not in loaves, but in the shape of big wreaths like exaggerated crullers, out of bags of dirty bed-tick. There is no use disguising the fact: they look like and they probably are old mattresses mustered into service under the pressure of a rush of trade. Stale bread was the one article the health officers, after a raid on the market, once reported as "not unwholesome." It was only disgusting. Here is a brawny butcher, sleeves rolled up above the elbows and clay pipe in mouth, skinning a kid that hangs from his hook. They will tell you with a laugh at the Elizabeth Street police station that only a few days ago when a dead goat had been reported lying in Pell Street it was mysteriously missing by the time the offal-cart came to take it away. It turned out that an Italian had carried it off in his sack to a wake or feast of some sort in one of the back alleys.

On either side of the narrow entrance to Bandit's Roost, one of the most notorious of these, is a shop that is a fair sample of the sort of invention necessity is the mother of in "the Bend." It is not enough that trucks and ash-barrels have provided four distinct lines of shops that are not down on the insurance maps, to accommodate the crowds. Here have the very hallways been made into shops. Three feet wide by four deep, they have just room for one, the shop-keeper, who, himself within, does his business outside, his wares displayed on a board hung across what was once the hall door. Back of the rear wall of this unique shop a hole has been punched from the hall into the alley and the tenants go that way. One of the shops is a "tobacco bureau,"[50] presided over by an unknown saint, done in yellow and red — there is not a shop, a stand, or an ash-barrel doing duty for a counter, that has not its patron saint — the other is a fish-stand full of slimy, odd-looking creatures, fish that never swam in American waters, or if they did, were never seen on an American fish-stand, and snails. Big, awkward sausages, anything but appetizing, hang in the grocer's door-way, knocking against the customer's head as if to remind him that they are there waiting to be bought. What they are I never had the courage to ask. Down the street comes a file of women carrying enormous bundles of fire-wood on their heads, loads of decaying vegetables from the market wagons in their aprons, and each a baby at the breast supported by a sort of sling that prevents it from tumbling down. The women do all the carry-ing, all the work one sees going on in "the Bend." The men sit or stand in the streets, on trucks, or in the open doors of the saloons smoking black clay pipes, talking and gesticulating as if forever on the point of coming to blows. Near a particularly boisterous group, a really pretty girl with a string of amber beads twisted artlessly in the knot of her raven hair has been bargaining long and earnestly with an old granny, who presides over a wheel-barrow load of second-hand stockings and faded cotton yarn, industriously darning the biggest holes while she extols the virtues of her stock. One of the rude swains, with patched overalls tucked into his boots, to whom the girl's eyes have strayed more than once, steps up and gallantly offers to pick her out the handsomest pair, whereat she laughs and pushes him away with a gesture which he interprets as an invitation to stay; and he does, evidently to the satisfaction of the beldame, who forth-with raises her prices fifty per cent. without being detected by the girl.

---

[50] Small shop that sells tobacco products and other sundries. — ED.

The Bend.

Red bandannas and yellow kerchiefs are everywhere; so is the Italian tongue, infinitely sweeter than the harsh gutturals of the Russian Jew around the corner. So are the "ristorantes" of innumerable Pasquales; half of the people in "the Bend" are christened Pasquale, or get the name in some other way. When the police do not know the name of an escaped murderer, they guess at Pasquale and send the name out on alarm; in nine cases out of ten it fits. So are the "banks" that hang out their shingle as tempting bait on every hand. There are half a dozen in the single block, steamship agencies, employment offices, and savings-banks, all in one. So are the toddling youngsters, bow-legged half of them, and so are no end of mothers, present and prospective, some of them scarce yet in their teens. Those who are not in the street are hanging half way out of the windows, shouting at some one below. All "the Bend" must be, if not altogether, at least half out of doors when the sun shines.

In the street, where the city wields the broom, there is at least an effort at cleaning up. There has to be, or it would be swamped in filth overrunning from the courts and alleys where the rag-pickers live. It requires more than ordinary courage to explore these on a hot day. The undertaker has to do it then, the police always. Right here, in this tenement on the east side of the street, they found little Antonia Candia, victim of fiendish cruelty, "covered," says the account found in the records of the Society for the Prevention of Cruelty to Children, "with sores, and her hair matted with dried blood." Abuse is the normal condition of "the Bend," murder its everyday crop, with the tenants not always the criminals. In this block between Bayard, Park, Mulberry, and Baxter Streets, "the Bend" proper, the late Tenement House Commission counted 155 deaths of children[51] in a specimen year (1882). Their per centage of the total mortality in the block was 68.28, while for the whole city the proportion was only 46.20. The infant mortality in any city or place as compared with the whole number of deaths is justly considered a good barometer of its general sanitary condition. Here, in this tenement, No. $59\frac{1}{2}$, next to Bandit's Roost, fourteen persons died that year, and eleven of them were children; in No. 61 eleven, and eight of them not yet five years old. According to the records in the Bureau of Vital Statistics only thirty-nine people lived in No. $59\frac{1}{2}$ in the year 1888, nine of them little children. There were five baby funerals in that house the same year. Out of the alley itself, No. 59, nine dead were carried in 1888, five in baby coffins. Here is the record of the year for the whole block, as furnished by the Registrar of Vital Statistics, Dr. Roger S. Tracy:

Deaths and Death-rates in 1888 on Baxter and Mulberry Streets, between Park and Bayard Streets

	POPULATION			DEATH			DEATH-RATE		
	Five years old and over	Under five years	Total	Five years old and over	Under five years	Total	Five years old and over	Under five years	General
Baxter Street	1,918	315	2,233	26	46	72	13.56	146.02	32.24
Mulberry Street	2,788	629	3,417	44	86	130	15.78	136.70	38.05
Total	4,706	944	5,650	70	132	202	14.87	139.83	35.75

The general death-rate for the whole city that year was 26.27.

[51] The term child means in the mortality tables a person under five years of age. Children five years old and over figure in the tables as adults.

Bandits' Roost.

These figures speak for themselves, when it is shown that in the model tenement across the way at Nos. 48 and 50, where the same class of people live in greater swarms (161, according to the record), but under good management, and in decent quarters, the hearse called that year only twice, once for a baby. The agent of the Christian people who built that tenement will tell you that Italians are good tenants, while the owner of the alley will oppose every order to put his property in repair with the claim that they are the worst of a bad lot. Both are right, from their different stand-points. It is the stand-point that makes the difference — and the tenant.

What if I were to tell you that this alley, and more tenement property in "the Bend," all of it notorious for years as the vilest and worst to be found anywhere, stood associated on the tax-books all through the long struggle to make its owners responsible, which has at last resulted in a qualified victory for the law, with the name of an honored family, one of the "oldest and best," rich in possessions and in influence, and high in the councils of the city's government? It would be but the plain truth. Nor would it be the only instance by very many that stand recorded on the Health Department's books of a kind that has come near to making the name of landlord as odious in New York as it has become in Ireland.

Bottle Alley is around the corner in Baxter Street; but it is a fair specimen of its kind, wherever found. Look into any of these houses, everywhere the same piles of rags, of malodorous bones and musty paper, all of which the sanitary police flatter themselves they have banished to the dumps and the warehouses. Here is a "flat" of "parlor" and two pitch-dark coops called bedrooms. Truly, the bed is all there is room for. The family tea-kettle is on the stove, doing duty for the time being as a wash-boiler. By night it will have returned to its proper use again, a practical illustration of how poverty in "the Bend" makes both ends meet. One, two, three beds are there, if the old boxes and heaps of foul straw can be called by that name; a broken stove with crazy pipe from which the smoke leaks at every joint, a table of rough boards propped up on boxes, piles of rubbish in the corner. The closeness and smell are appalling. How many people sleep here? The woman with the red bandanna shakes her head sullenly, but the bare-legged girl with the bright face counts on her fingers — five, six!

"Six, sir!" Six grown people and five children.

"Only five," she says with a smile, swathing the little one on her lap in its cruel bandage. There is another in the cradle — actually a cradle. And how much the rent?

Nine and a half, and "please, sir! he won't put the paper on."

"He" is the landlord. The "paper" hangs in musty shreds on the wall.

Well do I recollect the visit of a health inspector to one of these tenements on a July day when the thermometer outside was climbing high in the nineties; but inside, in that awful room, with half a dozen persons washing, cooking, and sorting rags, lay the dying baby alongside the stove, where the doctor's thermometer ran up to 115°! Perishing for the want of a breath of fresh air in this city of untold charities! Did not the manager of the Fresh Air Fund[52] write to the pastor of an Italian Church only last year[53] that "no one asked for Italian children," and hence he could not send any to the country?

Half a dozen blocks up Mulberry Street there is a rag-picker's settlement, a sort of overflow from "the Bend," that exists to-day in all its pristine nastiness. Something like forty families are packed into five old two-story and attic houses that were built to hold five, and out in the yards additional crowds are, or were until very recently, accommodated in sheds built of all sorts of old boards and used as drying racks for the Italian tenants' "stock." I found them empty when I visited the settlement while writing this. The last two tenants had just left. Their fate was characteristic. The "old man," who lived in the corner coop, with barely room to crouch beside the stove — there would not have been room for him to sleep had not age crooked his frame to fit his house — had been taken to the "crazy house," and the woman who was his neighbor and had lived in her shed for years had simply disappeared. The agent and the other tenants "guessed," doubtless correctly, that she might be found on the "island," but she was decrepit anyhow from rheumatism, and "not much good," and no one took the trouble to inquire for her. They had all they could do attending to their own business and raising the rent. No wonder; I found that for one front room and two "bedrooms" in the shameful old wrecks of buildings the tenant was paying $10 a month, for the back-room and one bedroom $9, and for the attic rooms, according to size, from $3.75 to $5.50.

There is a standing quarrel between the professional — I mean now the official — sanitarian and the unsalaried agitator for sanitary reform over the question of overcrowded tenements. The one puts the number a little vaguely at four or five hundred, while the other asserts that there are thirty-two thousand, the whole number of houses classed as tenements at the census of two years ago, taking no account of the better kind of flats. It depends on the angle from which one sees it which is right. At best the term overcrowding is a relative one, and the scale of official measurement conveniently sliding. Under the pressure of the Italian influx the standard of breathing space required for an adult by the health officers has been cut down from six to four hundred cubic feet. The "needs of the situation" is their plea, and no more perfect argument could be advanced for the reformer's position.

It is in "the Bend" the sanitary policeman locates the bulk of his four hundred, and the sanitary reformer gives up the task in despair. Of its

<hr>

[52] Organization established in 1877 by Willard Parsons that offered rural summer vacations to impoverished city children. — ED.

[53] See City Mission Report, February, 1890, page 77.

Bottle Alley.

vast homeless crowds the census takes no account. It is their instinct to shun the light, and they cannot be corralled in one place long enough to be counted. But the houses can, and the last count showed that in "the Bend" district, between Broadway and the Bowery and Canal and Chatham Streets, in a total of four thousand three hundred and sixty-seven "apartments" only nine were for the moment vacant, while in the old

Lodgers in a Crowded Bayard Street Tenement — "Five Cents a Spot."

"Africa," west of Broadway, that receives the overflow from Mulberry Street and is rapidly changing its character, the notice "standing room only" is up. Not a single vacant room was found there. Nearly a hundred and fifty "lodgers" were driven out of two adjoining Mulberry Street tenements, one of them aptly named "the House of Blazes," during that census. What squalor and degradation inhabit these dens the health officers know. Through the long summer days their carts patrol "the Bend," scattering disinfectants in streets and lanes, in sinks and cellars, and hidden hovels where the tramp burrows. From midnight till far into the small hours of the morning the policeman's thundering rap on closed doors is heard, with his stern command, *"Apri port'!"*[54] on his rounds gathering evidence of illegal overcrowding. The doors are opened unwill-

[54] "Open the door!" (French) — ED.

ingly enough — but the order means business, and the tenant knows it even if he understands no word of English — upon such scenes as the one presented in the picture. It was photographed by flashlight on just such a visit. In a room not thirteen feet either way slept twelve men and women, two or three in bunks set in a sort of alcove, the rest on the floor. A kerosene lamp burned dimly in the fearful atmosphere, probably to guide other and later arrivals to their "beds," for it was only just past midnight. A baby's fretful wail came from an adjoining hall-room, where, in the semi-darkness, three recumbent figures could be made out. The "apartment" was one of three in two adjoining buildings we had found, within half an hour, similarly crowded. Most of the men were lodgers, who slept there for five cents a spot.

Another room on the top floor, that had been examined a few nights before, was comparatively empty. There were only four persons in it, two men, an old woman, and a young girl. The landlord opened the door with alacrity, and exhibited with a proud sweep of his hand the sacrifice he had made of his personal interests to satisfy the law. Our visit had been anticipated. The policeman's back was probably no sooner turned than the room was reopened for business.

Chapter VII

A Raid on the Stale-beer Dives

Midnight roll-call was over in the Elizabeth Street police-station, but the reserves were held under orders. A raid was on foot, but whether on the Chinese fan-tan games,[55] on the opium joints of Mott and Pell Streets, or on dens of even worse character, was a matter of guess-work in the men's room. When the last patrolman had come in from his beat, all doubt was dispelled by the brief order "To the Bend!" The stale-beer dives were the object of the raid. The policemen buckled their belts tighter, and with expressive grunts of disgust took up their march toward Mulberry Street. Past the heathen temples[56] of Mott Street — there was some fun to be gotten out of a raid *there* — they trooped, into "the Bend," sending here and there a belated tramp scurrying in fright toward healthier quarters,

---

[55] Chinese gambling game in which objects are placed under a bowl and bets are made on the number of objects remaining after the total is counted off in fours. — ED.

[56] Chinese houses of worship. — ED.

and halted at the mouth of one of the hidden alleys. Squads were told off and sent to make a simultaneous descent on all the known tramps' burrows in the block. Led by the sergeant, ours — I went along as a kind of war correspondent — groped its way in single file through the narrow rift between slimy walls to the tenements in the rear. Twice during our trip we stumbled over tramps, both women, asleep in the passage. They were quietly passed to the rear, receiving sundry prods and punches on the trip, and headed for the station in the grip of a policeman as a sort of advance guard of the coming army. After what seemed half a mile of groping in the dark we emerged finally into the alley proper, where light escaping through the cracks of closed shutters on both sides enabled us to make out the contour of three rickety frame tenements. Snatches of ribald songs and peals of coarse laughter reached us from now this, now that of the unseen burrows.

"School is in," said the Sergeant drily as we stumbled down the worn steps of the next cellar-way. A kick of his boot-heel sent the door flying into the room.

A room perhaps a dozen feet square, with walls and ceiling that might once have been clean — assuredly the floor had not in the memory of man, if indeed there was other floor than hard-trodden mud — but were now covered with a brown crust that, touched with the end of a club, came off in shuddering showers of crawling bugs, revealing the blacker filth beneath. Grouped about a beer-keg that was propped on the wreck of a broken chair, a foul and ragged host of men and women, on boxes, benches, and stools. Tomato-cans filled at the keg were passed from hand to hand. In the centre of the group a sallow, wrinkled hag, evidently the ruler of the feast, dealt out the hideous stuff. A pile of copper coins rattled in her apron, the very pennies received with such showers of blessings upon the giver that afternoon; the faces of some of the women were familiar enough from the streets as those of beggars forever whining for a penny, "to keep a family from starving." Their whine and boisterous hilarity were alike hushed now. In sullen, cowed submission they sat, evidently knowing what to expect. At the first glimpse of the uniform in the open door some in the group, customers with a record probably, had turned their heads away to avoid the searching glance of the officer; while a few, less used to such scenes, stared defiantly.

A single stride took the sergeant into the middle of the room, and with a swinging blow of his club he knocked the faucet out of the keg and the half-filled can from the boss hag's hand. As the contents of both splashed upon the floor, half a dozen of the group made a sudden dash, and with shoulders humped above their heads to shield their skulls against the dreaded locust[57] broke for the door. They had not counted upon the policemen outside. There was a brief struggle, two or three heavy thumps, and the runaways were brought back to where their comrades crouched in dogged silence.

"Thirteen!" called the sergeant, completing his survey. "Take them out. 'Revolvers' all but one. Good for six months on the island, the whole lot." The exception was a young man not much if any over twenty, with a hard look of dissipation on his face. He seemed less unconcerned than the rest, but tried hard to make up for it by putting on the boldest air he could. "Come down early," commented the officer, shoving him along with his stick. "There is need of it. They don't last long at this. That stuff is brewed to kill at long range."

At the head of the cellar-steps we encountered a similar procession from farther back in the alley, where still another was forming to take up its march to the station. Out in the street was heard the tramp of the hosts already pursuing that well-trodden path, as with a fresh complement of men we entered the next stale-beer alley. There were four dives in one cellar here. The filth and the stench were utterly unbearable; even the sergeant turned his back and fled after scattering the crowd with his club and starting them toward the door. The very dog in the alley preferred the cold flags[58] for a berth to the stifling cellar. We found it lying outside. Seventy-five tramps, male and female, were arrested in the four small rooms. In one of them, where the air seemed thick enough to cut with a knife, we found a woman, a mother with a new-born babe on a heap of dirty straw. She was asleep and was left until an ambulance could be called to take her to the hospital.

Returning to the station with this batch, we found every window in the building thrown open to the cold October wind, and the men from the sergeant down smoking the strongest cigars that could be obtained by way of disinfecting the place. Two hundred and seventy-five tramps had been jammed into the cells to be arraigned next morning in the police court on the charge of vagrancy, with the certain prospect of six months "on the Island." Of the sentence at least they were sure. As to the length of the men's stay the experienced official at the desk was sceptical, it being then within a month of an important election. If tramps have nothing else to call their own they have votes, and votes that are for sale cheap for cash. About election time this gives them a "pull," at least by proxy. The sergeant observed, as if it were the most natural thing in the

---

[57] An alcoholic beverage that combines liquor and snuff, specifically beer and cigar ash. — ED.

[58] Flagstones. — ED.

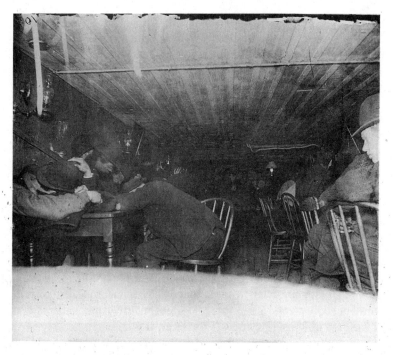

An All-Night Two-Cent Restaurant, in "The Bend."

world, that he had more than once seen the same tramp sent to Black-well's Island twice in twenty-four hours for six months at a time.

As a thief never owns to his calling, however devoid of moral scruples, preferring to style himself a speculator, so this real home-product of the slums, the stale-beer dive, is known about "the Bend" by the more dignified name of the two-cent restaurant. Usually, as in this instance, it is in some cellar giving on a back alley. Doctored, unlicensed beer is its chief ware. Sometimes a cup of "coffee" and a stale roll may be had for two cents. The men pay the score. To the women — unutterable horror of the suggestion — the place is free. The beer is collected from the kegs put on the sidewalk by the saloon-keeper to await the brewer's cart, and is touched up with drugs to put a froth on it. The privilege to sit all night on a chair, or sleep on a table, or in a barrel, goes with each round of drinks. Generally an Italian, sometimes a negro, occasionally a woman, "runs" the dive. Their customers, alike homeless and hopeless in their utter wretchedness, are the professional tramps, and these only. The meanest thief is infinitely above the stale-beer level. Once upon that plane there is no escape. To sink below it is impossible; no one ever rose from it. One night spent in a stale-beer dive is like the traditional putting on of the uniform of the caste, the discarded rags of an old tramp. That stile once crossed, the lane has no longer a turn; and contrary to the proverb, it is usually not long either.

With the gravitation of the Italian tramp landlord toward the old stronghold of the African on the West Side, a share of the stale-beer traffic has left "the Bend;" but its headquarters will always remain there, the real home of trampdom, just as Fourteenth Street is its limit. No real tramp crosses that frontier after nightfall and in the daytime only to beg. Repulsive as the business is, its profits to the Italian dive-keeper are considerable; in fact, barring a slight outlay in the ingredients that serve to give "life" to the beer-dregs, it is all profit. The "banker" who curses the Italian colony does not despise taking a hand in it, and such a thing as a stale-beer trust on a Mulberry Street scale may yet be among the possibilities. One of these bankers, who was once known to the police as the keeper of one notorious stale-beer dive and the active backer of others, is to-day an extensive manufacturer of macaroni, the owner of several big tenements and other real estate; and the capital, it is said, has all come out of his old business. Very likely it is true.

On hot summer nights it is no rare experience when exploring the worst of the tenements in "the Bend" to find the hallways occupied by rows of "sitters," tramps whom laziness or hard luck has prevented from earning enough by their day's "labor" to pay the admission fee to a stale-beer dive, and who have their reasons for declining the hospitality of the police station lodging-rooms. Huddled together in loathsome files, they squat there over night, or until an inquisitive policeman breaks up the congregation with his club, which in Mulberry Street has always free swing. At that season the woman tramp predominates. The men, some of them at least, take to the railroad track and to camping out when the nights grow warm, returning in the fall to prey on the city and to recruit their ranks from the lazy, the shiftless, and the unfortunate. Like a foul loadstone, "the Bend" attracts and brings them back, no matter how far they have wandered. For next to idleness the tramp loves rum; next to rum stale beer, its equivalent of the gutter. And the first and last go best together.

As "sitters" they occasionally find a job in the saloons about Chatham and Pearl Streets on cold winter nights, when the hallway is not practicable, that enables them to pick up a charity drink now and then and a bite of an infrequent sandwich. The barkeeper permits them to sit about the stove and by shivering invite the sympathy of transient customers. The dodge works well, especially about Christmas and election time, and the sitters are able to keep comfortably filled up to the advantage of their host. But to look thoroughly miserable they must keep awake. A tramp placidly dozing at the fire would not be an object of sympathy. To make sure that they do keep awake, the wily bartender makes them sit constantly swinging one foot like the pendulum of a clock. When it stops the slothful "sitter" is roused with a kick and "fired out." It is said by those who profess to know that habit has come to the rescue of oversleepy tramps and that the old rounders can swing hand or foot in their sleep without betraying themselves. In some saloons "sitters" are let in at these seasons in fresh batches every hour.

On one of my visits to "the Bend" I came across a particularly ragged and disreputable tramp, who sat smoking his pipe on the rung of a ladder with such evident philosophic contentment in the busy labor of a score of rag-pickers all about him, that I bade him sit for a picture, offering him ten cents for the job. He accepted the offer with hardly a nod, and sat patiently watching me from his perch until I got ready for work. Then he took the pipe out of his mouth and put it in his pocket, calmly declaring that it was not included in the contract, and that it was worth a quarter to have it go in the picture. The pipe, by the way, was of clay, and of the two-for-a-cent kind. But I had to give in. The man, scarce ten seconds employed at honest labor, even at sitting down, at which he was an undoubted expert, had gone on strike. He knew his rights and the value of "work," and was not to be cheated out of either.

Whence these tramps, and why the tramping? are questions oftener asked than answered. Ill-applied charity and idleness answer the first query. They are the whence, and to a large extent the why also. Once started on the career of a tramp, the man keeps to it because it is the laziest. Tramps and toughs profess the same doctrine, that the world owes them a living, but from stand-points that tend in different directions. The tough does not become a tramp, save in rare instances, when old and broken down. Even then usually he is otherwise disposed of. The devil has various ways of taking care of his own. Nor is the tramps' army recruited from any certain class. All occupations and most grades of society yield to it their contingent of idleness. Occasionally, from one cause or another, a recruit of a better stamp is forced into the ranks; but the first acceptance of alms puts a brand on the able-bodied man which his moral nature rarely holds out to efface. He seldom recovers his lost caste. The evolution is gradual, keeping step with the increasing shabbiness of his clothes and corresponding loss of self-respect, until he reaches the bottom in "the Bend."

The Tramp.

Of the tough the tramp doctrine that the world owes him a living makes a thief; of the tramp a coward. Numbers only make him bold unless he has to do with defenceless women. In the city the policemen keep him straight enough. The women rob an occasional clothesline when no one is looking, or steal the pail and scrubbing brush with which they are set to clean up in the station-house lodging-rooms after their night's sleep. At the police station the roads of the tramp and the tough again converge.

In mid-winter, on the coldest nights, the sanitary police corral the tramps here and in their lodging-houses and vaccinate them, despite their struggles and many oaths that they have recently been "scraped." The station-house is the sieve that sifts out the chaff from the wheat, if there be any wheat there. A man goes from his first night's sleep on the hard slab of a police station lodging-room to a deck-hand's berth on an outgoing steamer, to the recruiting office, to any work that is honest, or he goes "to the devil or the dives, same thing," says my friend, the Sergeant, who knows.

Chapter VIII

The Cheap Lodging-houses

When it comes to the question of numbers with this tramps' army, another factor of serious portent has to be taken into account: the cheap lodging-houses. In the caravanseries[59] that line Chatham Street and the Bowery, harboring nightly a population as large as that of many a thriving town, a home-made article of tramp and thief is turned out that is attracting the increasing attention of the police, and offers a field for the missionary's labors beside which most others seem of slight account. Within a year they have been stamped as nurseries of crime by the chief of the Secret Police,[60] the sort of crime that feeds especially on idleness and lies ready to the hand of fatal opportunity. In the same strain one of the justices on the police court bench sums up his long experience as a committing magistrate: "The ten-cent lodging-houses more than counter-balance the good done by the free reading-room, lectures, and all other agencies of reform. Such lodging-houses have caused more destitution, more beggary and crime than any other agency I know of." A very slight acquaintance with the subject is sufficient to convince the observer that neither authority overstates the fact. The two officials had reference, however, to two different grades of lodging-houses. The cost of a night's lodging makes the difference. There is a wider gap between the "hotel" — they are all hotels — that charges a quarter and the one that furnishes

[59] Specifically a large inn designed for the caravans traveling throughout the Near East. Riis uses the term to describe the lodging houses on the Lower East Side. — ED.

[60] Inspector Byrnes on Lodging-houses, in the North American Review, September, 1889.

a bed for a dime than between the bridal suite and the everyday hall bedroom of the ordinary hostelry.

The metropolis is to lots of people like a lighted candle to the moth. It attracts them in swarms that come year after year with the vague idea that they can get along here if anywhere; that something is bound to turn up among so many. Nearly all are young men, unsettled in life, many — most of them, perhaps — fresh from good homes, beyond a doubt with honest hopes of getting a start in the city and making a way for themselves. Few of them have much money to waste while looking around, and the cheapness of the lodging offered is an object. Fewer still know anything about the city and its pitfalls. They have come in search of crowds, of "life," and they gravitate naturally to the Bowery, the great democratic highway of the city, where the twenty-five-cent lodging-houses take them in. In the alleged reading-rooms of these great barracks, that often have accommodations, such as they are, for two, three, and even four hundred guests, they encounter three distinct classes of associates: the great mass adventurers like themselves, waiting there for something to turn up; a much smaller class of respectable clerks or mechanics, who, too poor or too lonely to have a home of their own, live this way from year to year; and lastly the thief in search of recruits for his trade. The sights the young stranger sees and the company he keeps in the Bowery are not of a kind to strengthen any moral principle he may have brought away from home, and by the time his money is gone, with no work yet in sight, and he goes down a step, a long step, to the fifteen-cent lodging-house, he is ready for the tempter whom he finds waiting for him there, reinforced by the contingent of ex-convicts returning from the prisons after having served out their sentences for robbery or theft. Then it is that the something he has been waiting for turns up. The police returns have the record of it. "In nine cases out of ten," says Inspector Byrnes, "he turns out a thief, or a burglar, if, indeed, he does not sooner or later become a murderer." As a matter of fact, some of the most atrocious of recent murders have been the result of schemes of robbery hatched in these houses, and so frequent and bold have become the depredations of the lodging-house thieves, that the authorities have been compelled to make a public demand for more effective laws that shall make them subject at all times to police regulation.

Inspector Byrnes observes that in the last two or three years at least four hundred young men have been arrested for petty crimes that originated in the lodging-houses, and that in many cases it was their first step in crime. He adds his testimony to the notorious fact that three-fourths of the young men called on to plead to generally petty offences in the courts are under twenty years of age, poorly clad, and without means. The bearing of the remark is obvious. One of the, to the police, well-known thieves who lived, when out of jail, at the Windsor, a well-known lodging-house in the Bowery, went to Johnstown[61] after the flood and was shot and killed there while robbing the dead.

An idea of just how this particular scheme of corruption works, with an extra touch of infamy thrown in, may be gathered from the story of David Smith, the "New York Fagin,"[62] who was convicted and sent to prison last year through the instrumentality of the Society for the Prevention of Cruelty to Children. Here is the account from the Society's last report:

> The boy, Edward Mulhearn, fourteen years old, had run away from his home in Jersey City, thinking he might find work and friends in New York. He may have been a trifle wild. He met Smith on the Bowery and recognized him as an acquaintance. When Smith offered him a supper and bed he was only too glad to accept. Smith led the boy to a vile lodging-house on the Bowery, where he introduced him to his "pals" and swore he would make a man of him before he was a week older. Next day he took the unsuspecting Edward all over the Bowery and Grand Street, showed him the sights and drew his attention to the careless way the ladies carried their bags and purses and the easy thing it was to get them. He induced Edward to try his hand. Edward tried and won. He was richer by three dollars! It did seem easy. "Of course it is," said his companion. From that time Smith took the boy on a number of thieving raids, but he never seemed to become adept enough to be trusted out of range of the "Fagin's" watchful eye. When he went out alone he generally returned empty-handed. This did not suit Smith. It was then he conceived the idea of turning this little inferior thief into a superior beggar. He took the boy into his room and burned his arms with a hot iron. The boy screamed and entreated in vain. The merciless wretch pressed the iron deep into the tender flesh, and afterward applied acid to the raw wound.
>
> Thus prepared, with his arm inflamed, swollen, and painful, Edward was sent out every day by this fiend, who never let him out of his sight, and threatened to burn his arm off if he did not beg money enough. He was instructed to tell people the wound had been caused by acid falling upon his arm at the works. Edward was now too much under the man's influence to resist or disobey him. He begged hard and handed Smith the pennies faithfully. He received in return bad food and worse treatment.

---

[61] City in southwestern Pennsylvania that was struck by a catastrophic flood in 1889. — ED.

[62] An adult who teaches children how to be criminals. The name comes from a character in the Charles Dickens novel *Oliver Twist.* — ED.

Bunks in a Seven-Cent Lodging-House, Pell Street.

The reckoning came when the wretch encountered the boy's father, in search of his child, in the Bowery, and fell under suspicion of knowing more than he pretended of the lad's whereabouts. He was found in his den with a half dozen of his chums revelling on the proceeds of the boy's begging for the day.

The twenty-five cent lodging-house keeps up the pretence of a bed-room, though the head-high partition enclosing a space just large enough to hold a cot and a chair and allow the man room to pull off his clothes is the shallowest of all pretences. The fifteen-cent bed stands boldly forth without screen in a room full of bunks with sheets as yellow and blankets as foul. At the ten-cent level the locker for the sleeper's clothes disappears. There is no longer need of it. The tramp limit is reached, and there is nothing to lock up save, on general principles, the lodger. Usually the ten- and seven-cent lodgings are different grades of the same abomination. Some sort of an apology for a bed, with mattress and blanket, represents the aristocratic purchase of the tramp who, by a lucky stroke of beggary, has exchanged the chance of an empty box or ash-barrel for shelter on the quality floor of one of these "hotels." A strip of canvas, strung between rough timbers, without covering of any kind, does for the couch of the seven-cent lodger who prefers the questionable comfort of a red-hot stove close to his elbow to the revelry of the stale-beer dive. It is not the most secure perch in the world. Uneasy sleepers roll off at intervals, but they have not far to fall to the next tier of bunks, and the commotion that ensues is speedily quieted by the boss and his club. On cold winter nights, when every bunk had its tenant, I have stood in such a lodging-room more than once, and listening to the snoring of the sleepers like the regular strokes of an engine, and the slow creaking of the beams under their restless weight, imagined myself on shipboard and experienced the very real nausea of sea-sickness. The one thing that did not favor the deception was the air; its character could not be mistaken.

The proprietor of one of these seven-cent houses was known to me as a man of reputed wealth and respectability. He "ran" three such establishments and made, it was said, $8,000 a year clear profit on his investment. He lived in a handsome house quite near to the stylish precincts of Murray Hill, where the nature of his occupation was not suspected. A notice that was posted on the wall of the lodgers' room suggested at least an effort to maintain his up-town standing in the slums. It read: "No swearing or loud talking after nine o'clock." Before nine no exceptions were taken to the natural vulgarity of the place; but that was the limit.

There are no licensed lodging-houses known to me which charge less than seven cents for even such a bed as this canvas strip, though there are unlicensed ones enough where one may sleep on the floor for five cents a spot, or squat in a sheltered hallway for three. The police station lodging-house, where the soft side of a plank is the regulation couch, is next in order. The manner in which this police bed is "made up" is interesting in its simplicity. The loose planks that make the platform are simply turned over, and the job is done, with an occasional coat of whitewash thrown in to sweeten things. I know of only one easier way, but, so far as I am informed, it has never been introduced in this country. It used to be practised, if report spoke truly, in certain old-country towns. The "bed" was represented by clothes-lines stretched across the room upon which the sleepers hung by the arm-pits for a penny a night. In the morning the boss woke them up by simply untying the line at one end and letting it go with its load; a labor-saving device certainly, and highly successful in attaining the desired end.

According to the police figures, 4,974,025 separate lodgings were furnished last year by these dormitories, between two and three hundred in number, and, adding the 147,634 lodgings furnished by the station-houses, the total of the homeless army was 5,121,659, an average of over fourteen thousand homeless men[63] for every night in the year! The health officers, professional optimists always in matters that trench upon their official jurisdiction, insist that the number is not quite so large as here given. But, apart from any slight discrepancy in the figures, the more important fact remains that last year's record of lodgers is an all round increase over the previous year's of over three hundred thousand, and that this has been the ratio of growth of the business during the last three years, the period of which Inspector Byrnes complains as turning out so many young criminals with the lodging-house stamp upon them. More than half of the lodging-houses are in the Bowery district, that is to say, the Fourth, Sixth, and Tenth Wards, and they harbor nearly three-fourths of their crowds. The calculation that more than nine thousand homeless young men lodge nightly along Chatham Street and the Bowery, between the City Hall and the Cooper Union, is probably not far out of the way. The City Missionary finds them there far less frequently than the thief in need of helpers. Appropriately enough, nearly one-fifth of all the pawn-shops in the city and one-sixth of all the saloons are located here, while twenty-seven per cent. of all the arrests on the police books have been credited to the district for the last two years.

About election time, especially in Presidential elections, the lodging-houses come out strong on the side of the political boss who has the biggest "barrel."[64] The victory in political contests, in the three wards I have mentioned of all others, is distinctly to the general with the strongest battalions, and the lodging-houses are his favorite recruiting ground. The colonization of voters is an evil of the first magnitude, none the less because both parties smirch their hands with it, and for that reason next to hopeless. Honors are easy, where the two "machines,"[65] intrenched in their strongholds, outbid each other across the Bowery in open rivalry as to who shall commit the most flagrant frauds at the polls. Semi-occasion-

[63] Deduct 69,111 women lodgers in the police stations.

[64] Short for "pork-barrel"; a government project that gives an elected official valuable "pork" with which he can please his constituents. — ED.

[65] Political organizations like Tammany Hall that controlled municipal affairs in many nineteenth-century American cities. — ED.

ally a champion offender is caught and punished, as was, not long ago, the proprietor of one of the biggest Bowery lodging-houses. But such scenes are largely spectacular, if not prompted by some hidden motive of revenge that survives from the contest. Beyond a doubt Inspector Byrnes speaks by the card[66] when he observes that "usually this work is done in the interest of some local political boss, who stands by the owner of the house, in case the latter gets into trouble." For standing by, read twisting the machinery of outraged justice so that its hand shall fall not too heavily upon the culprit, or miss him altogether. One of the houses that achieved profitable notoriety in this way in many successive elections, a notorious tramps' resort in Houston Street, was lately given up, and has most appropriately been turned into a bar-factory, thus still contributing, though in a changed form, to the success of "the cause." It must be admitted that the black tramp who herds in the West Side "hotels" is more discriminating in this matter of electioneering than his white brother. He at least exhibits some real loyalty in invariably selling his vote to the Republican bidder for a dollar, while he charges the Democratic boss a dollar and a half. In view of the well-known facts, there is a good deal of force in the remark made by a friend of ballot reform during the recent struggle over that hotly contested issue, that real ballot reform will do more to knock out cheap lodging-houses than all the regulations of police and health officers together.

The experiment made by a well-known stove manufacturer a winter or two ago in the way of charity might have thrown much desired light on the question of the number of tramps in the city, could it have been carried to a successful end. He opened a sort of breakfast shop for the idle and unemployed in the region of Washington Square, offering to all who had no money a cup of coffee and a roll for nothing. The first morning he had a dozen customers, the next about two hundred. The number kept growing until one morning, at the end of two weeks, found by actual count 2,014 shivering creatures in line waiting their turn for a seat at his tables. The shop was closed that day. It was one of the rare instances of too great a rush of custom wrecking a promising business, and the great problem remained unsolved.

---

[66] With accuracy; by the script. — ED.

Chapter IX

Chinatown

Between the tabernacles of Jewry and the shrines of the Bend, Joss has cheekily planted his pagan worship of idols, chief among which are the celestial worshipper's own gain and lusts. Whatever may be said about the Chinaman being a thousand years behind the age on his own shores, here he is distinctly abreast of it in his successful scheming to "make it pay." It is doubtful if there is anything he does not turn to a paying account, from his religion down, or up, as one prefers. At the risk of distressing some well-meaning, but, I fear, too trustful people, I state it in advance as my opinion, based on the steady observation of years, that all attempts to make an effective Christian of John Chinaman will remain abortive in this generation; of the next I have, if anything, less hope. Ages of senseless idolatry, a mere grub-worship, have left him without the essential qualities for appreciating the gentle teachings of a faith whose motive and unselfish spirit are alike beyond his grasp. He lacks the handle of a strong faith in something, anything, however wrong, to catch him by. There is nothing strong about him, except his passions when aroused. I am convinced that he adopts Christianity, when he adopts it at all, as he puts on American clothes, with what the politicians would call an ulterior motive, some sort of gain in the near prospect — washing, a Christian wife perhaps, anything he happens to rate for the moment above his cherished pigtail. It may be that I judge him too harshly. Exceptions may be found. Indeed, for the credit of the race, I hope there are such. But I am bound to say my hope is not backed by lively faith.

Chinatown as a spectacle is disappointing. Next-door neighbor to the Bend, it has little of its outdoor stir and life, none of its gayly-colored rags or picturesque filth and poverty. Mott Street is clean to distraction: the laundry stamp is on it, though the houses are chiefly of the conventional tenement-house type, with nothing to rescue them from the everyday dismal dreariness of their kind save here and there a splash of dull red or yellow, a sign, hung endways and with streamers of red flannel tacked on, that announces in Chinese characters that Dr. Chay Yen Chong sells Chinese herb medicines, or that Won Lung & Co. — queer contradiction — take in washing, or deal out tea and groceries. There are some gimcracks[67] in the second story fire-escape of one of the houses, signifying

---

[67] Showy ornaments. — ED.

that Joss or a club has a habitation there. An American patent medicine[68] concern has seized the opportunity to decorate the back-ground with its cabalistic trade-mark, that in this company looks as foreign as the rest. Doubtless the privilege was bought for cash. It will buy anything in Chinatown, Joss himself included, as indeed, why should it not? He was bought for cash across the sea and came here under the law that shuts out the live Chinaman, but lets in his dead god on payment of the statutory duty on bric-à-brac. Red and yellow are the holiday colors of Chinatown as of the Bend, but they do not lend brightness in Mott Street as around the corner in Mulberry. Rather, they seem to descend to the level of the general dulness, and glower at you from doors and windows, from the telegraph pole that is the official organ of Chinatown and from the store signs, with blank, unmeaning stare, suggesting nothing, asking no questions, and answering none. Fifth Avenue is not duller on a rainy day than Mott Street to one in search of excitement. Whatever is on foot goes on behind closed doors. Stealth and secretiveness are as much part of the Chinaman in New York as the cat-like tread of his felt shoes. His business, as his domestic life, shuns the light, less because there is anything to conceal than because that is the way of the man. Perhaps the attitude of American civilization toward the stranger, whom it invited in, has taught him that way. At any rate, the very doorways of his offices and shops are fenced off by queer, forbidding partitions suggestive of a continual state of siege. The stranger who enters through the crooked approach is received with sudden silence, a sullen stare, and an angry "Vat you vant?" that breathes annoyance and distrust.

Trust not him who trusts no one, is as safe a rule in Chinatown as out of it. Were not Mott Street overawed in its isolation, it would not be safe to descend this open cellar-way, through which come the pungent odor of burning opium and the clink of copper coins on the table. As it is, though safe, it is not profitable to intrude. At the first foot-fall of leather soles on the steps the hum of talk ceases, and the group of celestials,[69] crouching over their game of fan tan, stop playing and watch the comer with ugly looks. Fan tan is their ruling passion. The average Chinaman, the police will tell you, would rather gamble than eat any day, and they have ample experience to back them. Only the fellow in the bunk smokes away, indifferent to all else but his pipe and his own enjoyment. It is a mistake to assume that Chinatown is honeycombed with opium "joints."

---

[68] Products advertised for their medicinal value which were generally of little if any value. — ED.

[69] Those of another world; used here by Riis to refer unfavorably to the Chinese. — ED.

There are a good many more outside of it than in it. The celestials do not monopolize the pipe. In Mott Street there is no need of them. Not a Chinese home or burrow there but has its bunk and its lay-out, where they can be enjoyed safe from police interference. The Chinaman smokes opium as Caucasians smoke tobacco, and apparently with little worse effect upon himself. But woe unto the white victim upon which his pitiless drug gets its grip!

The bloused pedlars who, with arms buried half to the elbow in their trousers' pockets, lounge behind their stock of watermelon seed and sugar-cane, cut in lengths to suit the purse of the buyer, disdain to offer the barbarian their wares. Chinatown, that does most things by contraries, rules it holiday style to carry its hands in its pockets, and its denizens follow the fashion, whether in blue blouse, in gray, or in brown, with shining and braided pig-tail dangling below the knees, or with hair cropped short above a coat collar of "Melican"[70] cut. All kinds of men are met, but no women — none at least with almond eyes. The reason is simple: there are none. A few, a very few, Chinese merchants have wives of their own color, but they are seldom or never seen in the street. The "wives" of Chinatown are of a different stock that comes closer home.

From the teeming tenements to the right and left of it come the white slaves of its dens of vice and their infernal drug, that have infused into the "Bloody Sixth" Ward a subtler poison than ever the stale-beer dives knew, or the "sudden death" of the Old Brewery.[71] There are houses, dozens of them, in Mott and Pell Streets, that are literally jammed, from the "joint" in the cellar to the attic, with these hapless victims of a passion which, once acquired, demands the sacrifice of every instinct of decency to its insatiate desire. There is a church in Mott Street, at the entrance to Chinatown, that stands as a barrier between it and the tenements beyond. Its young men have waged unceasing war upon the monstrous wickedness for years, but with very little real result. I have in mind a house in Pell Street that has been raided no end of times by the police, and its population emptied upon Blackwell's Island, or into the reformatories, yet is to-day honeycombed with scores of the conventional households of the Chinese quarter: the men worshippers of Joss; the women, all white, girls hardly yet grown to womanhood, worshipping nothing save the pipe that has enslaved them body and soul. Easily tempted from homes that have no claim upon the name, they rarely or never return. Mott Street gives

[70] Riis's attempt to write *American* the way he hears the word pronounced by the Chinese. — ED.

[71] Abandoned factory that became one of New York's worst tenements. — ED.

up its victims only to the Charity Hospital or the Potter's Field. Of the depth of their fall no one is more thoroughly aware than these girls themselves; no one less concerned about it. The calmness with which they discuss it, while insisting illogically upon the fiction of a marriage that deceives no one, is disheartening. Their misery is peculiarly fond of company, and an amount of visiting goes on in these households that makes it extremely difficult for the stranger to untangle them. I came across a company of them "hitting the pipe" together, on a tour through their dens one night with the police captain of the precinct. The girls knew him, called him by name, offered him a pipe, and chatted with him about the incidents of their acquaintance, how many times he had "sent them up," and their chances of "lasting" much longer. There was no shade of regret in their voices, nothing but utter indifference and surrender.

One thing about them was conspicuous: their scrupulous neatness. It is the distinguishing mark of Chinatown, outwardly and physically. It is not altogether by chance the Chinaman has chosen the laundry as his distinctive field. He is by nature as clean as the cat, which he resembles in his traits of cruel cunning and savage fury when aroused. On this point of cleanliness he insists in his domestic circle, yielding in others with crafty submissiveness to the caprice of the girls, who "boss" him in a very independent manner, fretting vengefully under the yoke they loathe, but which they know right well they can never shake off, once they have put the pipe to their lips and given Mott Street a mortgage upon their souls for all time. To the priest, whom they call in when the poison racks the body, they pretend that they are yet their own masters; but he knows that it is an idle boast, least of all believed by themselves. As he walks with them the few short steps to the Potter's Field, he hears the sad story he has heard told over and over again, of father, mother, home and friends given up for the accursed pipe, and stands hopeless and helpless before the colossal evil for which he knows no remedy.

The frequent assertions of the authorities that at least no girls under age are wrecked on this Chinese shoal, are disproved by the observation of those who go frequently among these dens, though the smallest girl will invariably, and usually without being asked, insist that she is sixteen, and so of age to choose the company she keeps. Such assertions are not to be taken seriously. Even while I am writing, the morning returns from one of the precincts that pass through my hands report the arrest of a Chinaman for "inveigling little girls into his laundry," one of the hundred outposts of Chinatown that are scattered all over the city, as the outer threads of the spider's web that holds its prey fast. Reference to case No.

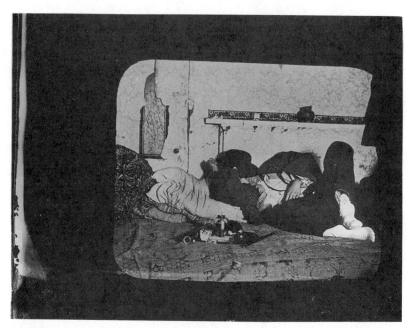

In a Chinese Joint.

39,499 in this year's report of the Society for the Prevention of Cruelty to Children, will discover one of the much travelled roads to Chinatown. The girl whose story it tells was thirteen, and one of six children abandoned by a dissipated father. She had been discharged from an Eighth Avenue store, where she was employed as cash girl, and, being afraid to tell her mother, floated about until she landed in a Chinese laundry. The judge heeded her tearful prayer, and sent her home with her mother, but she was back again in a little while despite all promises of reform.

Her tyrant knows well that she will come, and patiently bides his time. When her struggles in the web have ceased at last, he rules no longer with gloved hand. A specimen of celestial logic from the home circle at this period came home to me with a personal application one evening when I attempted, with a policeman, to stop a Chinaman whom we found beating his white "wife" with a broom-handle in a Mott Street cellar. He was angry at our interference, and declared vehemently that she was "bad."

"S'ppose your wifee bad, you no lickee her?" he asked, as if there could be no appeal from such a common-sense proposition as that. My assurance that I did not, that such a thing could not occur to me, struck him dumb with amazement. He eyed me a while in stupid silence, poked the linen in his tub, stole another look, and made up his mind. A gleam of intelligence shone in his eye, and pity and contempt struggled in his voice. "Then, I guess, she lickee you," he said.

No small commotion was caused in Chinatown once upon the occasion of an expedition I undertook, accompanied by a couple of police detectives, to photograph Joss. Some conscienceless wag spread the report, after we were gone, that his picture was wanted for the Rogues' Gallery at Headquarters. The insult was too gross to be passed over without atonement of some sort. Two roast pigs made matters all right with his offended majesty of Mott Street, and with his attendant priests, who bear a very practical hand in the worship by serving as the divine stomach, as it were. They eat the good things set before their rice-paper master, unless, as once happened, some sacrilegious tramp sneaks in and gets ahead of them. The practical way in which these people combine worship with business is certainly admirable. I was told that the scrawl covering the wall on both sides of the shrine stood for the names of the pillars of the church or club — the Joss House is both — that they might have their reward in this world, no matter what happened to them in the next. There was another inscription overhead that needed no interpreter. In familiar English letters, copied bodily from the trade dollar, was the sentiment: "In God we trust." The priest pointed to it with undisguised pride and attempted an explanation, from which I gathered that the inscription was intended as a diplomatic courtesy, a delicate international compliment to the "Melican Joss," the almighty dollar.

Chinatown has enlisted the telegraph for the dissemination of public intelligence, but it has got hold of the contrivance by the wrong end. As the wires serve us in newspaper-making, so the Chinaman makes use of the pole for the same purpose. The telegraph pole, of which I spoke as the real official organ of Chinatown, stands not far from the Joss House[72] in Mott Street, in full view from Chatham Square. In it centres the real life of the colony, its gambling news. Every day yellow and red notices are posted upon it by unseen hands, announcing that in such and such a cellar a fan tan game will be running that night, or warning the faithful that a raid is intended on this or that game through the machination of a rival interest. A constant stream of plotting and counter-plotting makes up the round of Chinese social and political existence. I do not pretend to understand the exact political structure of the colony, or its internal government. Even discarding as idle the stories of a secret cabal with

---

[72] Chinese house of worship. — ED.

"The Official Organ of Chinatown."

power over life and death, and authority to enforce its decrees, there is evidence enough that the Chinese consider themselves subject to the laws of the land only when submission is unavoidable, and that they are governed by a code of their own, the very essence of which is rejection of all other authority except under compulsion. If now and then some horrible crime in the Chinese colony, a murder of such hideous ferocity as one I have a very vivid recollection of, where the murderer stabbed his victim (both Chinamen, of course) in the back with a meat-knife, plunging it in to the hilt no less than seventeen times, arouses the popular prejudice to a suspicion that it was "ordered," only the suspected themselves are to blame, for they appear to rise up as one man to shield the criminal. The difficulty of tracing the motive of the crime and the murderer is extreme, and it is the rarest of all results that the police get on the track of either. The obstacles in the way of hunting down an Italian murderer are as nothing to the opposition encountered in Chinatown. Nor is the failure of the pursuit wholly to be ascribed to the familiar fact that to Caucasian eyes "all Chinamen look alike," but rather to their acting "alike," in a body, to defeat discovery at any cost.

Withal the police give the Chinese the name of being the "quietest people down there," meaning in the notoriously turbulent Sixth Ward; and they are. The one thing they desire above all is to be let alone, a very natural wish perhaps, considering all the circumstances. If it were a laudable or even an allowable ambition that prompts it, they might be humored with advantage, probably, to both sides. But the facts show too plainly that it is not, and that in their very exclusiveness and reserve they are a constant and terrible menace to society, wholly regardless of their influence upon the industrial problems which their presence confuses. The severest official scrutiny, the harshest repressive measures are justifiable in Chinatown, orderly as it appears on the surface, even more than in the Bend, and the case is infinitely more urgent. To the peril that threatens there all the senses are alert, whereas the poison that proceeds from Mott Street puts mind and body to sleep, to work out its deadly purpose in the corruption of the soul.

This again may be set down as a harsh judgment. I may be accused of inciting persecution of an unoffending people. Far from it. Granted, that the Chinese are in no sense a desirable element of the population, that they serve no useful purpose here, whatever they may have done elsewhere in other days, yet to this it is a sufficient answer that they are here, and that, having let them in, we must make the best of it. This is a time for very plain speaking on this subject. Rather than banish the Chinaman, I would have the door opened wider — for his wife; make it a condition of his coming or staying that he bring his wife with him. Then, at least, he might not be what he now is and remains, a homeless stranger among us. Upon this hinges the real Chinese question, in our city at all events, as I see it. To assert that the victims of his drug and his base passions would go to the bad anyhow, is begging the question. They might and they might not. The chance is the span between life and death. From any other form of dissipation than that for which Chinatown stands there is recovery; for the victims of any other vice, hope. For these there is neither hope nor recovery; nothing but death — moral, mental, and physical death.

Chapter X

Jewtown

The tenements grow taller, and the gaps in their ranks close up rapidly as we cross the Bowery and, leaving Chinatown and the Italians behind, invade the Hebrew quarter. Baxter Street, with its interminable rows of old clothes shops and its brigades of pullers-in[73] — nicknamed "the Bay" in honor, perhaps, of the tars[74] who lay to there after a cruise to stock up their togs,[75] or maybe after the "schooners" of beer plentifully bespoke in that latitude — Bayard Street, with its synagogues and its crowds, gave us a foretaste of it. No need of asking here where we are. The jargon of the street, the signs of the sidewalk, the manner and dress of the people, their unmistakable physiognomy, betray their race at every step. Men with queer skull-caps, venerable beard, and the outlandish long-skirted kaftan of the Russian Jew, elbow the ugliest and the handsomest women in the land. The contrast is startling. The old women are hags; the young, houris. Wives and mothers at sixteen, at thirty they are old. So thoroughly has the chosen people crowded out the Gentiles in the Tenth Ward that,

---

[73] People employed by shopowners to persuade passersby to come into their shops and purchase their goods. — ED.
[74] Slang term for sailor. — ED.
[75] Slang term for clothes. — ED.

when the great Jewish holidays come around every year, the public schools in the district have practically to close up. Of their thousands of pupils scarce a handful come to school. Nor is there any suspicion that the rest are playing hookey. They stay honestly home to celebrate. There is no mistaking it: we are in Jewtown.

It is said that nowhere in the world are so many people crowded together on a square mile as here. The average five-story tenement adds a story or two to its stature in Ludlow Street and an extra building on the rear lot, and yet the sign "To Let" is the rarest of all there. Here is one seven stories high. The sanitary policeman whose beat this is will tell you that it contains thirty-six families, but the term has a widely different meaning here and on the avenues. In this house, where a case of small-pox was reported, there were fifty-eight babies and thirty-eight children that were over five years of age. In Essex Street two small rooms in a six-story tenement were made to hold a "family" of father and mother, twelve children and six boarders. The boarder plays as important a part in the domestic economy of Jewtown as the lodger in the Mulberry Street Bend. These are samples of the packing of the population that has run up the record here to the rate of three hundred and thirty thousand per square mile. The densest crowding of Old London, I pointed out before, never got beyond a hundred and seventy-five thousand. Even the alley is crowded out. Through dark hallways and filthy cellars, crowded, as is every foot of the street, with dirty children, the settlements in the rear are reached. Thieves know how to find them when pursued by the police, and the tramps that sneak in on chilly nights to fight for the warm spot in the yard over some baker's oven. They are out of place in this hive of busy industry, and they know it. It has nothing in common with them or with their philosophy of life, that the world owes the idler a living. Life here means the hardest kind of work almost from the cradle. The world as a debtor has no credit in Jewtown. Its promise to pay wouldn't buy one of the old hats that are hawked about Hester Street, unless backed by security representing labor done at lowest market rates. But this army of workers must have bread. It is cheap and filling, and bakeries abound. Wherever they are in the tenements the tramp will skulk in, if he can. There is such a tramps' roost in the rear of a tenement near the lower end of Ludlow Street, that is never without its tenants in winter. By a judicious practice of flopping over on the stone pavement at intervals and thus warming one side at a time, and with an empty box to put the feet in, it is possible to keep reasonably comfortable there even on a rainy night. In summer the yard is the only one in the neighborhood that does not do duty as a public dormitory.

A Tramp's Nest in Ludlow Street.

Thrift is the watchword of Jewtown, as of its people the world over. It is at once its strength and its fatal weakness, its cardinal virtue and its foul disgrace. Become an over-mastering passion with these people who come here in droves from Eastern Europe to escape persecution, from which freedom could be bought only with gold, it has enslaved them in bondage worse than that from which they fled. Money is their God. Life itself is of little value compared with even the leanest bank account. In no other spot does life wear so intensely bald and materialistic an aspect as in Ludlow Street. Over and over again I have met with instances of these Polish or Russian Jews deliberately starving themselves to the point of physical exhaustion, while working night and day at a tremendous pressure to save a little money. An avenging Nemesis pursues this headlong hunt for wealth; there is no worse paid class anywhere. I once put the question to one of their own people, who, being a pawnbroker, and an unusually intelligent and charitable one, certainly enjoyed the advantage of a practical view of the situation: "Whence the many wretchedly poor people in such a colony of workers, where poverty, from a misfortune, has become a reproach, dreaded as the plague?"

"Immigration," he said, "brings us a lot. In five years it has averaged twenty-five thousand a year, of which more than seventy per cent. have stayed in New York. Half of them require and receive aid from the Hebrew Charities[76] from the very start, lest they starve. That is one explanation. There is another class than the one that cannot get work:

[76] Organization designed specifically, but not exclusively, to serve the needs of Eastern European Jewish immigrants. — ED.

those who have had too much of it; who have worked and hoarded and lived, crowded together like pigs, on the scantiest fare and the worst to be got, bound to save whatever their earnings, until, worn out, they could work no longer. Then their hoards were soon exhausted. That is their story." And I knew that what he said was true.

Penury and poverty are wedded everywhere to dirt and disease, and Jewtown is no exception. It could not well be otherwise in such crowds, considering especially their low intellectual status. The managers of the Eastern Dispensary,[77] which is in the very heart of their district, told the whole story when they said: "The diseases these people suffer from are not due to intemperance or immorality, but to ignorance, want of suitable food, and the foul air in which they live and work."[78] The homes of the Hebrew quarter are its workshops also. Reference will be made to the economic conditions under which they work in a succeeding chapter. Here we are concerned simply with the fact. You are made fully aware of it before you have travelled the length of a single block in any of these East Side streets, by the whir of a thousand sewing-machines, worked at high pressure from earliest dawn till mind and muscle give out together. Every member of the family, from the youngest to the oldest, bears a hand, shut in the qualmy rooms, where meals are cooked and clothing washed and dried besides, the live-long day. It is not unusual to find a dozen persons — men, women, and children — at work in a single small room. The fact accounts for the contrast that strikes with wonder the observer who comes across from the Bend. Over there the entire population seems possessed of an uncontrollable impulse to get out into the street; here all its energies appear to be bent upon keeping in and away from it. Not that the streets are deserted. The overflow from these tenements is enough to make a crowd anywhere. The children alone would do it. Not old enough to work and no room for play, that is their story. In the home the child's place is usurped by the lodger, who performs the service of the Irishman's pig — pays the rent. In the street the army of hucksters crowd him out. Typhus fever[79] and small-pox are bred here, and help solve the question what to do with him. Filth diseases both, they sprout naturally among the hordes that bring the germs with them from across the sea, and whose first instinct is to hide their sick lest

[77] Incorporated in 1832, the Eastern Dispensary, located in the Lower East Side, was one of several dispensaries designed to provide the poor with free medical and surgical services. — ED.

[78] Report of Eastern Dispensary for 1889.

[79] Contagious fever that plagued the poorer inhabitants of nineteenth-century cities. — ED.

the authorities carry them off to the hospital to be slaughtered, as they firmly believe. The health officers are on constant and sharp lookout for hidden fever-nests. Considering that half of the ready-made clothes that are sold in the big stores, if not a good deal more than half, are made in these tenement rooms, this is not excessive caution. It has happened more than once that a child recovering from small-pox, and in the most contagious stage of the disease, has been found crawling among heaps of half-finished clothing that the next day would be offered for sale on the counter of a Broadway store; or that a typhus fever patient has been discovered in a room whence perhaps a hundred coats had been sent home that week, each one with the wearer's death-warrant, unseen and unsuspected, basted in the lining.

The health officers call the Tenth the typhus ward; in the office where deaths are registered it passes as the "suicide ward," for reasons not hard to understand; and among the police as the "crooked ward," on account of the number of "crooks," petty thieves and their allies, the "fences," receivers of stolen goods, who find the dense crowds congenial. The nearness of the Bowery, the great "thieves' highway," helps to keep up the supply of these, but Jewtown does not support its dives. Its troubles with the police are the characteristic crop of its intense business rivalries. Oppression, persecution, have not shorn the Jew of his native combativeness one whit. He is as ready to fight for his rights, or what he considers his rights, in a business transaction — synonymous generally with his advantage — as if he had not been robbed of them for eighteen hundred years. One strong impression survives with him from his days of bondage: the power of the law. On the slightest provocation he rushes off to invoke it for his protection. Doubtless the sensation is novel to him, and therefore pleasing. The police at the Eldridge Street station are in a constant turmoil over these everlasting fights. Somebody is always denouncing somebody else, and getting his enemy or himself locked up; frequently both, for the prisoner, when brought in, has generally as plausible a story to tell as his accuser, and as hot a charge to make. The day closes on a wild conflict of rival interests. Another dawns with the prisoner in court, but no complainant. Over night the case has been settled on a business basis, and the police dismiss their prisoner in deep disgust.

These quarrels have sometimes a comic aspect. Thus, with the numerous dancing-schools that are scattered among the synagogues, often keeping them company in the same tenement. They are generally kept by some man who works in the daytime at tailoring, cigarmaking, or something else. The young people in Jewtown are inordinately fond of

A Market Scene in the Jewish Quarter.

dancing, and after their day's hard work will flock to these "schools" for a night's recreation. But even to their fun they carry their business preferences, and it happens that a school adjourns in a body to make a general raid on the rival establishment across the street, without the ceremony of paying the admission fee. Then the dance breaks up in a general fight, in which, likely enough, someone is badly hurt. The police come in, as usual, and ring down the curtain.

Bitter as are his private feuds, it is not until his religious life is invaded that a real inside view is obtained of this Jew, whom the history of Christian civilization has taught nothing but fear and hatred. There are two or three missions in the district conducting a hopeless propagandism for the Messiah whom the Tenth Ward rejects, and they attract occasional crowds, who come to hear the Christian preacher as the Jews of old gathered to hear the apostles expound the new doctrine. The result is often strikingly similar. "For once," said a certain well-known minister of an uptown church to me, after such an experience, "I felt justified in comparing myself to Paul preaching salvation to the Jews. They kept still until I spoke of Jesus Christ as the Son of God. Then they got up and fell to arguing among themselves and to threatening me, until it looked as if they meant to take me out in Hester Street and stone me." As at Jerusalem, the Chief Captain was happily at hand with his centurions, in the person of a sergeant and three policemen, and the preacher was rescued. So, in all matters pertaining to their religious life that tinges all their customs, they stand, these East Side Jews, where the new day that dawned on Calvary left them standing, stubbornly refusing to see the light. A visit to a Jewish house of mourning is like bridging the gap of two thousand years. The inexpressibly sad and sorrowful wail for the dead, as it swells and rises in the hush of all sounds of life, comes back from the ages like a mournful echo of the voice of Rachel[80] "weeping for her children and refusing to be comforted, because they are not."

Attached to many of the synagogues, which among the poorest Jews frequently consist of a scantily furnished room in a rear tenement, with a few wooden stools or benches for the congregation, are Talmudic schools that absorb a share of the growing youth. The school-master is not rarely a man of some attainments who has been stranded there, his native instinct for money-making having been smothered in the process that has made of him a learned man. It was of such a school in Eldridge Street that the wicked Isaac Iacob, who killed his enemy, his wife, and himself in one day, was janitor. But the majority of the children seek the public schools, where they are received sometimes with some misgivings on the part of the teachers, who find it necessary to inculcate lessons of cleanliness in the worst cases by practical demonstration with wash-bowl and soap. "He took hold of the soap as if it were some animal," said one of these teachers to me after such an experiment upon a new pupil, "and wiped three fingers across his face. He called that washing." In the Allen Street public school the experienced principal has embodied among the elementary lessons, to keep constantly before the children the duty that clearly lies next to their hands, a characteristic exercise. The question is asked daily from the teacher's desk: "What must I do to be healthy?" and the whole school responds:

> I must keep my skin clean,
> Wear clean clothes,
> Breathe pure air,
> And live in the sunlight.

It seems little less than biting sarcasm to hear them say it, for to not a few of them all these things are known only by name. In their everyday life there is nothing even to suggest any of them. Only the demand of

---

[80] The wife of Jacob and the mother of the Jewish people. — ED.

religious custom has power to make their parents clean up at stated intervals, and the young naturally are no better. As scholars, the children of the most ignorant Polish Jew keep fairly abreast of their more favored playmates, until it comes to mental arithmetic, when they leave them behind with a bound. It is surprising to see how strong the instinct of dollars and cents is in them. They can count, and correctly, almost before they can talk.

Within a few years the police captured on the East Side a band of firebugs who made a business of setting fire to tenements for the insurance on their furniture. There has, unfortunately, been some evidence in the past year that another such conspiracy is on foot. The danger to which these fiends expose their fellow-tenants is appalling. A fire-panic at night in a tenement, by no means among the rare experiences in New York, with the surging, half-smothered crowds on stairs and fire-escapes, the frantic mothers and crying children, the wild struggle to save the little that is their all, is a horror that has few parallels in human experience.

I cannot think without a shudder of one such scene in a First Avenue tenement. It was in the middle of the night. The fire had swept up with sudden fury from a restaurant on the street floor, cutting off escape. Men and women threw themselves from the windows, or were carried down senseless by the firemen. Thirteen half-clad, apparently lifeless bodies were laid on the floor of an adjoining coal-office, and the ambulance surgeons worked over them with sleeves rolled up to the elbows. A half-grown girl with a baby in her arms walked about among the dead and dying with a stunned, vacant look, singing in a low, scared voice to the child. One of the doctors took her arm to lead her out, and patted the cheek of the baby soothingly. It was cold. The baby had been smothered with its father and mother; but the girl, her sister, did not know it. Her reason had fled.

Thursday night and Friday morning are bargain days in the "Pig-market."[81] Then is the time to study the ways of this peculiar people to the best advantage. A common pulse beats in the quarters of the Polish Jews and in the Mulberry Bend, though they have little else in common. Life over yonder in fine weather is a perpetual holiday, here a veritable tread-mill of industry. Friday brings out all the latent color and picturesqueness of the Italians, as of these Semites. The crowds and the common poverty are the bonds of sympathy between them. The Pig-market is in Hester Street, extending either way from Ludlow Street, and up and down the side streets two or three blocks, as the state of trade

---

[81] Huge bazaar at which all sorts of goods are bought and sold. — ED.

demands. The name was given to it probably in derision, for pork is the one ware that is not on sale in the Pig-market. There is scarcely anything else that can be hawked from a wagon that is not to be found, and at ridiculously low prices. Bandannas and tin cups at two cents, peaches at a cent a quart, "damaged" eggs for a song, hats for a quarter, and spectacles, warranted to suit the eye, at the optician's who has opened shop on a Hester Street door-step, for thirty-five cents; frowsy-looking chickens and half-plucked geese, hung by the neck and protesting with wildly strutting feet even in death against the outrage, are the great staple of the market. Half or a quarter of a chicken can be bought here by those who cannot afford a whole. It took more than ten years of persistent effort on the part of the sanitary authorities to drive the trade in live fowl from the streets to the fowl-market on Gouverneur Slip, where the killing is now done according to Jewish rite by priests detailed for the purpose by the chief rabbi. Since then they have had a characteristic rumpus, that involved the entire Jewish community, over the fees for killing and the mode of collecting them. Here is a woman churning horse-radish on a machine she has chained and padlocked to a tree on the sidewalk, lest someone steal it. Beside her a butcher's stand with cuts at prices the avenues never dreamed of. Old coats are hawked for fifty cents, "as good as new," and "pants" — there are no trousers in Jewtown, only pants — at anything that can be got. There is a knot of half a dozen "pants" pedlars in the middle of the street, twice as many men of their own race fingering their wares and plucking at the seams with the anxious scrutiny of would-be buyers, though none of them has the least idea of investing in a pair. Yes, stop! This baker, fresh from his trough, bare-headed and with bare arms, has made an offer: for this pair thirty cents; a dollar and forty was the price asked. The pedlar shrugs his shoulders, and turns up his hands with a half pitying, wholly indignant air. What does the baker take him for? Such pants — . The baker has turned to go. With a jump like a panther's, the man with the pants has him by the sleeve. Will he give eighty cents? Sixty? Fifty? So help him, they are dirt cheap at that. Lose, will he, on the trade, lose all the profit of his day's pedling. The baker goes on unmoved. Forty then? What, not forty? Take them then for thirty, and wreck the life of a poor man. And the baker takes them and goes, well knowing that at least twenty cents of the thirty, two hundred per cent., were clear profit, if indeed the "pants" cost the pedlar anything.

The suspender pedlar is the mystery of the Pig-market, omnipresent and unfathomable. He is met at every step with his wares dangling over his shoulder, down his back, and in front. Millions of suspenders thus perambulate Jewtown all day on a sort of dress parade. Why suspenders,

The Old Clo'e's Man — In the Jewish Quarter.

is the puzzle, and where do they all go to? The "pants" of Jewtown hang down with a common accord, as if they had never known the support of suspenders. It appears to be as characteristic a trait of the race as the long beard and the Sabbath silk hat of ancient pedigree. I have asked again and again. No one has ever been able to tell me what becomes of the suspenders of Jewtown. Perhaps they are hung up as bric-à-brac in its homes, or laid away and saved up as the equivalent of cash. I cannot tell. I only know that more suspenders are hawked about the Pig-market every day than would supply the whole of New York for a year, were they all bought and turned to use.

The crowds that jostle each other at the wagons and about the sidewalk shops, where a gutter plank on two ash-barrels does duty for a counter! Pushing, struggling, babbling, and shouting in foreign tongues, a veritable Babel of confusion. An English word falls upon the ear almost with a sense of shock, as something unexpected and strange. In the midst of it all there is a sudden wild scattering, a hustling of things from the street into dark cellars, into back-yards and by-ways, a slamming and locking of doors hidden under the improvised shelves and counters. The health officers' cart is coming down the street, preceded and followed by stalwart policemen, who shovel up with scant ceremony the eatables — musty bread, decayed fish and stale vegetables — indifferent to the curses that are showered on them from stoops and windows, and carry them off to the dump. In the wake of the wagon, as it makes its way to the East River after the raid, follow a line of despoiled hucksters shouting defiance from a safe distance. Their clamor dies away with the noise of the market. The endless panorama of the tenements, rows upon rows, between stony streets, stretches to the north, to the south, and to the west as far as the eye reaches.

Chapter XI

The Sweaters [82] *of Jewtown*

Anything like an exhaustive discussion of the economical problem presented by the Tenth Ward[83] is beset by difficulties that increase in precise proportion to the efforts put forth to remove them. I have too vivid a recollection of weary days and nights spent in those stewing tenements, trying to get to the bottom of the vexatious question only to find myself in the end as far from the truth as at the beginning, asking with rising wrath Pilate's question, "What is truth?" to attempt to weary the reader by dragging him with me over that sterile and unprofitable ground. Nor are these pages the place for such a discussion. In it, let me confess it at once and have done with it, I should be like the blind leading the blind; between the real and apparent poverty, the hidden hoards and the

---

[82] The workers who labor in sweatshops. — ED.

[83] I refer to the Tenth Ward always as typical. The district embraced in the discussion really includes the Thirteenth Ward, and in a growing sense large portions of the Seventh and contiguous wards as well.

unhesitating mendacity of these people, where they conceive their interests to be concerned in one way or another, the reader and I would fall together into the ditch of doubt and conjecture in which I have found company before.

The facts that lie on the surface indicate the causes as clearly as the nature of the trouble. In effect both have been already stated. A friend of mine who manufactures cloth once boasted to me that nowadays, on cheap clothing, New York "beats the world." "To what," I asked, "do you attribute it?" "To the cutter's long knife[84] and the Polish Jew," he said. Which of the two has cut deepest into the workman's wages is not a doubtful question. Practically the Jew has monopolized the business since the battle between East Broadway and Broadway ended in a complete victory for the East Side and cheap labor, and transferred to it the control of the trade in cheap clothing. Yet, not satisfied with having won the field, he strives as hotly with his own for the profit of half a cent as he fought with his Christian competitor for the dollar. If the victory is a barren one, the blame is his own. His price is not what he can get, but the lowest he can live for and underbid his neighbor. Just what that means we shall see. The manufacturer knows it, and is not slow to take advantage of his knowledge. He makes him hungry for work by keeping it from him as long as possible; then drives the closest bargain he can with the sweater.

Many harsh things have been said of the "sweater," that really apply to the system in which he is a necessary, logical link. It can at least be said of him that he is no worse than the conditions that created him. The sweater is simply the middleman, the sub-contractor, a workman like his fellows, perhaps with the single distinction from the rest that he knows a little English; perhaps not even that, but with the accidental possession of two or three sewing-machines, or of credit enough to hire them, as his capital, who drums up work among the clothing-houses. Of workmen he can always get enough. Every ship-load from German ports brings them to his door in droves, clamoring for work. The sun sets upon the day of the arrival of many a Polish Jew, finding him at work in an East Side tenement, treading the machine and "learning the trade." Often there are two, sometimes three, sets of sweaters on one job. They work with the rest when they are not drumming up trade, driving their "hands" as they drive their machine, for all they are worth, and making a profit on their work, of course, though in most cases not nearly as extravagant a

---

[84] An invention that cuts many garments at once, where the scissors could cut only a few.

percentage, probably, as is often supposed. If it resolves itself into a margin of five or six cents, or even less, on a dozen pairs of boys' trousers, for instance, it is nevertheless enough to make the contractor with his thrifty instincts independent. The workman growls, not at the hard labor or poor pay, but over the pennies another is coining out of his sweat, and on the first opportunity turns sweater himself, and takes his revenge by driving an even closer bargain than his rival tyrant, thus reducing his profits.

The sweater knows well that the isolation of the workman in his helpless ignorance is his sure foundation, and he has done what he could — with merciless severity where he could — to smother every symptom of awakening intelligence in his slaves. In this effort to perpetuate his despotism he has had the effectual assistance of his own system and the sharp competition that keep the men on starvation wages; of their constitutional greed, that will not permit the sacrifice of temporary advantage, however slight, for permanent good, and above all, of the hungry hordes of immigrants to whom no argument appeals save the cry for bread. Within very recent times he has, however, been forced to partial surrender by the organization of the men to a considerable extent into trades unions, and by experiments in co-operation, under intelligent leadership, that presage the sweater's doom. But as long as the ignorant crowds continue to come and to herd in these tenements, his grip can never be shaken off. And the supply across the seas is apparently inexhaustible. Every fresh persecution of the Russian or Polish Jew on his native soil starts greater hordes hitherward to confound economical problems, and recruit the sweater's phalanx. The curse of bigotry and ignorance reaches half-way across the world, to sow its bitter seed in fertile soil in the East Side tenements. If the Jew himself was to blame for the resentment he aroused over there, he is amply punished. He gathers the first-fruits of the harvest here.

The bulk of the sweater's work is done in the tenements, which the law that regulates factory labor does not reach. To the factories themselves that are taking the place of the rear tenements in rapidly growing numbers, letting in bigger day-crowds than those the health officers banished, the tenement shops serve as a supplement through which the law is successfully evaded. Ten hours is the legal work-day in the factories, and nine o'clock the closing hour at the latest. Forty-five minutes at least must be allowed for dinner, and children under sixteen must not be employed unless they can read and write English; none at all under fourteen. The very fact that such a law should stand on the statute book, shows how desperate the plight of these people. But the tenement has defeated its benevolent purpose. In it the child works unchallenged from the day he is old enough to pull a thread. There is no such thing as a dinner hour; men and women eat while they work, and the "day" is lengthened at both ends far into the night. Factory hands take their work with them at the close of the lawful day to eke out their scanty earnings by working overtime at home. Little chance on this ground for the campaign of education that alone can bring the needed relief; small wonder that there are whole settlements on this East Side where English is practically an unknown tongue, though the people be both willing and anxious to learn. "When shall we find time to learn?" asked one of them of me once. I owe him the answer yet.

Take the Second Avenue Elevated Railroad at Chatham Square and ride up half a mile through the sweaters' district. Every open window of the big tenements, that stand like a continuous brick wall on both sides of the way, gives you a glimpse of one of these shops as the train speeds by. Men and women bending over their machines, or ironing clothes at the window, half-naked. Proprieties do not count on the East Side; nothing counts that cannot be converted into hard cash. The road is like a big gangway through an endless work-room where vast multitudes are forever laboring. Morning, noon, or night, it makes no difference; the scene is always the same. At Rivington Street let us get off and continue our trip on foot. It is Sunday evening west of the Bowery. Here, under the rule of Mosaic law, the week of work is under full headway, its first day far spent. The hucksters' wagons are absent or stand idle at the curb; the saloons admit the thirsty crowds through the side-door labelled "Family Entrance;" a tin sign in a store-window announces that a "Sunday School" gathers in stray children of the new dispensation; but beyond these things there is little to suggest the Christian Sabbath. Men stagger along the sidewalk groaning under heavy burdens of unsewn garments, or enormous black bags stuffed full of finished coats and trousers. Let us follow one to his home and see how Sunday passes in a Ludlow Street tenement.

Up two flights of dark stairs, three, four, with new smells of cabbage, of onions, of frying fish, on every landing, whirring sewing machines behind closed doors betraying what goes on within, to the door that opens to admit the bundle and the man. A sweater, this, in a small way. Five men and a woman, two young girls, not fifteen, and a boy who says unasked that he is fifteen, and lies in saying it, are at the machines sewing knickerbockers, "knee-pants" in the Ludlow Street dialect. The floor is littered ankle-deep with half-sewn garments. In the alcove, on a couch of many dozens of "pants" ready for the finisher, a bare-legged baby with pinched face is asleep. A fence of piled-up clothing keeps him from rolling off on the floor. The faces, hands, and arms to the elbows of everyone in the room are black with the color of the cloth on which they are working. The boy and the woman alone look up at our entrance. The girls shoot sidelong glances, but at a warning look from the man with the bundle they tread their machines more energetically than ever. The men do not appear to be aware even of the presence of a stranger.

They are "learners," all of them, says the woman, who proves to be the wife of the boss, and have "come over" only a few weeks ago. She is disinclined to talk at first, but a few words in her own tongue from our guide[85] set her fears, whatever they are, at rest and she grows almost talkative. The learners work for week's wages, she says. How much do they earn? She shrugs her shoulders with an expressive gesture. The workers themselves, asked in their own tongue, say indifferently, as though the question were of no interest: from two to five dollars. The children — there are four of them — are not old enough to work. The oldest is only six. They turn out one hundred and twenty dozen "knee-pants" a week, for which the manufacturer pays seventy cents a dozen. Five cents a dozen is the clear profit, but her own and her husband's work brings the family earnings up to twenty-five dollars a week, when they have work all the time. But often half the time is put in looking for it. They work no longer than to nine o'clock at night, from daybreak. There are ten machines in the room; six are hired at two dollars a month. For the two shabby, smoke-begrimed rooms, one somewhat larger than ordinary, they pay twenty dollars a month. She does not complain, though "times are not what they were, and it costs a good deal to live." Eight dollars a week for the family of six and two boarders. How do they do it? She laughs, as she goes over the bill of fare, at the silly question: Bread, fifteen cents a day, of milk two quarts a day at four cents a quart, one pound of meat for dinner at twelve cents, butter one pound a week at "eight cents a quarter of a pound." Coffee, potatoes, and pickles complete the list. At the least calculation, probably, this sweater's family hoards up thirty dollars a month, and in a few years will own a tenement somewhere and profit by the example set by their landlord in rent-collecting. It is the way the savings of Jewtown are universally invested, and with the natural talent of its people for commercial speculation the investment is enormously profitable.

---

[85] I was always accompanied on these tours of inquiry by one of their own people who knew of and sympathized with my mission. Without that precaution my errand would have been fruitless; even with him it was often nearly so.

"Knee-Pants" at Forty-Five Cents a Dozen — A Ludlow Street Sweater's Shop.

On the next floor, in a dimly lighted room with a big red-hot stove to keep the pressing irons ready for use, is a family of man, wife, three children, and a boarder. "Knee-pants" are made there too, of a still lower grade. Three cents and a half is all he clears, says the man, and lies probably out of at least two cents. The wife makes a dollar and a half finishing, the man about nine dollars at the machine. The boarder pays sixty-five cents a week. He is really only a lodger, getting his meals outside. The rent is two dollars and twenty-five cents a week, cost of living five dollars. Every floor has at least two, sometimes four, such shops. Here is one with a young family for which life is bright with promise. Husband and wife work together; just now the latter, a comely young woman, is eating her dinner of dry bread and green pickles. Pickles are favorite food in Jewtown. They are filling, and keep the children from crying with hunger. Those who have stomachs like ostriches[86] thrive in spite of them and grow strong — plain proof that they are good to eat. The rest? "Well,

---

[86] A distended "ostrich" like stomach is a sign of malnutrition. — ED.

they die," says our guide, dryly. No thought of untimely death comes to disturb this family with life all before it. In a few years the man will be a prosperous sweater. Already he employs an old man as ironer at three dollars a week, and a sweet-faced little Italian girl as finisher at a dollar and a half. She is twelve, she says, and can neither read nor write; will probably never learn. How should she? The family clears from ten to eleven dollars a week in brisk times, more than half of which goes into the bank.

A companion picture from across the hall. The man works on the machine for his sweater twelve hours a day, turning out three dozen "knee-pants," for which he receives forty-two cents a dozen. The finisher who works with him gets ten, and the ironer eight cents a dozen; buttonholes are extra, at eight to ten cents a hundred. This operator has four children at his home in Stanton Street, none old enough to work, and a sick wife. His rent is twelve dollars a month; his wages for a hard week's work less than eight dollars. Such as he, with their consuming desire for money thus smothered, recruit the ranks of the anarchists, won over by the promise of a general "divide";[87] and an enlightened public sentiment turns up its nose at the vicious foreigner for whose perverted notions there is no room in this land of plenty.

Turning the corner into Hester Street, we stumble upon a nest of cloak-makers in their busy season. Six months of the year the cloak-maker is idle, or nearly so. Now is his harvest. Seventy-five cents a cloak, all complete, is the price in this shop. The cloak is of cheap plush, and might sell for eight or nine dollars over the store-counter. Seven dollars is the weekly wage of this man with wife and two children, and nine dollars and a half rent to pay per month. A boarder pays about a third of it. There was a time when he made ten dollars a week and thought himself rich. But wages have come down fearfully in the last two years. Think of it: "come down" to this. The other cloak-makers aver that they can make as much as twelve dollars a week, when they are employed, by taking their work home and sewing till midnight. One exhibits his account-book with a Ludlow Street sweater. It shows that he and his partner, working on first-class garments for a Broadway house in the four busiest weeks of the season, made together from $15.15 to $19.20 a week by striving from 6 A.M. to 11 P.M., that is to say, from $7.58 to $9.60 each.[88] The sweater on this work probably made as much as fifty per cent. at least on their labor. Not far away is a factory in a rear yard where the factory inspector reports

---

[87] A conflict between economic classes, specifically the wealthy and the poor. — ED.

[88] The strike of the cloakmakers last summer, that ended in victory, raised their wages considerably, at least for the time being.

teams of tailors making men's coats at an average of twenty-seven cents a coat, all complete except buttons and button-holes.

Turning back, we pass a towering double tenement in Ludlow Street, owned by a well-known Jewish liquor dealer and politician, a triple combination that bodes ill for his tenants. As a matter of fact, the cheapest "apartment," three rear rooms on the sixth floor, only one of which deserves the name, is rented for $13 a month. Here is a reminder of the Bend, a hallway turned into a shoemaker's shop. Two hallways side by side in adjoining tenements would be sinful waste in Jewtown, when one would do as well by knocking a hole in the wall. But this shoemaker knows a trick the Italian's ingenuity did not suggest. He has his "flat" as well as his shop there. A curtain hung back of his stool in the narrow passage half conceals his bed that fills it entirely from wall to wall. To get into it he has to crawl over the footboard, and he must come out the same way. Expedients more odd than this are born of the East Side crowding. In one of the houses we left, the coal-bin of a family on the fourth floor was on the roof of the adjoining tenement. A quarter of a ton of coal was being dumped there while we talked with the people.

We have reached Broome Street. The hum of industry in this six-story tenement on the corner leaves no doubt of the aspect Sunday wears within it. One flight up, we knock at the nearest door. The grocer, who keeps the store, lives on the "stoop," the first floor in East Side parlance. In this room a suspender-maker sleeps and works with his family of wife and four children. For a wonder there are no boarders. His wife and eighteen years old daughter share in the work, but the girl's eyes are giving out from the strain. Three months in the year, when work is very brisk, the family makes by united efforts as high as fourteen and fifteen dollars a week. The other nine months it averages from three to four dollars. The oldest boy, a young man, earns from four to six dollars in an Orchard Street factory, when he has work. The rent is ten dollars a month for the room and a miserable little coop of a bedroom where the old folks sleep. The girl makes her bed on the lounge in the front room; the big boys and the children sleep on the floor. Coal at ten cents a small pail, meat at twelve cents a pound, one and a half pound of butter a week at thirty-six cents, and a quarter of a pound of tea in the same space of time, are items of their house-keeping account as given by the daughter. Milk at four and five cents a quart, "according to quality." The sanitary authorities know what that means, know how miserably inadequate is the fine of fifty or a hundred dollars for the murder done in cold blood by the wretches who poison the babes of these tenements with the stuff that is half water, or swill. Their defence is that the demand is for "cheap milk." Scarcely a wonder that this suspender-maker will hardly be able to save up the *dot* for his daughter, without which she stands no chance of marrying in Jewtown, even with her face that would be pretty had it a healthier tinge.

Up under the roof three men are making boys' jackets at twenty cents a piece, of which the sewer takes eight, the ironer three, the finisher five cents, and the button-hole-maker two and a quarter, leaving a cent and three-quarters to pay for the drumming up, the fetching and bringing back of the goods. They bunk together in a room for which they pay eight dollars a month. All three are single here, that is: their wives are on the other side yet, waiting for them to earn enough to send for them. Their breakfast, eaten at the work-bench, consists of a couple of rolls at a cent a piece, and a draught of water, milk when business has been very good, a square meal at noon in a restaurant, and the morning meal over again at night. This square meal, that is the evidence of a very liberal disposition on the part of the consumer, is an affair of more than ordinary note; it may be justly called an institution. I know of a couple of restaurants at the lower end of Orchard Street that are favorite resorts for the Polish Jews, who remember the injunction that the ox that treadeth out the corn shall not be muzzled. Being neighbors, they are rivals of course, and cutting under. When I was last there one gave a dinner of soup, meat-stew, bread, pie, pickles, and a "schooner" of beer for thirteen cents; the other charged fifteen cents for a similar dinner, but with two schooners of beer and a cigar, or a cigarette, as the extra inducement. The two cents had won the day, however, and the thirteen-cent restaurant did such a thriving business that it was about to spread out into the adjoining store to accommodate the crowds of customers. At this rate the lodger of Jewtown can "live like a lord," as he says himself, for twenty-five cents a day, including the price of his bed, that ranges all the way from thirty to forty and fifty cents a week, and save money, no matter what his earnings. He does it, too, so long as work is to be had at any price, and by the standard he sets up Jewtown must abide.

It has thousands upon thousands of lodgers who help to pay its extortionate rents. At night there is scarce a room in all the district that has not one or more of them, some above half a score, sleeping on cots, or on the floor. It is idle to speak of privacy in these "homes." The term carries no more meaning with it than would a lecture on social ethics to an audience of Hottentots.[89] The picture is not overdrawn. In fact, in presenting the home life of these people I have been at some pains to avoid the extreme of privation, taking the cases just as they came to hand

[89] Tribe of bushmen living in South Africa. — ED.

on the safer middle-ground of average earnings. Yet even the direst apparent poverty in Jewtown, unless dependent on absolute lack of work, would, were the truth known, in nine cases out of ten have a silver lining in the shape of a margin in bank.

These are the economical conditions that enable my manufacturing friend to boast that New York can "beat the world" on cheap clothing. In support of his claim he told me that a single Bowery firm last year sold fifteen thousand suits at $1.95 that averaged in cost 1.12\frac{1}{2}$. With the material at fifteen cents a yard, he said, children's suits of assorted sizes can be sold at wholesale for seventy-five cents, and boys' cape overcoats at the same price. They are the same conditions that have perplexed the committee of benevolent Hebrews in charge of Baron de Hirsch's[90] munificent gift of ten thousand dollars a month for the relief of the Jewish poor in New York. To find proper channels through which to pour this money so that it shall effect its purpose without pauperizing, and without perpetuating the problem it is sought to solve, by attracting still greater swarms, is indeed no easy task. Colonization[91] has not in the past been a success with these people. The great mass of them are too gregarious to take kindly to farming, and their strong commercial instinct hampers the experiment. To herd them in model tenements, though it relieve the physical suffering in a measure, would be to treat a symptom of the disease rather than strike at its root, even if land could be got cheap enough where they gather to build on a sufficiently large scale to make the plan a success. Trade schools for manual training could hardly be made to reach the adults, who in addition would have to be supported for months while learning. For the young this device has proved most excellent under the wise management of the United Hebrew Charities, an organization that gathers to its work the best thought and effort of many of our most public-spirited citizens. One, or all, of these plans may be tried, probably will. I state but the misgivings as to the result of some of the practical minds that have busied themselves with the problem. Its keynote evidently is the ignorance of the immigrants. They must be taught the language of the country they have chosen as their home, as the first and most necessary step. Whatever may follow, that is essential, absolutely vital. That done, it may well be that the case in its new aspect will not be nearly so hard to deal with.

---

[90] Baron Maurice de Hirsch (1831–1896). Wealthy Austrian philanthropist. — ED.

[91] Baron de Hirsch's plan to settle Jewish immigrants in rural areas of the United States and encourage them to establish farming communities. — ED.

Evening has worn into night as we take up our homeward journey through the streets, now no longer silent. The thousands of lighted windows in the tenements glow like dull red eyes in a huge stone wall. From every door multitudes of tired men and women pour forth for a half-hour's rest in the open air before sleep closes the eyes weary with incessant working. Crowds of half-naked children tumble in the street and on the sidewalk, or doze fretfully on the stone steps. As we stop in front of a tenement to watch one of these groups, a dirty baby in a single brief garment — yet a sweet, human little baby despite its dirt and tatters — tumbles off the lowest step, rolls over once, clutches my leg with unconscious grip, and goes to sleep on the flagstones, its curly head pillowed on my boot.

Chapter XII

The Bohemians — Tenement-house Cigarmaking

Evil as the part is which the tenement plays in Jewtown as the pretext for circumventing the law that was made to benefit and relieve the tenant, we have not far to go to find it in even a worse rôle. If the tenement is here continually dragged into the eye of public condemnation and scorn, it is because in one way or another it is found directly responsible for, or intimately associated with, three-fourths of the miseries of the poor. In the Bohemian quarter it is made the vehicle for enforcing upon a proud race a slavery as real as any that ever disgraced the South. Not content with simply robbing the tenant, the owner, in the dual capacity of landlord and employer, reduces him to virtual serfdom by making his becoming *his* tenant, on such terms as he sees fit to make, the condition of employment at wages likewise of his own making. It does not help the case that this landlord employer, almost always a Jew, is frequently of the thrifty Polish race just described.

Perhaps the Bohemian quarter is hardly the proper name to give to the colony, for though it has distinct boundaries it is scattered over a wide area on the East Side, in wedge-like streaks that relieve the monotony of the solid German population by their strong contrasts. The two races mingle no more on this side of the Atlantic than on the rugged slopes of the Bohemian mountains; the echoes of the thirty years' war[92] ring in New York, after two centuries and a half, with as fierce a hatred as the gigantic combat bred among the vanquished Czechs. A chief reason for this is doubtless the complete isolation of the Bohemian immigrant. Several causes operate to bring this about: his singularly harsh and unattractive language, which he can neither easily himself unlearn nor impart to others, his stubborn pride of race, and a popular prejudice which has forced upon him the unjust stigma of a disturber of the public peace and an enemy of organized labor. I greatly mistrust that the Bohemian on our shores is a much-abused man. To his traducer, who casts up anarchism against him, he replies that the last census (1880) shows his people to have the fewest criminals of all in proportion to numbers. In New York a Bohemian criminal is such a rarity that the case of two firebugs of several years ago is remembered with damaging distinctness. The accusation that he lives like the "rat" he is, cutting down wages by his underpaid labor, he throws back in the teeth of the trades unions with the counter-charge that they are the first cause of his attitude to the labor question.

A little way above Houston Street the first of his colonies is encountered, in Fifth Street and thereabouts. Then for a mile and a half scarce a Bohemian is to be found, until Thirty-eighth Street is reached. Fifty-fourth and Seventy-third Streets in their turn are the centres of populous Bohemian settlements. The location of the cigar factories, upon which he depends for a living, determines his choice of home, though there is less choice about it than with any other class in the community, save perhaps the colored people. Probably more than half of all the Bohemians in this city are cigarmakers, and it is the herding of these in great numbers in the so-called tenement factories, where the cheapest grade of work is done at the lowest wages, that constitutes at once their greatest hardship and the chief grudge of other workmen against them. The manufacturer who owns, say, from three or four to a dozen or more tenements contiguous to his shop, fills them up with these people, charging them outrageous rents, and demanding often even a preliminary deposit of five dollars "key money";[93] deals them out tobacco by the week, and devotes the rest of his energies to the paring down of wages to within a peg or two of the point where the tenant rebels in desperation. When he does rebel, he is given the alternative of submission, or eviction with entire loss of

---

[92] A series of wars fought between 1618 and 1648 that led to the end of the Habsburg dominance of Europe. — ED.

[93] A deposit required of renters for which the landlord will exchange the apartment key. — ED.

employment. His needs determine the issue. Usually he is not in a position to hesitate long. Unlike the Polish Jew, whose example of untiring industry he emulates, he has seldom much laid up against a rainy day. He is fond of a glass of beer, and likes to live as well as his means will permit. The shop triumphs, and fetters more galling than ever are forged for the tenant. In the opposite case, the newspapers have to record the throwing upon the street of a small army of people, with pitiful cases of destitution and family misery.

Men, women and children work together seven days in the week in these cheerless tenements to make a living for the family, from the break of day till far into the night. Often the wife is the original cigarmaker from the old home, the husband having adopted her trade here as a matter of necessity, because, knowing no word of English, he could get no other work. As they state the cause of the bitter hostility of the trades unions, she was the primary bone of contention in the day of the early Bohemian immigration. The unions refused to admit the women, and, as the support of the family depended upon her to a large extent, such terms as were offered had to be accepted. The manufacturer has ever since industriously fanned the antagonism between the unions and his hands, for his own advantage. The victory rests with him, since the Court of Appeals decided that the law, passed a few years ago, to prohibit cigarmaking in tenements was unconstitutional, and thus put an end to the struggle. While it lasted, all sorts of frightful stories were told of the shocking conditions under which people lived and worked in these tenements, from a sanitary point of view especially, and a general impression survives to this day that they are particularly desperate. The Board of Health, after a careful canvass, did not find them so then. I am satisfied from personal inspection, at a much later day, guided in a number of instances by the union cigarmakers themselves to the tenements which they considered the worst, that the accounts were greatly exaggerated. Doubtless the people are poor, in many cases very poor; but they are not uncleanly, rather the reverse; they live much better than the clothing-makers in the Tenth Ward, and in spite of their sallow look, that may be due to the all-pervading smell of tobacco, they do not appear to be less healthy than other in-door workers. I found on my tours of investigation several cases of consumption, of which one at least was said by the doctor to be due to the constant inhalation of tobacco fumes. But an examination of the death records in the Health Department does not support the claim that the Bohemian cigarmakers are peculiarly prone to that disease. On the contrary, the Bohemian percentage of deaths from consumption appears quite low. This, however, is a line of scientific inquiry which I leave to others to pursue, along with the more involved problem whether the falling off in the number of children, sometimes quite noticeable in the Bohemian settlements, is, as has been suggested, dependent upon the character of the parents' work. The sore grievances I found were the miserable wages and the enormous rents exacted for the minimum of accommodation. And surely these stand for enough of suffering.

Take a row of houses in East Tenth Street as an instance. They contained thirty-five families of cigarmakers, with probably not half a dozen persons in the whole lot of them, outside of the children, who could speak a word of English, though many had been in the country half a lifetime. This room with two windows giving on the street, and a rear attachment without windows, called a bedroom by courtesy, is rented at $12.25 a month. In the front room man and wife work at the bench from six in the morning till nine at night. They make a team, stripping the tobacco leaves together; then he makes the filler, and she rolls the wrapper on and finishes the cigar. For a thousand they receive $3.75, and can turn out together three thousand cigars a week. The point has been reached where the rebellion comes in, and the workers in these tenements are just now on a strike, demanding $5.00 and $5.50 for their work. The manufacturer having refused, they are expecting hourly to be served with notice to quit their homes, and the going of a stranger among them excites their resentment, until his errand is explained. While we are in the house, the ultimatum of the "boss" is received. He will give $3.75 a thousand, not another cent. Our host is a man of seeming intelligence, yet he has been nine years in New York and knows neither English nor German. Three bright little children play about the floor.

His neighbor on the same floor has been here fifteen years, but shakes his head when asked if he can speak English. He answers in a few broken syllables when addressed in German. With $11.75 rent to pay for like accommodation, he has the advantage of his oldest boy's work besides his wife's at the bench. Three properly make a team, and these three can turn out four thousand cigars a week, at $3.75. This Bohemian has a large family; there are four children, too small to work, to be cared for. A comparison of the domestic bills of fare in Tenth and in Ludlow Streets results in the discovery that this Bohemian's butcher's bill for the week, with meat at twelve cents a pound as in Ludlow Street, is from two dollars and a half to three dollars. The Polish Jew fed as big a family on one pound of meat a day. The difference proves to be typical. Here is a suite of three rooms, two dark, three flights up. The ceiling is partly down in one of the rooms. "It is three months since we asked the landlord to fix it," says the oldest son, a very intelligent lad who has learned English in the evening school. His father has not had that advantage, and has sat at his bench, deaf and dumb to the world about him except his own, for six years. He has improved his time and become an expert at his trade. Father, mother and son together, a full team, make from fifteen to sixteen dollars a week.

A man with venerable beard and keen eyes answers our questions through an interpreter, in the next house. Very few brighter faces would be met in a day's walk among American mechanics, yet he has in nine years learned no syllable of English. German he probably does not want to learn. His story supplies the explanation, as did the stories of the others. In all that time he has been at work grubbing to earn bread. Wife and he by constant labor make three thousand cigars a week, earning $11.25 when there is no lack of material; when in winter they receive from the manufacturer tobacco for only two thousand, the rent of $10 for two rooms, practically one with a dark alcove, has nevertheless to be paid in full, and six mouths to be fed. He was a blacksmith in the old country, but cannot work at his trade here because he does not understand "Engliska." If he could, he says, with a bright look, he could do better work than he sees done here. It would seem happiness to him to knock off at 6 o'clock instead of working, as he now often has to do, till midnight. But how? He knows of no Bohemian blacksmith who can understand him; he should starve. Here, with his wife, he can make a living at least. "Aye," says she, turning, from listening, to her household duties, "it would be nice for sure to have father work at his trade." Then what a home she could make for them, and how happy they would be. Here is an unattainable ideal, indeed, of a workman in the most prosperous city in the world! There is genuine, if unspoken, pathos in the soft tap she gives her husband's hand as she goes about her work with a half-suppressed little sigh.

The very ash-barrels that stand in front of the big rows of tenements in Seventy-first and Seventy-third Streets advertise the business that is carried on within. They are filled to the brim with the stems of stripped tobacco leaves. The rank smell that waited for us on the corner of the block follows us into the hallways, penetrates every nook and cranny of the houses. As in the settlement farther down town, every room here has its work-bench with its stumpy knife and queer pouch of bed-tick, worn brown and greasy, fastened in front the whole length of the bench to receive the scraps of waste. This landlord-employer at all events gives three rooms for $12.50, if two be dark, one wholly and the other getting some light from the front room. The mother of the three bare-footed little children we met on the stairs was taken to the hospital the other day when she could no longer work. She will never come out alive. There is no waste in these tenements. Lives, like clothes, are worn through and out before

Bohemian Cigarmakers at Work in Their Tenement.

put aside. Her place at the bench is taken already by another who divides with the head of the household his earnings of $15.50 a week. He has just come out successful of a strike that brought the pay of these tenements up to $4.50 per thousand cigars. Notice to quit had already been served on them, when the employer decided to give in, frightened by the prospective loss of rent. Asked how long he works, the man says: "from they can see till bed-time." Bed-time proves to be eleven o'clock. Seventeen hours a day, seven days in the week, at thirteen cents an hour for the two, six cents and a half for each! Good average earnings for a tenement-house cigarmaker in summer. In winter it is at least one-fourth less. In spite of it all, the rooms are cleanly kept. From the bedroom farthest back the woman brings out a pile of moist tobacco-leaves to be stripped. They are kept there, under cover lest they dry and crack, from Friday to Friday, when an accounting is made and fresh supplies given out. The people sleep there too, but the smell, offensive to the unfamiliar nose, does not bother them. They are used to it.

In a house around the corner that is not a factory-tenement, lives now the cigarmaker I spoke of as suffering from consumption which the doctor said was due to the tobacco-fumes. Perhaps the lack of healthy exercise had as much to do with it. His case is interesting from its own stand-point. He too is one with a — for a Bohemian — large family. Six children sit at his table. By trade a shoemaker, for thirteen years he helped his wife make cigars in the manufacturer's tenement. She was a very good hand, and until his health gave out two years ago they were able to make from $17 to $25 a week, by lengthening the day at both ends. Now that he can work no more, and the family under the doctor's orders has moved away from the smell of tobacco, the burden of its support has fallen upon her alone, for none of the children is old enough to help. She has work in the shop at eight dollars a week, and this must go round; it is all there is. Happily, this being a tenement for revenue only, unmixed with cigars, the rent is cheaper: seven dollars for two bright rooms on the top floor. No housekeeping is attempted. A woman in Seventy-second Street supplies their meals, which the wife and mother fetches in a basket, her husband being too weak. Breakfast of coffee and hard-tack, or black bread, at twenty cents for the whole eight; a good many, the little woman says with a brave, patient smile, and there is seldom anything to spare, but ———. The invalid is listening, and the sentence remains unfinished. What of dinner? One of the children brings it from the cook. Oh! it is a good dinner, meat, soup, greens and bread, all for thirty cents. It is the principal family meal. Does she come home for dinner? No; she cannot leave the shop, but gets a bite at her bench. The question: A bite of what? seems as merciless as the surgeon's knife, and she winces under it as one shrinks from physical pain. Bread, then. But at night they all have supper together — sausage and bread. For ten cents they can eat all they want. Can they not? she says, stroking the hair of the little boy at her knee; his eyes glisten hungrily at the thought, as he nods stoutly in support of his mother. Only, she adds, the week the rent is due, they have to shorten rations to pay the landlord.

But what of his being an Anarchist, this Bohemian — an infidel — I hear somebody say. Almost one might be persuaded by such facts as these — and they are everyday facts, not fancy — to retort: what more natural? With every hand raised against him in the old land and the new, in the land of his hoped-for freedom, what more logical than that his should be turned against society that seems to exist only for his oppression? But the charge is not half true. Naturally the Bohemian loves peace, as he loves music and song. As someone has said: He does not seek war, but when attacked knows better how to die than how to surrender. The Czech is the Irishman of Central Europe, with all his genius and his strong passions, with the same bitter traditions of landlord-robbery, perpetuated here where he thought to forget them; like him ever and on principle in the opposition, "agin the government" wherever he goes. Among such a people, ground by poverty until their songs have died in curses upon their oppressors, hopelessly isolated and ignorant of our language and our laws, it would not be hard for bad men at any time to lead a few astray. And this is what has been done. Yet, even with the occasional noise made by the few, the criminal statistics already alluded to quite dispose of the charge that they incline to turbulence and riot. So it is with the infidel propaganda, the legacy perhaps of the fierce contention through hundreds of years between Catholics and Protestants on Bohemia's soil, of bad faith and savage persecutions in the name of the Christians' God that disgrace its history. The Bohemian clergyman, who spoke for his people at the Christian Conference held in Chickering Hall two years ago, took even stronger ground. "They are Roman Catholics by birth, infidels by necessity, and Protestants by history and inclination," he said. Yet he added his testimony in the same breath to the fact that, though the Freethinkers had started two schools in the immediate neighborhood of his church to counteract its influence, his flock had grown in a few years from a mere handful at the start to proportions far beyond his hopes, gathering in both Anarchists and Freethinkers, and making good church members of them.

Thus the whole matter resolves itself once more into a question of education, all the more urgent because these people are poor, miserably poor almost to a man. "There is not," said one of them, who knew thoroughly what he was speaking of, "there is not one of them all, who, if he were to sell all he was worth to-morrow, would have money enough to buy a house and lot in the country."

Chapter XIII

The Color Line in New York

The color line must be drawn through the tenements to give the picture its proper shading. The landlord does the drawing, does it with an absence of pretence, a frankness of despotism, that is nothing if not brutal. The Czar of all the Russias is not more absolute upon his own soil than the New York landlord in his dealings with colored tenants. Where he permits them to live, they go; where he shuts the door, stay out. By his grace they exist at all in certain localities; his ukase[94] banishes them from others. He accepts the responsibility, when laid at his door, with unruffled complacency. It is business, he will tell you. And it is. He makes the prejudice in which he traffics pay him well, and that, as he thinks it quite superfluous to tell you, is what he is there for.

That his pencil does not make quite as black a mark as it did, that the hand that wields it does not bear down as hard as only a short half dozen years ago, is the hopeful sign of an awakening public conscience under the stress of which the line shows signs of wavering. But for this the landlord deserves no credit. It has come, is coming about despite him. The line may not be wholly effaced while the name of the negro, alone among the world's races, is spelled with a small n. Natural selection will have more or less to do beyond a doubt in every age with dividing the races; only so, it may be, can they work out together their highest destiny. But with the despotism that deliberately assigns to the defenceless Black the lowest level for the purpose of robbing him there that has nothing to do. Of such slavery, different only in degree from the other kind that held him as a chattel, to be sold or bartered at the will of his master, this century, if signs fail not, will see the end in New York.

Ever since the war New York has been receiving the overflow of colored population from the Southern cities. In the last decade this migration has grown to such proportions that it is estimated that our Blacks have quite doubled in number since the Tenth Census.[95] Whether the exchange has been of advantage to the negro may well be questioned. Trades of which he had practical control in his Southern home are not open to him here. I know that it may be answered that there is no industrial proscription of color; that it is a matter of choice. Perhaps so. At all events he does not choose then. How many colored carpenters or masons has anyone seen at work in New York? In the South there are enough of them and, if the testimony of the most intelligent of their people is worth anything, plenty of them have come here. As a matter of fact the colored man takes in New York, without a struggle, the lower level of menial service for which his past traditions and natural love of ease perhaps as yet fit him best. Even the colored barber is rapidly getting to be a thing of the past. Along shore, at any unskilled labor, he works unmolested; but he does not appear to prefer the job. His sphere thus defined, he naturally takes his stand among the poor, and in the homes

[94] An order from the Russian czar that had the force of law. The term was also used to describe any order made by an absolute authority. — ED.

[95] First carried out in 1790, the U.S. Census appears every ten years. Riis is referring to the Census of 1880. — ED.

of the poor. Until very recent times — the years since a change was wrought can be counted on the fingers of one hand — he was practically restricted in the choice of a home to a narrow section on the West Side, that nevertheless had a social top and bottom to it — the top in the tenements on the line of Seventh Avenue as far north as Thirty-second Street, where he was allowed to occupy the houses of unsavory reputation which the police had cleared and for which decent white tenants could not be found; the bottom in the vile rookeries of Thompson Street and South Fifth Avenue, the old "Africa" that is now fast becoming a modern Italy. To-day there are black colonies in Yorkville and Morrisania. The encroachment of business and the Italian below, and the swelling of the population above, have been the chief agents in working out his second emancipation, a very real one, for with his cutting loose from the old tenements there has come a distinct and gratifying improvement in the tenant, that argues louder than theories or speeches the influence of vile surroundings in debasing the man. The colored citizen whom this year's census man found in his Ninety-ninth Street "flat" is a very different individual from the "nigger" his predecessor counted in the black-and-tan slums of Thompson and Sullivan Streets. There is no more clean and orderly community in New York than the new settlement of colored people that is growing up on the East Side from Yorkville to Harlem.

Cleanliness is the characteristic of the negro in his new surroundings, as it was his virtue in the old. In this respect he is immensely the superior of the lowest of the whites, the Italians and the Polish Jews, below whom he has been classed in the past in the tenant scale. Nevertheless, he has always had to pay higher rents than even these for the poorest and most stinted rooms. The exceptions I have come across, in which the rents, though high, have seemed more nearly on a level with what was asked for the same number and size of rooms in the average tenement, were in the case of tumble-down rookeries in which no one else would live, and were always coupled with the condition that the landlord should "make no repairs." It can readily be seen that his profits were scarcely curtailed by his "humanity." The reason advanced for this systematic robbery is that white people will not live in the same house with colored tenants, or even in a house recently occupied by negroes, and that consequently its selling value is injured. The prejudice undoubtedly exists, but it is not lessened by the house agents, who have set up the maxim "once a colored house, always a colored house."

There is method in the maxim, as shown by an inquiry made last year by the *Real Estate Record*. It proved agents to be practically unanimous in the endorsement of the negro as a clean, orderly, and "profitable" tenant. Here is the testimony of one of the largest real estate firms in the city: "We would rather have negro tenants in our poorest class of tenements than the lower grades of foreign white people. We find the former cleaner than the latter, and they do not destroy the property so much. We also get higher prices. We have a tenement on Nineteenth Street, where we get $10 for two rooms which we could not get more than $7.50 for from white tenants previously. We have a four-story tenement on our books on Thirty-third Street, between Sixth and Seventh Avenues, with four rooms per floor — a parlor, two bedrooms, and a kitchen. We get $20 for the first floor, $24 for the second, $23 for the third and $20 for the fourth, in all $87 or $1,044 per annum. The size of the building is only 21 + 55." Another firm declared that in a specified instance they had saved fifteen to twenty per cent. on the gross rentals since they changed from white to colored tenants. Still another gave the following case of a front and rear tenement that had formerly been occupied by tenants of a "low European type," who had been turned out on account of filthy habits and poor pay. The negroes proved cleaner, better, and steadier tenants. Instead, however, of having their rents reduced in consequence, the comparison stood as follows:

Rents under White Tenants				**Rents under Colored Tenants**		
			Per month			Per month
Front —	1st floor (store, etc.)		$21	Front —	1st floor (store, etc.)	$21
	2d		13		2d	14
	3d		13		3d	14
	4th (and rear)		21		4th	14
Rear —	2d		12	Rear —	2d	12
	3d		12		3d	13
	4th (see front)		—		4th	13
Rear house —	1st		8	Rear house — 1st		10
	2d		10		2d	12
	3d		9		3d	11
	4th		8		4th	10
Total			$127	Total		$144

An increased rental of $17 per month, or $204 a year, and an advance of nearly thirteen and one-half per cent. on the gross rental "in favor" of the colored tenant. Profitable, surely!

I have quoted these cases at length in order to let in light on the quality of this landlord despotism that has purposely confused the public mind, and for its own selfish ends is propping up a waning prejudice. It will be cause for congratulation if indeed its time has come at last. Within a year, I am told by one of the most intelligent and best informed of our colored citizens, there has been evidence, simultaneous with the colored hegira from the low down-town tenements, of a movement toward less exorbitant rents. I cannot pass from this subject without adding a leaf from my own experience that deserves a place in this record, though, for the credit of humanity, I hope as an extreme case. It was last Christmas that I had occasion to visit the home of an old colored woman in Sixteenth Street, as the almoner of generous friends out of town who wished me to buy her a Christmas dinner. The old woman lived in a wretched shanty, occupying two mean, dilapidated rooms at the top of a sort of hen-ladder that went by the name of stairs. For these she paid ten dollars a month out of her hard-earned wages as a scrubwoman. I did not find her in and, being informed that she was "at the agent's," went around to hunt her up. The agent's wife appeared, to report that Ann was out. Being in a hurry it occurred to me that I might save time by making her employer the purveyor of my friend's bounty, and proposed to entrust the money, two dollars, to her to be expended for Old Ann's benefit. She fell in with the suggestion at once, and confided to me in the fullness of her heart that she liked the plan, inasmuch as "I generally find her a Christmas dinner myself, and this money — she owes Mr. ——— (her husband, the agent) a lot of rent." Needless to state that there was a change of programme then and there, and that Ann was saved from the sort of Christmas cheer that woman's charity would have spread before her. When I had the old soul comfortably installed in her own den, with a chicken and "fixin's" and a bright fire in her stove, I asked her how much she owed of her rent. Her answer was that she did not really owe anything, her month not being quite up, but that the amount yet unpaid was — two dollars!

Poverty, abuse, and injustice alike the negro accepts with imperturbable cheerfulness. His philosophy is of the kind that has no room for repining. Whether he lives in an Eighth Ward barrack or in a tenement with a brown-stone front and pretensions to the title of "flat," he looks at the sunny side of life and enjoys it. He loves fine clothes and good living a good deal more than he does a bank account. The proverbial rainy day it would be rank ingratitude, from his point of view, to look for when the sun shines unclouded in a clear sky. His home surroundings, except when he is utterly depraved, reflect his blithesome temper. The poorest negro housekeeper's room in New York is bright with gaily-colored prints of his beloved "Abe Linkum," General Grant, President Garfield, Mrs. Cleveland, and other national celebrities, and cheery with flowers and singing birds. In the art of putting the best foot foremost, of disguising his poverty by making a little go a long way, our negro has no equal. When a fair share of prosperity is his, he knows how to make life and home very pleasant to those about him. Pianos and parlor furniture abound in the uptown homes of colored tenants and give them a very prosperous air. But even where the wolf howls at the door, he makes a bold and gorgeous front. The amount of "style" displayed on fine Sundays on Sixth and Seventh Avenues by colored holiday-makers would turn a pessimist black with wrath. The negro's great ambition is to rise in the social scale to which his color has made him a stranger and an outsider, and he is quite willing to accept the shadow for the substance where that is the best he can get. The claw-hammer coat and white tie of a waiter in a first-class summer hotel, with the chance of taking his ease in six months of winter, are to him the next best thing to mingling with the white quality he serves, on equal terms. His festive gatherings, pre-eminently his cake-walks,[96] at which a sugared and frosted cake is the proud prize of the couple with the most aristocratic step and carriage, are comic mixtures of elaborate ceremonial and the joyous abandon of the natural man. With all his ludicrous incongruities, his sensuality and his lack of moral accountability, his superstition and other faults that are the effect of temperament and of centuries of slavery, he has his eminently good points. He is loyal to the backbone, proud of being an American and of his new-found citizenship.[97] He is at least as easily moulded for good as for evil. His churches are crowded to the doors on Sunday nights when the colored colony turns out to worship. His people own church property in this city upon which they have paid half a million dollars out of the depth of their poverty, with comparatively little assistance from their white brethren. He is both willing and anxious to learn, and his intellectual status is distinctly improving. If his emotions are not very deeply rooted, they are at least sincere while they last, and until the tempter gets the upper hand again.

Of all the temptations that beset him, the one that troubles him and the police most is his passion for gambling. The game of policy is a kind of unlawful penny lottery specially adapted to his means, but patronized extensively by poor white players as well. It is the meanest of swindles, but reaps for its backers rich fortunes wherever colored people congregate. Between the fortune-teller and the policy shop,[98] closely allied frauds always, the wages of many a hard day's work are wasted by the negro; but the loss causes him few regrets. Penniless, but with undaunted faith in his ultimate "luck," he looks forward to the time when he shall

---

[96] A type of dance popular in the black community. — ED.

[97] African Americans were legally entitled to vote only after Fifteenth Amendment of the United States Constitution was adopted in 1870. — ED.

[98] Shop in which "numbers" are played. — ED.

A Black-and-Tan Dive in "Africa."

once more be able to take a hand at "beating policy."[99] When periodically the negro's lucky numbers, 4–11–44, come out on the slips of the alleged daily drawings, that are supposed to be held in some far-off Western town, intense excitement reigns in Thompson Street and along the Avenue, where someone is always the winner. An immense impetus is given then to the bogus business that has no existence outside of the cigar stores and candy shops where it hides from the law, save in some cunning Bowery "broker's" back office, where the slips are printed and the "winnings" apportioned daily with due regard to the backer's interests.

It is a question whether "Africa" has been improved by the advent of the Italian, with the tramp from the Mulberry Street Bend in his train. The moral turpitude of Thompson Street has been notorious for years, and the mingling of the three elements does not seem to have wrought any change for the better. The border-land where the white and black races meet in common debauch, the aptly-named black-and-tan saloon,

[99] Hitting the number. — ED.

has never been debatable ground from a moral stand-point. It has always been the worst of the desperately bad. Than this commingling of the utterly depraved of both sexes, white and black, on such ground, there can be no greater abomination. Usually it is some foul cellar dive, perhaps run by the political "leader" of the district, who is "in with" the police. In any event it gathers to itself all the lawbreakers and all the human wrecks within reach. When a fight breaks out during the dance a dozen razors are handy in as many boot-legs, and there is always a job for the surgeon and the ambulance. The black "tough" is as handy with the razor in a fight as his peaceably inclined brother is with it in pursuit of his honest trade.[100] As the Chinaman hides his knife in his sleeve and the Italian his stiletto in the bosom, so the negro goes to the ball with a razor in his boot-leg, and on occasion does as much execution with it as both of the others together. More than three-fourths of the business the police have with the colored people in New York arises in the black-and-tan district, now no longer fairly representative of their color.

I have touched briefly upon such facts in the negro's life as may serve to throw light on the social condition of his people in New York. If, when the account is made up between the races, it shall be claimed that he falls short of the result to be expected from twenty-five years of freedom, it may be well to turn to the other side of the ledger and see how much of the blame is borne by the prejudice and greed that have kept him from rising under a burden of responsibility to which he could hardly be equal. And in this view he may be seen to have advanced much farther and faster than before suspected, and to promise, after all, with fair treatment, quite as well as the rest of us, his white-skinned fellow-citizens, had any right to expect.

Chapter XIV

The Common Herd

There is another line not always so readily drawn in the tenements, yet the real boundary line of the Other Half: the one that defines the "flat." The law does not draw it at all, accounting all flats tenements without distinction. The health officer draws it from observation, lumping all those which in his judgment have nothing, or not enough, to give them claim upon the name, with the common herd, and his way is, perhaps, on

[100] Barbering. — ED.

the whole, the surest and best. The outside of the building gives no valuable clew. Brass and brown-stone go well sometimes with dense crowds and dark and dingy rooms; but the first attempt to enter helps draw the line with tolerable distinctness. A locked door is a strong point in favor of the flat. It argues that the first step has been taken to secure privacy, the absence of which is the chief curse of the tenement. Behind a locked door the hoodlum is not at home, unless there be a jailor in place of a janitor to guard it. Not that the janitor and the door-bell are infallible. There may be a tenement behind a closed door; but never a "flat" without it. The hall that is a highway for all the world by night and by day is the tenement's proper badge. The Other Half ever receives with open doors.

With this introduction we shall not seek it long anywhere in the city. Below Houston Street the door-bell in our age is as extinct as the dodo. East of Second Avenue, and west of Ninth Avenue as far up as the Park, it is practically an unknown institution. The nearer the river and the great workshops the more numerous the tenements. The kind of work carried on in any locality to a large extent determines their character. Skilled and well-paid labor puts its stamp on a tenement even in spite of the open door, and usually soon supplies the missing bell. Gas-houses,[101] slaughter-houses and the docks, that attract the roughest crowds and support the vilest saloons, invariably form slum-centres. The city is full of such above the line of Fourteenth Street, that is erroneously supposed by some to fence off the good from the bad, separate the chaff from the wheat. There is nothing below that line that can outdo in wickedness Hell's Kitchen, in the region of three-cent whiskey, or its counterpoise at the other end of Thirty-ninth Street, on the East River, the home of the infamous Rag Gang. Cherry Street is not "tougher" than Battle Row in East Sixty-third Street, or "the village" at Twenty-ninth Street and First Avenue, where stores of broken bricks, ammunition for the nightly conflicts with the police, are part of the regulation outfit of every tenement. The Mulberry Street Bend is scarce dirtier than Little Italy in Harlem. Even across the Harlem River, Frog Hollow challenges the admiration of the earlier slums for the boldness and pernicious activity of its home gang. There are enough of these sore spots. We shall yet have occasion to look into the social conditions of some of them; were I to draw a picture of them here as they are, the subject, I fear, would outgrow alike the limits of this book and the reader's patience.

It is true that they tell only one side of the story; that there is another to tell. A story of thousands of devoted lives, laboring earnestly to make

---

[101] A building in which gas is made for heating and light. — ED.

The Open Door.

the most of their scant opportunities for good; of heroic men and women striving patiently against fearful odds and by their very courage coming off victors in the battle with the tenement; of womanhood pure and undefiled. That it should blossom in such an atmosphere is one of the unfathomable mysteries of life. And yet it is not an uncommon thing to find sweet and innocent girls, singularly untouched by the evil around them, true wives and faithful mothers, literally "like jewels in a swine's snout," in the worst of the infamous barracks. It is the experience of all who have intelligently observed this side of life in a great city, not to be explained — unless on the theory of my friend, the priest in the Mulberry Street Bend, that inherent purity revolts instinctively from the naked brutality of vice as seen in the slums — but to be thankfully accepted as the one gleam of hope in an otherwise hopeless desert.

But the relief is not great. In the dull content of life bred on the tenement-house dead level there is little to redeem it, or to calm apprehension for a society that has nothing better to offer its toilers; while the patient efforts of the lives finally attuned to it to render the situation tolerable, and the very success of these efforts, serve only to bring out in stronger contrast the general gloom of the picture by showing how much farther they might have gone with half a chance. Go into any of the "respectable" tenement neighborhoods — the fact that there are not more than two saloons on the corner, nor over three or four in the block

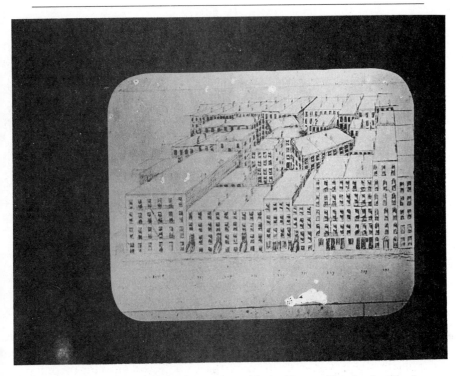

Bird's-Eye View of an East Side Tenement Block. (From a Drawing by Charles I. Wingate, Esq.)

will serve as a fair guide — where live the great body of hard-working Irish and German immigrants and their descendants, who accept naturally the conditions of tenement life, because for them there is nothing else in New York; be with and among its people until you understand their ways, their aims, and the quality of their ambitions, and unless you can content yourself with the scriptural promise that the poor we shall have always with us, or with the menagerie view that, if fed, they have no cause of complaint, you shall come away agreeing with me that, humanly speaking, life there does not seem worth the living. Take at random one of these uptown tenement blocks, not of the worst nor yet of the most prosperous kind, within hail of what the newspapers would call a "fine residential section." These houses were built since the last cholera scare made people willing to listen to reason. The block is not like the one over on the East Side in which I actually lost my way once. There were thirty or forty rear houses in the heart of it, three or four on every lot, set at all sorts of angles, with odd, winding passages, or no passage at all, only "runways" for the thieves and toughs of the neighborhood. These yards are clear. There is air there, and it is about all there is. The view between brick walls outside is that of a stony street; inside, of rows of unpainted board fences, a bewildering maze of clothes-posts and lines; underfoot, a desert of brown, hard-baked soil from which every blade of grass, every stray weed, every speck of green, has been trodden out, as must inevitably be every gentle thought and aspiration above the mere wants of the body in those whose moral natures such home surroundings are to nourish. In self-defence, you know, all life eventually accommodates itself to its environment, and human life is no exception. Within the house there is nothing to supply the want thus left unsatisfied. Tenement-houses have no æsthetic resources. If any are to be brought to bear on them, they must come from the outside. There is the common hall with doors opening softly on every landing as the strange step is heard on the stairs, the air-shaft that seems always so busy letting out foul stenches from below that it has no time to earn its name by bringing down fresh air, the squeaking pumps that hold no water, and the rent that is never less than one week's wages out of the four, quite as often half of the family earnings.

Why complete the sketch? It is drearily familiar already. Such as it is, it is the frame in which are set days, weeks, months, and years of unceasing toil, just able to fill the mouth and clothe the back. Such as it is, it is the world, and all of it, to which these weary workers return nightly to feed heart and brain after wearing out the body at the bench, or in the shop. To it come the young with their restless yearnings, perhaps to pass on the threshold one of the daughters of sin, driven to the tenement by the police when they raided her den, sallying forth in silks and fine attire after her day of idleness. These in their coarse garments — girls with the love of youth for beautiful things, with this hard life before them — who shall save them from the tempter? Down in the street the saloon, always bright and gay, gathering to itself all the cheer of the block, beckons the boys. In many such blocks the census-taker found two thousand men, women, and children, and over, who called them home.

The picture is faithful enough to stand for its class wherever along both rivers the Irish brogue is heard. As already said, the Celt falls most readily victim to tenement influences since shanty-town and its original free-soil-ers have become things of the past. If he be thrifty and shrewd his progress thenceforward is along the plane of the tenement, on which he soon assumes to manage without improving things. The German has an advantage over his Celtic neighbor in his strong love for flowers, which not all the tenements on the East Side have power to smother. His garden goes with him wherever he goes. Not that it represents any high moral principle in the man; rather perhaps the capacity for it. He turns his saloon into a shrubbery as soon as his back-yard. But wherever he puts it in a tenement block it does the work of a dozen police clubs. In proportion as it spreads the neighborhood takes on a more orderly character. As the green dies out of the landscape and increases in political importance, the police find more to do. Where it disappears altogether from sight, lapsing into a mere sentiment, police-beats are shortened and the force patrols double at night. Neither the man nor the sentiment is wholly responsible for this. It is the tenement unadorned that is. The changing of Tompkins Square from a sand lot into a beautiful park put an end for good and all to the "Bread or Blood" riots[102] of which it used to be the scene, and transformed a nest of dangerous agitators into a harmless, beer-craving band of Anarchists. They have scarcely been heard of since. Opponents of the small parks system as a means of relieving the congested population of tenement districts, please take note.

With the first hot nights in June police despatches, that record the killing of men and women by rolling off roofs and window-sills while asleep, announce that the time of greatest suffering among the poor is at hand. It is in hot weather, when life indoors is well-nigh unbearable with cooking, sleeping, and working, all crowded into the small rooms together, that the tenement expands, reckless of all restraint. Then a strange and picturesque life moves upon the flat roofs. In the day and early evening mothers air their babies there, the boys fly their kites from the house-tops, undismayed by police regulations, and the young men and girls court and pass the growler. In the stifling July nights, when the big barracks are like fiery furnaces, their very walls giving out absorbed heat, men and women lie in restless, sweltering rows, panting for air and sleep. Then every truck in the street, every crowded fire-escape, becomes a bedroom, infinitely preferable to any the house affords. A cooling shower on such a night is hailed as a heaven-sent blessing in a hundred thousand homes.

Life in the tenements in July and August spells death to an army of little ones whom the doctor's skill is powerless to save. When the white badge of mourning[103] flutters from every second door, sleepless mothers walk the streets in the gray of the early dawn, trying to stir a cooling breeze to fan the brow of the sick baby. There is no sadder sight than this patient devotion striving against fearfully hopeless odds. Fifty "summer

---

[102] Revolutionary political rallies, the most violent of which occured in July 1877. — ED.
[103] Sign that someone in the apartment had died. — ED

doctors,"[104] especially trained to this work, are then sent into the tenements by the Board of Health, with free advice and medicine for the poor. Devoted women follow in their track with care and nursing for the sick. Fresh-air excursions run daily out of New York on land and water; but despite all efforts the grave-diggers in Calvary work over-time, and little coffins are stacked mountain-high on the deck of the Charity Commissioners' boat when it makes its semi-weekly trips to the city cemetery.

Under the most favorable circumstances, an epidemic, which the well-to-do can afford to make light of as a thing to be got over or avoided by reasonable care, is excessively fatal among the children of the poor, by reason of the practical impossibility of isolating the patient in a tenement. The measles, ordinarily a harmless disease, furnishes a familiar example. Tread it ever so lightly on the avenues, in the tenements it kills right and left. Such an epidemic ravaged three crowded blocks in Elizabeth Street on the heels of the grippe[105] last winter, and, when it had spent its fury, the death-maps in the Bureau of Vital Statistics looked as

---

[104] Physicians who were part of the city's Summer Corps. Established in the summer of 1876, the Corps employed numerous doctors every August to serve the medical needs of the tenement poor. — ED.

[105] Influenza. — ED.

if a black hand had been laid across those blocks over-shadowing in part the contiguous tenements in Mott Street, and with the thumb covering a particularly packed settlement of half a dozen houses in Mulberry Street. The track of the epidemic through these teeming barracks was as clearly defined as the track of a tornado through a forest district. There were houses in which as many as eight little children had died in five months. The records showed that respiratory diseases, the common heritage of the grippe and the measles, had caused death in most cases, discovering the trouble to be, next to the inability to check the contagion in those crowds, in the poverty of the parents and the wretched home conditions that made proper care of the sick impossible. The fact was emphasized by the occurrence here and there of a few isolated deaths from diphtheria and scarlet fever. In the case of these diseases, considered more dangerous to the public health, the health officers exercised summary powers of removal to the hospital where proper treatment could be had, and the result was a low death-rate.

These were tenements of the tall, modern type. A little more than a year ago, when a census was made of the tenements and compared with the mortality tables, no little surprise and congratulation was caused by the discovery that as the buildings grew taller the death-rate fell. The reason is plain, though the reverse had been expected by most people. The biggest tenements have been built in the last ten years of sanitary reform rule, and have been brought, in all but the crowding, under its laws. The old houses that from private dwellings were made into tenements, or were run up to house the biggest crowds in defiance of every moral and physical law, can be improved by no device short of demolition. They will ever remain the worst.

That ignorance plays its part, as well as poverty and bad hygienic surroundings, in the sacrifice of life is of course inevitable. They go usually hand in hand. A message came one day last spring summoning me to a Mott Street tenement in which lay a child dying from some unknown disease. With the "charity doctor" I found the patient on the top floor, stretched upon two chairs in a dreadfully stifling room. She was gasping in the agony of peritonitis that had already written its death-sentence on her wan and pinched face. The whole family, father, mother, and four ragged children, sat around looking on with the stony resignation of helpless despair that had long since given up the fight against fate as useless. A glance around the wretched room left no doubt as to the cause of the child's condition. "Improper nourishment," said the doctor, which, translated to suit the place, meant starvation. The father's hands were crippled from lead poisoning. He had not been able to work for a year. A

In Poverty Gap, West Twenty-Eighth Street. An English Coal-Heaver's Home.[106]

contagious disease of the eyes, too long neglected, had made the mother and one of the boys nearly blind. The children cried with hunger. They had not broken their fast that day, and it was then near noon. For months the family had subsisted on two dollars a week from the priest, and a few loaves and a piece of corned beef which the sisters sent them on Saturday. The doctor gave direction for the treatment of the child, knowing that it

[106] Suspicions of murder, in the case of a woman who was found dead, covered with bruises after a day's running fight with her husband, in which the beer-jug had been the bone of contention, brought me to this house, a ramshackle tenement on the tail-end of a lot over near the North River docks. The family in the picture lived above the rooms where the dead woman lay on a bed of straw, overrun by rats, and had been uninterested witnesses of the affray that was an everyday occurrence in the house. A patched and shaky stairway led up to their bare and miserable room, in comparison with which a white-washed prison-cell seemed a real palace. A heap of old rags, in which the baby slept serenely, served as the common sleeping-bunk of father, mother, and children — two bright and pretty girls, singularly out of keeping in their clean, if coarse, dresses, with their surroundings. The father, a slow going, honest English coal-heaver, earned on the average five dollars a week, "when work was fairly brisk," at the docks. But there were long seasons when it was very "slack," he said, doubtfully. Yet the prospect did not seem to discourage them. The mother, a pleasant-faced woman, was cheerful, even light-hearted. Her smile seemed the most sadly hopeless of all in the utter wretchedness of the place, cheery though it was meant to be and really was. It seemed doomed to certain disappointment — the one thing there that was yet to know a greater depth of misery.

was possible only to alleviate its sufferings until death should end them, and left some money for food for the rest. An hour later, when I returned, I found them feeding the dying child with ginger ale, bought for two cents a bottle at the pedlar's cart down the street. A pitying neighbor had proposed it as the one thing she could think of as likely to make the child forget its misery. There was enough in the bottle to go round to the rest of the family. In fact, the wake had already begun; before night it was under way in dead earnest.

Every once in a while a case of downright starvation gets into the newspapers and makes a sensation. But this is the exception. Were the whole truth known, it would come home to the community with a shock that would rouse it to a more serious effort than the spasmodic undoing of its purse-strings. I am satisfied from my own observation that hundreds of men, women, and children are every day slowly starving to death in the tenements with my medical friend's complaint of "improper nourishment." Within a single week I have had this year three cases of insanity, provoked directly by poverty and want. One was that of a mother who in the middle of the night got up to murder her child, who was crying for food; another was the case of an Elizabeth Street truck-driver whom the newspapers never heard of. With a family to provide for, he had been unable to work for many months. There was neither food, nor a scrap of anything upon which money could be raised, left in the house; his mind gave way under the combined physical and mental suffering. In the third case I was just in time with the police to prevent the madman from murdering his whole family. He had the sharpened hatchet in his pocket when we seized him. He was an Irish laborer, and had been working in the sewers until the poisonous gases destroyed his health. Then he was laid off, and scarcely anything had been coming in all winter but the oldest child's earnings as cash-girl in a store, $2.50 a week. There were seven children to provide for, and the rent of the Mulberry Street attic in which the family lived was $10 a month. They had borrowed as long as anybody had a cent to lend. When at last the man got an odd job that would just buy the children bread, the week's wages only served to measure the depth of their misery. "It came in so on the tail-end of everything," said his wife in telling the story, with unconscious eloquence. The outlook worried him through sleepless nights until it destroyed his reason. In his madness he had only one conscious thought: that the town should not take the children. "Better that I take care of them myself," he repeated to himself as he ground the axe to an edge. Help came in abundance from many almost as poor as they when the desperate straits of the family became known through his arrest. The readiness of the poor to share what little they have with those who have even less is one of the few moral virtues of the tenements. Their enormous crowds touch elbow in a closeness of sympathy that is scarcely to be understood out of them, and has no parallel except among the unfortunate women whom the world scorns as outcasts. There is very little professed sentiment about it to draw a sentimental tear from the eye of romantic philanthropy. The hard fact is that the instinct of self-preservation impels them to make common cause against the common misery.

No doubt intemperance bears a large share of the blame for it; judging from the stand-point of the policeman perhaps the greater share. Two such entries as I read in the police returns on successive days last March, of mothers in West Side tenements, who in their drunken sleep lay upon and killed their infants, go far to support such a position. And they are far from uncommon. But my experience has shown me another view of it, a view which the last report of the Society for Improving the Condition of the Poor seems more than half inclined to adopt in allotting to "intemperance the cause of distress, or distress the cause of intemperance," forty per cent. of the cases it is called upon to deal with. Even if it were all true, I should still load over upon the tenement the heaviest responsibility. A single factor, the scandalous scarcity of water in the hot summer when the thirst of the million must be quenched, if not in that in something else, has in the past years more than all other causes encouraged drunkenness among the poor. But to my mind there is a closer connection between the wages of the tenements and the vices and improvidence of those who dwell in them than, with the guilt of the tenement upon our heads, we are willing to admit even to ourselves. Weak tea with a dry crust is not a diet to nurse moral strength. Yet how much better might the fare be expected to be in the family of this "widow with seven children, very energetic and prudent" — I quote again from the report of the Society for the Improvement of the Condition of the Poor — whose "eldest girl was employed as a learner in a tailor's shop at small wages, and one boy had a place as 'cash' in a store. There were two other little boys who sold papers and sometimes earned one dollar. The mother finishes pantaloons and can do three pairs in a day, thus earning thirty-nine cents. Here is a family of eight persons with rent to pay and an income of less than six dollars a week."

And yet she was better off in point of pay than this Sixth Street mother, who "had just brought home four pairs of pants to finish, at seven cents a pair. She was required to put the canvas in the bottom, basting and sewing three times around; to put the linings in the waistbands; to tack three pockets, three corners to each; to put on two stays and eight buttons, and make six button-holes; to put the buckle on the back strap and sew on the ticket, all for seven cents." Better off than the "church-going mother of six children," and with a husband sick to death, who to support the family made shirts, averaging an income of one dollar and twenty cents a week, while her oldest girl, aged thirteen, was "employed down-town cutting out Hamburg edgings at one dollar and a half a week — two and a half cents per hour for ten hours of steady labor — making the total income of the family two dollars and seventy cents per week." Than the Harlem woman, who was "making a brave effort to support a sick husband and two children by taking in washing at thirty-five cents for the lot of fourteen large pieces, finding coal, soap, starch, and bluing[107] herself, rather than depend on charity in any form." Specimen wages of the tenements these, seemingly inconsistent with the charge of improvidence.

But the connection on second thought is not obscure. There is nothing in the prospect of a sharp, unceasing battle for the bare necessaries of life to encourage looking ahead, everything to discourage the effort. Improvidence and wastefulness are natural results. The instalment plan secures to the tenant who lives from hand to mouth his few comforts; the evil day of reckoning is put off till a to-morrow that may never come. When it does come, with failure to pay and the loss of hard-earned dollars, it simply adds another hardship to a life measured from the cradle by such incidents. The children soon catch the spirit of this sort of thing. I remember once calling at the home of a poor washer-woman living in an East Side tenement, and finding the door locked. Some children in the hallway stopped their play and eyed me attentively while I knocked. The biggest girl volunteered the information that Mrs. Smith was out; but while I was thinking of how I was to get a message to her, the child put a question of her own: "Are you the spring man[108] or the clock man?" When I assured her that I was neither one nor the other, but had brought work for her mother, Mrs. Smith, who had been hiding from the instalment collector, speedily appeared.

Perhaps of all the disheartening experiences of those who have devoted lives of unselfish thought and effort, and their number is not so small as often supposed, to the lifting of this great load, the indifference of those they would help is the most puzzling. They will not be helped. Dragged by main force out of their misery, they slip back again on the first opportunity, seemingly content only in the old rut. The explanation

[107] Bleaching or whitening. — ED.
[108] Probably the man who repairs and replaces bedsprings. He also removes bedbugs from the springs. — ED.

was supplied by two women of my acquaintance in an Elizabeth Street tenement, whom the city missionaries had taken from their wretched hovel and provided with work and a decent home somewhere in New Jersey. In three weeks they were back, saying that they preferred their dark rear room to the stumps out in the country. But to me the oldest, the mother, who had struggled along with her daughter making cloaks at half a dollar apiece, twelve long years since the daughter's husband was killed in a street accident and the city took the children, made the bitter confession: "We do get so kind o' downhearted living this way, that we have to be where something is going on, or we just can't stand it." And there was sadder pathos to me in her words than in the whole long story of their struggle with poverty; for unconsciously she voiced the sufferings of thousands, misjudged by a happier world, deemed vicious because they are human and unfortunate.

It is a popular delusion, encouraged by all sorts of exaggerated stories when nothing more exciting demands public attention, that there are more evictions in the tenements of New York every year "than in all Ireland." I am not sure that it is doing much for the tenant to upset this fallacy. To my mind, to be put out of a tenement would be the height of good luck. The fact is, however, that evictions are not nearly as common in New York as supposed. The reason is that in the civil courts, the judges of which are elected in their districts, the tenant-voter has solid ground to stand upon at last. The law that takes his side to start with is usually twisted to the utmost to give him time and save him expense. In the busiest East Side court, that has been very appropriately dubbed the "Poor Man's Court," fully five thousand dispossess warrants are issued in a year, but probably not fifty evictions take place in the district. The landlord has only one vote, while there may be forty voters hiring his rooms in the house, all of which the judge takes into careful account as elements that have a direct bearing on the case. And so they have — on his case. There are sad cases, just as there are "rounders"[109] who prefer to be moved at the landlord's expense and save the rent, but the former at least are unusual enough to attract more than their share of attention.

If his very poverty compels the tenant to live at a rate if not in a style that would beggar a Vanderbilt,[110] paying four prices for everything he needs, from his rent and coal down to the smallest item in his housekeeping account, fashion, no less inexorable in the tenements than on the avenue, exacts of him that he must die in a style that is finally and utterly

---

[109] One who makes the rounds of numerous bars. — ED.

[110] One of America's richest families; Cornelius Vanderbilt (1794–1877) amassed a fortune as a financier. — ED.

Dispossessed.

ruinous. The habit of expensive funerals — I know of no better classification for it than along with the opium habit and similar grievous plagues of mankind — is a distinctively Irish inheritance, but it has taken root among all classes of tenement dwellers, curiously enough most firmly among the Italians, who have taken amazingly to the funeral coach, perhaps because it furnishes the one opportunity of their lives for a really grand turn-out with a free ride thrown in. It is not at all uncommon to find the hoards of a whole lifetime of hard work and self-denial squandered on the empty show of a ludicrous funeral parade and a display of flowers that ill comports with the humble life it is supposed to exalt. It is easier to understand the wake as a sort of consolation cup for the survivors for whom there is — as one of them, doubtless a heathenish pessimist, put it to me once — "no such luck." The press and the pulpit have denounced the wasteful practice that often entails bitter want upon the relatives of the one buried with such pomp, but with little or no apparent result. Rather, the undertaker's business prospers more than ever in the tenements since the genius of politics has seen its way clear to make capital out of the dead voter as well as of the living, by making him the means of a useful "show of strength" and count of noses.

The Trench in the Potter's Field.

One free excursion awaits young and old whom bitter poverty has denied the poor privilege of the choice of the home in death they were denied in life, the ride up the Sound to the Potter's Field, charitably styled the City Cemetery. But even there they do not escape their fate. In the common trench of the Poor Burying Ground they lie packed three stories deep, shoulder to shoulder, crowded in death as they were in life, to "save space;" for even on that desert island the ground is not for the exclusive possession of those who cannot afford to pay for it. There is an odd coincidence in this, that year by year the lives that are begun in the gutter, the little nameless waifs whom the police pick up and the city adopts as its wards, are balanced by the even more forlorn lives that are ended in the river. I do not know how or why it happens, or that it is more than a mere coincidence. But there it is. Year by year the balance is struck — a few more, a few less — substantially the same when the record is closed.

Chapter XV

The Problem of the Children

The problem of the children becomes, in these swarms, to the last degree perplexing. Their very number makes one stand aghast. I have already given instances of the packing of the child population in East Side tenements. They might be continued indefinitely until the array would be enough to startle any community. For, be it remembered, these children with the training they receive — or do not receive — with the instincts they inherit and absorb in their growing up, are to be our future rulers, if our theory of government is worth anything. More than a working majority of our voters now register from the tenements. I counted the other day the little ones, up to ten years or so, in a Bayard Street tenement that for a yard has a triangular space in the centre with sides fourteen or fifteen feet long, just room enough for a row of ill-smelling closets at the base of the triangle and a hydrant at the apex. There was about as much light in this "yard" as in the average cellar. I gave up my self-imposed task in despair when I had counted one hundred and twenty-eight in forty families. Thirteen I had missed, or not found in. Applying the average for the forty to the whole fifty-three, the house contained one hundred and seventy children. It is not the only time I have had to give up such census work. I have in mind an alley — an inlet rather to a row of rear tenements — that is either two or four feet wide according as the wall of the crazy old building that gives on it bulges out or in. I tried to count the children that swarmed there, but could not. Sometimes I have doubted that anybody knows just how many there are about. Bodies of drowned children turn up in the rivers right along in summer whom no one seems to know anything about. When last spring some workmen, while moving a pile of lumber on a North River pier, found under the last plank the body of a little lad crushed to death, no one had missed a boy, though his parents afterward turned up. The truant officer assuredly does not know, though he spends his life trying to find out, somewhat illogically, perhaps, since the department that employs him admits that thousands of poor children are crowded out of the schools year by year for want of room. There was a big tenement in the Sixth Ward, now happily appropriated by the beneficent spirit of business that blots out so many foul spots in New York — it figured not long ago in the official reports as "an out-and-out hog-pen" — that had a record of one hundred and two arrests in four years among its four hundred and seventy-eight tenants, fifty-seven of them for drunken and disorderly conduct. I do not know how many children there were in it, but the inspector reported that he found only seven in the whole house who owned that they went to school. The rest gathered all the instruction they received running for beer for their elders. Some of them claimed the "flat" as their home as a mere matter of form. They slept in the streets at night. The official came upon a little party of four drinking beer out of the cover of a milk-can in the hallway. They were of the seven good boys and proved their claim to the title by offering him some.

The old question, what to do with the boy, assumes a new and serious phase in the tenements. Under the best conditions found there, it is not easily answered. In nine cases out of ten he would make an excellent mechanic, if trained early to work at a trade, for he is neither dull nor slow, but the short-sighted despotism of the trades unions has practically closed that avenue to him. Trade-schools, however excellent, cannot supply the opportunity thus denied him, and at the outset the boy stands condemned by his own to low and ill-paid drudgery, held down by the hand that of all should labor to raise him. Home, the greatest factor of all in the training of the young, means nothing to him but a pigeon-hole in a coop along with so many other human animals. Its influence is scarcely of the elevating kind, if it have any. The very games at which he takes a hand in the street become polluting in its atmosphere. With no steady hand to guide him, the boy takes naturally to idle ways. Caught in the street by the truant officer, or by the agents of the Children's Societies, peddling, perhaps, or begging, to help out the family resources, he runs the risk of being sent to a reformatory, where contact with vicious boys older than himself soon develops the latent possibilities for evil that lie hidden in him. The city has no Truant Home in which to keep him, and all efforts of the children's friends to enforce school attendance are paralyzed by this want. The risk of the reformatory is too great. What is done in the end is to let him take chances — with the chances all against him. The result is the rough young savage, familiar from the street. Rough as he is, if any one doubt that this child of common clay have in him the instinct of beauty, of love for the ideal of which his life has no embodiment, let him put the matter to the test. Let him take into a tenement block a handful of flowers from the fields and watch the brightened faces, the sudden abandonment of play and fight that go ever hand in hand where there is no elbow-room, the wild entreaty for "posies," the eager love with which the little messengers of peace are shielded, once possessed; then let him change his mind. I have seen an armful of daisies keep the peace of a block better than a policeman and his club, seen instincts awaken under their gentle appeal, whose very existence the soil in which they grew made seem a mockery. I have not forgotten the deputation of ragamuffins from a Mulberry Street alley that knocked at my office door one morning on a mysterious expedition for flowers, not for themselves, but for "a lady," and having obtained what they wanted, trooped off to bestow them, a ragged and dirty little band, with a solemnity that was quite unusual. It was not until an old man called the next day to thank me for the flowers that I found out they had decked the bier of a pauper, in the dark rear room where she lay waiting in her pine-board coffin for the city's hearse. Yet, as I knew, that dismal alley with its bare brick walls, between which no sun ever rose or set, was the world of those children. It filled their young lives. Probably not one of them had ever been out of the sight of it. They were too dirty, too ragged, and too generally disreputable, too well hidden in their slum besides, to come into line with the Fresh Air summer boarders.

With such human instincts and cravings, forever unsatisfied, turned into a haunting curse; with appetite ground to keenest edge by a hunger that is never fed, the children of the poor grow up in joyless homes to lives of wearisome toil that claims them at an age when the play of their happier fellows has but just begun. Has a yard of turf been laid and a vine been coaxed to grow within their reach, they are banished and barred out from it as from a heaven that is not for such as they. I came upon a couple of youngsters in a Mulberry Street yard a while ago that were chalking on the fence their first lesson in "writin'." And this is what they wrote: "Keeb of te Grass." They had it by heart, for there was not, I verily believe, a green sod within a quarter of a mile. Home to them is an empty name. Pleasure? A gentleman once catechized a ragged class in a down-town public school on this point, and recorded the result: Out of forty-eight boys twenty had never seen the Brooklyn Bridge that was scarcely five minutes' walk away, three only had been in Central Park, fifteen had known the joy of a ride in a horse-car. The street, with its ash-barrels and its dirt, the river that runs foul with mud, are their domain. What training they receive is picked up there. And they are apt pupils. If the mud and the dirt are easily reflected in their lives, what wonder? Scarce half-grown, such lads as these confront the world with the challenge to give them their due, too long withheld, or ———— . Our jails supply the answer to the alternative.

A little fellow who seemed clad in but a single rag was among the flotsam and jetsam stranded at Police Headquarters one day last summer. No one knew where he came from or where he belonged. The boy himself knew as little about it as anybody, and was the least anxious to have light shed on the subject after he had spent a night in the matron's nursery. The discovery that beds were provided for boys to sleep in there, and that he could have "a whole egg" and three slices of bread for breakfast put him on the best of terms with the world in general, and he decided that Headquarters was "a bully place." He sang "McGinty" all through, with Tenth Avenue variations, for the police, and then settled down to the serious business of giving an account of himself. The examination went on after this fashion:

"Where do you go to church, my boy?"

"We don't have no clothes to go to church." And indeed his appearance, as he was, in the door of any New York church would have caused a sensation.

"Well, where do you go to school, then?"

"I don't go to school," with a snort of contempt.

"Where do you buy your bread?"

"We don't buy no bread; we buy beer," said the boy, and it was eventually the saloon that led the police as a landmark to his "home." It was worthy of the boy. As he had said, his only bed was a heap of dirty straw on the floor, his daily diet a crust in the morning, nothing else.

Into the rooms of the Children's Aid Society were led two little girls whose father had "busted up the house" and put them on the street after their mother died. Another, who was turned out by her step-mother "because she had five of her own and could not afford to keep her," could not remember ever having been in church or Sunday-school, and only knew the name of Jesus through hearing people swear by it. She had no idea what they meant. These were specimens of the overflow from the tenements of our home-heathen that are growing up in New York's streets to-day, while tender-hearted men and women are busying themselves with the socks and the hereafter of well-fed little Hottentots thousands of miles away. According to Canon Taylor, of York, one hundred and nine missionaries in the four fields of Persia, Palestine,

Arabia, and Egypt spent one year and sixty thousand dollars in converting one little heathen girl. If there is nothing the matter with those missionaries, they might come to New York with a good deal better prospect of success.

By those who lay flattering unction to their souls in the knowledge that to-day New York has, at all events, no brood of the gutters of tender years that can be homeless long unheeded, let it be remembered well through what effort this judgment has been averted. In thirty-seven years the Children's Aid Society, that came into existence as an emphatic protest against the tenement corruption of the young, has sheltered quite three hundred thousand outcast, homeless, and orphaned children in its lodging-houses, and has found homes in the West for seventy thousand that had none. Doubtless, as a mere stroke of finance, the five millions and a half thus spent were a wiser investment than to have let them grow up thieves and thugs. In the last fifteen years of this tireless battle for the safety of the State the intervention of the Society for the Prevention of Cruelty to Children has been invoked for 138,891 little ones; it has thrown its protection around more than twenty-five thousand helpless children, and has convicted nearly sixteen thousand wretches of child-beating and abuse. Add to this the standing army of fifteen thousand dependent children in New York's asylums and institutions, and some idea is gained of the crop that is garnered day by day in the tenements, of the enormous force employed to check their inroads on our social life, and of the cause for apprehension that would exist did their efforts flag for ever so brief a time.

Nothing is now better understood than that the rescue of the children is the key to the problem of city poverty, as presented for our solution to-day; that character may be formed where to reform it would be a hopeless task.

The concurrent testimony of all who have to undertake it at a later stage: that the young are naturally neither vicious nor hardened, simply weak and undeveloped, except by the bad influences of the street, makes this duty all the more urgent as well as hopeful. Helping hands are held out on every side. To private charity the municipality leaves the entire care of its proletariat of tender years, lulling its conscience to sleep with liberal appropriations of money to foot the bills. Indeed, it is held by those whose opinions are entitled to weight that it is far too liberal a paymaster for its own best interests and those of its wards. It deals with the evil in the seed to a limited extent in gathering in the outcast babies from the streets. To the ripe fruit the gates of its prisons, its reformatories, and its workhouses are opened wide the year round. What the showing would be at this end of the line were it not for the barriers wise charity has thrown across the broad highway to ruin — is building day by day — may be measured by such results as those quoted above in the span of a single life.

Chapter XVI

Waifs of the City's Slums

First among these barriers is the Foundling Asylum.[111] It stands at the very outset of the waste of life that goes on in a population of nearly two millions of people; powerless to prevent it, though it gather in the outcasts by night and by day. In a score of years an army of twenty-five thousand of these forlorn little waifs have cried out from the streets of New York in arraignment of a Christian civilization under the blessings of which the instinct of motherhood even was smothered by poverty and want. Only the poor abandon their children. The stories of richly-dressed foundlings that are dished up in the newspapers at intervals are pure fiction. Not one instance of even a well-dressed infant having been picked up in the streets is on record. They come in rags, a newspaper often the only wrap, semi-occasionally one in a clean slip with some evidence of loving care; a little slip of paper pinned on, perhaps, with some such message as this I once read, in a woman's trembling hand: "Take care of Johnny, for God's sake. I cannot." But even that is the rarest of all happenings.

The city divides with the Sisters of Charity[112] the task of gathering them in. The real foundlings, the children of the gutter that are picked up by the police, are the city's wards. In midwinter, when the poor shiver in their homes, and in the dog-days when the fierce heat and foul air of the tenements smother their babies by thousands, they are found, sometimes three and four in a night, in hallways, in areas and on the doorsteps of the rich, with whose comfort in luxurious homes the wretched mother somehow connects her own misery. Perhaps, as the drowning man clutches at a straw, she hopes that these happier hearts may have love to spare even for her little one. In this she is mistaken. Unauthorized babies

---

[111] Institution responsible for the care of abandoned children. — ED.

[112] The Sisters of Charity of Saint Vincent de Paul. Established in the United States in 1809, the Sisters set up hospitals, orphanages, and nursing homes that were designed specifically to care for the poor. — ED.

especially are not popular in the abodes of the wealthy. It never happens outside of the story-books that a baby so deserted finds home and friends at once. Its career, though rather more official, is less romantic, and generally brief. After a night spent at Police Headquarters it travels up to the Infants' Hospital on Randall's Island in the morning, fitted out with a number and a bottle, that seldom see much wear before they are laid aside for a fresh recruit. Few outcast babies survive their desertion long. Murder is the true name of the mother's crime in eight cases out of ten. Of 508 babies received at the Randall's Island Hospital last year 333 died, 65.55 per cent. But of the 508 only 170 were picked up in the streets, and among these the mortality was much greater, probably nearer ninety per cent., if the truth were told. The rest were born in the hospitals. The high mortality among the foundlings is not to be marvelled at. The wonder is, rather, that any survive. The stormier the night, the more certain is the police nursery to echo with the feeble cries of abandoned babes. Often they come half dead from exposure. One live baby came in a little pine coffin which a policeman found an inhuman wretch trying to bury in an up-town lot. But many do not live to be officially registered as a charge upon the county. Seventy-two dead babies were picked up in the streets last year. Some of them were doubtless put out by very poor parents to save funeral expenses. In hard times the number of dead and live found-lings always increases very noticeably. But whether travelling by way of the Morgue or the Infants' Hospital, the little army of waifs meets, reunited soon, in the trench in the Potter's Field where, if no medical student is in need of a subject, they are laid in squads of a dozen.

Most of the foundlings come from the East Side, where they are left by young mothers without wedding-ring or other name than their own to bestow upon the baby, returning from the island hospital to face an unpitying world with the evidence of their shame. Not infrequently they wear the bed-tick regimentals of the Public Charities, and thus their origin is easily enough traced. Oftener no ray of light penetrates the gloom, and no effort is made to probe the mystery of sin and sorrow. This also is the policy pursued in the great Foundling Asylum of the Sisters of Charity in Sixty-eighth Street, known all over the world as Sister Irene's Asylum. Years ago the crib that now stands just inside the street door, under the great main portal, was placed outside at night; but it filled up too rapidly. The babies took to coming in little squads instead of in single file, and in self-defence the sisters were forced to take the cradle in. Now the mother must bring her child inside and put it in the crib where she is seen by the sister on guard. No effort is made to question her, or discover the child's antecedents, but she is asked to stay and nurse her own and another baby. If she refuses, she is allowed to depart unhindered. If willing, she enters at once into the great family of the good Sister who in twenty-one years has gathered as many thousand homeless babies into her fold. One was brought in when I was last in the asylum, in the middle of July, that received in its crib the number 20715. The death-rate is of course lowered a good deal where exposure of the child is prevented. Among the eleven hundred infants in the asylum it was something over nineteen per cent. last year; but among those actually received in the twelvemonth nearer twice that figure. Even the nineteen per cent., remarkably low for a Foundling Asylum, was equal to the startling death-rate of Gotham Court in the cholera scourge.

Four hundred and sixty mothers, who could not or would not keep their own babies, did voluntary penance for their sin in the asylum last year by nursing a strange waif besides their own until both should be strong enough to take their chances in life's battle. An even larger number than the eleven hundred were "pay babies," put out to be nursed by "mothers" outside the asylum. The money thus earned pays the rent of hundreds of poor families. It is no trifle, quite half of the quarter of a million dollars contributed annually by the city for the support of the asylum. The procession of these nurse-mothers, when they come to the asylum on the first Wednesday of each month to receive their pay and have the babies inspected by the sisters, is one of the sights of the city. The nurses, who are under strict supervision, grow to love their little charges and part from them with tears when, at the age of four or five, they are sent to Western homes to be adopted. The sisters carefully encourage the home-feeling in the child as their strongest ally in seeking its mental and moral elevation, and the toddlers depart happy to join their "papas and mammas" in the far-away, unknown home.

An infinitely more fiendish, if to surface appearances less deliberate, plan of child-murder than desertion has flourished in New York for years under the title of baby-farming. The name, put into plain English, means starving babies to death. The law has fought this most heinous of crimes by compelling the registry of all baby-farms. As well might it require all persons intending murder to register their purpose with time and place of the deed under the penalty of exemplary fines. Murderers do not hang out a shingle. "Baby-farms," said once Mr. Elbridge T. Gerry, the President of the Society charged with the execution of the law that was passed through his efforts, "are concerns by means of which persons, usually of disreputable character, eke out a living by taking two, or three, or four babies to board. They are the charges of outcasts, or illegitimate children. They feed them on sour milk, and give them paregoric to keep them quiet, until they die, when they get some young medical man without experience to sign a certificate to the Board of Health that the child died of inanition, and so the matter ends. The baby is dead, and there is no one to complain." A handful of baby-farms have been registered and licensed by the Board of Health with the approval of the Society for the Prevention of Cruelty to Children in the last five years, but none of this kind. The devil keeps the only complete register to be found anywhere. Their trace is found oftenest by the coroner or the police; sometimes they may be discovered hiding in the advertising columns of certain newspapers, under the guise of the scarcely less heartless traffic in helpless children that is dignified with the pretence of adoption — for cash. An idea of how this scheme works was obtained through the disclosures in a celebrated divorce case, a year or two ago. The society has among its records a very recent case[113] of a baby a week old (Baby "Blue Eyes") that was offered for sale — adoption, the dealer called it — in a newspaper. The agent bought it after some haggling for a dollar, and arrested the woman slave-trader; but the law was powerless to punish her for her crime. Twelve unfortunate women awaiting dishonored motherhood were found in her house.

One gets a glimpse of the frightful depths to which human nature, perverted by avarice bred of ignorance and rasping poverty, can descend, in the mere suggestion of systematic insurance *for profit* of children's lives. A woman was put on trial in this city last year for incredible cruelty in her treatment of a step-child. The evidence aroused a strong suspicion that a pitifully small amount of insurance on the child's life was one of the motives for the woman's savagery. A little investigation brought out the fact that three companies that were in the business of insuring children's lives, for sums varying from $17 up, had issued not less than a million such policies! The premiums ranged from five to twenty-five cents a week. What untold horrors this business may conceal was suggested by a formal agreement entered into by some of the companies, "for the purpose of preventing speculation in the insurance of children's lives." By the terms of this compact, "no higher premium than ten cents could be accepted on children under six years old." Barbarism forsooth! Did ever heathen cruelty invent a more fiendish plot than the one written down between the lines of this legal paper?

It is with a sense of glad relief that one turns from this misery to the brighter page of the helping hands stretched forth on every side to save the young and the helpless. New York is, I firmly believe, the most

[113] Society for the Prevention of Cruelty to Children, Case 42,028, May 16, 1889.

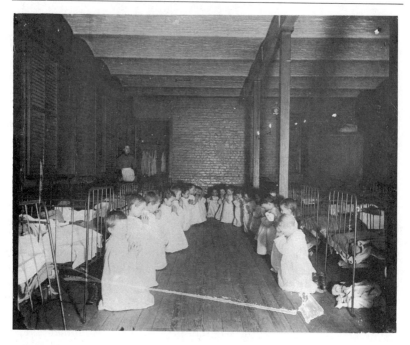

Prayer-Time in the Nursery — Five Points House of Industry.

charitable city in the world. Nowhere is there so eager a readiness to help, when it is known that help is worthily wanted; nowhere are such armies of devoted workers, nowhere such abundance of means ready to the hand of those who know the need and how rightly to supply it. Its poverty, its slums, and its suffering are the result of unprecedented growth with the consequent disorder and crowding, and the common penalty of metropolitan greatness. If the structure shows signs of being top-heavy, evidences are not wanting — they are multiplying day by day — that patient toilers are at work among the underpinnings. The Day Nurseries, the numberless Kindergartens and charitable schools in the poor quarters, the Fresh Air Funds, the thousand and one charities that in one way or another reach the homes and the lives of the poor with sweetening touch, are proof that if much is yet to be done, if the need only grows with the effort, hearts and hands will be found to do it in ever-increasing measure. Black as the cloud is it has a silver lining, bright with promise. New York is to-day a hundredfold cleaner, better, purer, city than it was even ten years ago.

Two powerful agents that were among the pioneers in this work of moral and physical regeneration stand in Paradise Park to-day as milestones on the rocky, uphill road. The handful of noble women, who braved the foul depravity of the Old Brewery to rescue its child victims, rolled away the first and heaviest bowlder, which legislatures and city councils had tackled in vain. The Five Points Mission and the Five Points House of Industry[114] have accomplished what no machinery of government availed to do. Sixty thousand children have been rescued by them from the streets and had their little feet set in the better way. Their work still goes on, increasing and gathering in the waifs, instructing and feeding them, and helping their parents with advice and more substantial aid. Their charity knows not creed or nationality. The House of Industry is an enormous nursery-school with an average of more than four hundred day scholars and constant boarders — "outsiders" and "insiders." Its influence is felt for many blocks around in that crowded part of the city. It is one of the most touching sights in the world to see a score of babies, rescued from homes of brutality and desolation, where no other blessing than a drunken curse was ever heard, saying their prayers in the nursery at bedtime. Too often their white night-gowns hide tortured little bodies and limbs cruelly bruised by inhuman hands. In the shelter of this fold they are safe, and a happier little group one may seek long and far in vain.

Chapter XVII

The Street Arab[115]

Not all the barriers erected by society against its nether life, not the labor of unnumbered societies for the rescue and relief of its outcast waifs, can dam the stream of homelessness that issues from a source where the very name of home is a mockery. The Street Arab is as much of an institution in New York as Newspaper Row,[116] to which he gravitates naturally, following his Bohemian instinct. Crowded out of the tenements to shift for himself, and quite ready to do it, he meets there the host of adventurous runaways from every State in the Union

---

[114] Founded by the Reverand Lewis M. Pease in 1850 and 1856. — ED.

[115] A child who lives on the streets. — ED.

[116] A stretch of Park Row where many of the city's newspaper offices were located. — ED.

and from across the sea, whom New York attracts with a queer fascination, as it attracts the older emigrants from all parts of the world. A census of the population in the Newsboys' Lodging-house on any night will show such an odd mixture of small humanity as could hardly be got together in any other spot. It is a mistake to think that they are helpless little creatures, to be pitied and cried over because they are alone in the world. The unmerciful "guying"[117] the good man would receive, who went to them with such a programme, would soon convince him that that sort of pity was wasted, and would very likely give him the idea that they were a set of hardened little scoundrels, quite beyond the reach of missionary effort.

But that would only be his second mistake. The Street Arab has all the faults and all the virtues of the lawless life he leads. Vagabond that he is, acknowledging no authority and owing no allegiance to anybody or anything, with his grimy fist raised against society whenever it tries to coerce him, he is as bright and sharp as the weasel, which, among all the predatory beasts, he most resembles. His sturdy independence, love of freedom and absolute self-reliance, together with his rude sense of justice that enables him to govern his little community, not always in accordance with municipal law or city ordinances, but often a good deal closer to the saving line of "doing to others as one would be done by" — these are strong handles by which those who know how can catch the boy and make him useful. Successful bankers, clergymen, and lawyers all over the country, statesmen in some instances of national repute, bear evidence in their lives to the potency of such missionary efforts. There is scarcely a learned profession, or branch of honorable business, that has not in the last twenty years borrowed some of its brightest light from the poverty and gloom of New York's streets.

Anyone, whom business or curiosity has taken through Park Row or across Printing House Square in the midnight hour, when the air is filled with the roar of great presses spinning with printers' ink on endless rolls of white paper the history of the world in the twenty-four hours that have just passed away, has seen little groups of these boys hanging about the newspaper offices; in winter, when snow is on the streets, fighting for warm spots around the grated vent-holes that let out the heat and steam from the underground press-rooms with their noise and clatter, and in summer playing craps and 7–11 on the curb for their hard-earned pennies, with all the absorbing concern of hardened gamblers. This is their beat. Here the agent of the Society for the Prevention of Cruelty to

---

[117] To tease or mock; to ridicule. — ED.

Children finds those he thinks too young for "business,"[118] but does not always capture them. Like rabbits in their burrows, the little ragamuffins sleep with at least one eye open, and every sense alert to the approach of danger: of their enemy, the policeman, whose chief business in life is to move them on, and of the agent bent on robbing them of their cherished freedom. At the first warning shout they scatter and are off. To pursue them would be like chasing the fleet-footed mountain goat in his rocky fastnesses. There is not an open door, a hidden turn or runway which they do not know, with lots of secret passages and short cuts no one else ever found. To steal a march on them is the only way. There is a coal chute from the sidewalk to the boiler-room in the sub-cellar of the Post Office which the Society's officer found the boys had made into a sort of toboggan slide to a snug berth in wintry weather. They used to slyly raise the cover in the street, slide down in single file, and snuggle up to the warm boiler out of harm's way, as they thought. It proved a trap, however. The agent slid down himself one cold night — there was no other way of getting there — and, landing right in the midst of the sleeping colony, had it at his mercy. After repeated raids upon their headquarters, the boys forsook it last summer, and were next found herding under the shore-end of one of the East River banana docks, where they had fitted up a regular club-room that was shared by thirty or forty homeless boys and about a million rats.

Newspaper Row is merely their headquarters. They are to be found all over the city, these Street Arabs, where the neighborhood offers a chance of picking up a living in the daytime and of "turning in" at night with a promise of security from surprise. In warm weather a truck in the street, a convenient out-house, or a dug-out in a hay-barge at the wharf make good bunks. Two were found making their nest once in the end of a big iron pipe up by the Harlem Bridge, and an old boiler at the East River served as an elegant flat for another couple, who kept house there with a thief the police had long sought, little suspecting that he was hiding under their very noses for months together. When the Children's Aid Society first opened its lodging-houses, and with some difficulty persuaded the boys that their charity was no "pious dodge" to trap them into a treasonable "Sunday-school racket," its managers overheard a laughable discussion among the boys in their unwontedly comfortable beds — perhaps the first some of them had ever slept in — as to the relative merits of the different styles of their everyday berths. Preferences were divided between the steam-grating and a sand-box; but the weight of the evidence

---

[118] Euphemism for the "business" of theft. — ED.

"Didn't Live Nowhere."

was decided to be in favor of the sand-box, because, as its advocate put it, "you could curl all up in it." The new "find" was voted a good way ahead of any previous experience, however. "My eyes, ain't it nice!" said one of the lads, tucked in under his blanket up to the chin, and the roomful of boys echoed the sentiment. The compact silently made that night between the Street Arabs and their hosts has never been broken. They have been fast friends ever since.

Whence this army of homeless boys? is a question often asked. The answer is supplied by the procession of mothers that go out and in at Police Headquarters the year round, inquiring for missing boys, often not until they have been gone for weeks and months, and then sometimes rather as a matter of decent form than from any real interest in the lad's fate. The stereotyped promise of the clerks who fail to find his name on the books among the arrests, that he "will come back when he gets hungry," does not always come true. More likely he went away because he was hungry. Some are orphans, actually or in effect, thrown upon the world when their parents were "sent up" to the island or to Sing Sing,[119] and somehow overlooked by the "Society," which thenceforth became the enemy to be shunned until growth and dirt and the hardships of the street, that make old early, offer some hope of successfully floating the lie that they are "sixteen." A drunken father explains the matter in other cases, as in that of John and Willie, aged ten and eight, picked up by the police. They "didn't live nowhere," never went to school, could neither read nor write. Their twelve-year-old sister kept house for the father, who turned the boys out to beg, or steal, or starve. Grinding poverty and hard work beyond the years of the lad; blows and curses for breakfast, dinner, and supper; all these are recruiting agents for the homeless army. Sickness in the house, too many mouths to feed:

"We wuz six," said an urchin of twelve or thirteen I came across in the Newsboys' Lodging House, "and we ain't got no father. Some on us had to go." And so he went, to make a living by blacking boots.[120] The going is easy enough. There is very little to hold the boy who has never known anything but a home in a tenement. Very soon the wild life in the streets holds him fast, and thenceforward by his own effort there is no escape. Left alone to himself, he soon enough finds a place in the police books, and there would be no other answer to the second question: "what becomes of the boy?" than that given by the criminal courts every day in the week.

But he is not left alone. Society in our day has no such suicidal intention. Right here, at the parting of the ways, it has thrown up the strongest of all its defences for itself and for the boy. What the Society for the Prevention of Cruelty to Children is to the baby-waif, the Children's Aid Society is to the homeless boy at this real turning-point in his career. The good it has done cannot easily be over-estimated. Its lodging-houses, its schools and its homes block every avenue of escape with their offer of shelter upon terms which the boy soon accepts, as on the whole cheap and fair. In the great Duane Street lodging-house for newsboys, they are succinctly stated in a "notice" over the door that reads thus: "Boys who swear and chew tobacco cannot sleep here." There is another unwritten condition, viz.: that the boy shall be really without a home; but upon this the managers wisely do not insist too obstinately, accepting without too close inquiry his account of himself where that seems advisable, well knowing that many a home that sends forth such lads far less deserves the name than the one they are able to give them.

---

[119] Prison located thirty miles north of Manhattan in Ossining, New York. — ED.
[120] Shining shoes. — ED.

Street Arabs in Sleeping Quarters.

With these simple preliminaries the outcast boy may enter. Rags do not count; to ignorance the door is only opened wider. Dirt does not survive long, once within the walls of the lodging-house. It is the settled belief of the men who conduct them that soap and water are as powerful moral agents in their particular field as preaching, and they have experience to back them. The boy may come and go as he pleases, so long as he behaves himself. No restraint of any sort is put on his independence. He is as free as any other guest at a hotel, and, like him, he is expected to pay for what he gets. How wisely the men planned who laid the foundation of this great rescue work and yet carry it on, is shown by no single feature of it better than by this. No pauper was ever bred within these houses. Nothing would have been easier with such material, or more fatal. But charity of the kind that pauperizes is furthest from their scheme. Self-help is its very key-note, and it strikes a response in the boy's sturdiest trait that raises him at once to a level with the effort made in his behalf. Recognized as an independent trader, capable of and bound to take care of himself, he is in a position to ask trust if trade has gone against him and he cannot pay cash for his "grub" and his bed, and to get it without question. He can even have the loan of the small capital required to start him in business with a boot-black's kit, or an armful of papers, if he is known or vouched for; but every cent is charged to him as carefully as though the transaction involved as many hundreds of dollars, and he is expected to pay back the money as soon as he has made enough to keep him going without it. He very rarely betrays the trust reposed in him. Quite on the contrary, around this sound core of self-help, thus encouraged, habits of thrift and ambitious industry are seen to grow up in a majority of instances. The boy is "growing" a character, and he goes out to the man's work in life with that which for him is better than if he had found a fortune.

Six cents for his bed, six for his breakfast of bread and coffee, and six for his supper of pork and beans, as much as he can eat, are the rates of the boys' "hotel" for those who bunk together in the great dormitories that sometimes hold more than a hundred berths, two tiers high, made of iron, clean and neat. For the "upper ten," the young financiers who early take the lead among their fellows, hire them to work for wages and add a share of their profits to their own, and for the lads who are learning a trade and getting paid by the week, there are ten-cent beds with a locker and with curtains hung about. Night schools and Sunday night meetings are held in the building and are always well attended, in winter especially, when the lodging-houses are crowded. In summer the tow-path and the country attract their share of the bigger boys. The "Sunday-school racket"

Getting Ready for Supper in the Newsboys' Lodging-House.

has ceased to have terror for them. They follow the proceedings with the liveliest interest, quick to detect cant of any sort, should any stray in. No one has any just conception of what congregational singing is until he has witnessed a roomful of these boys roll up their sleeves and start in on "He is the lily of the valley." The swinging trapeze in the gymnasium on the top floor is scarcely more popular with the boys than this tremendously vocal worship. The Street Arab puts his whole little soul into what interests him for the moment, whether it be pulverizing a rival who has done a mean trick to a smaller boy, or attending at the "gospel shop"[121] on Sundays. This characteristic made necessary some extra supervision when recently the lads in the Duane Street Lodging House "chipped in" and bought a set of boxing gloves. The trapeze suffered a temporary eclipse until this new toy had been tested to the extent of several miniature black eyes upon which soap had no effect, and sundry little scores had been settled that evened things up, as it were, for a fresh start.

[121] A church or chapel. — ED.

I tried one night, not with the best of success I confess, to photograph the boys in their wash-room, while they were cleaning up for supper. They were quite turbulent, to the disgust of one of their number who assumed, unasked, the office of general manager of the show, and expressed his mortification to me in very polite language. "If they would only behave, sir!" he complained, "you could make a good picture."

"Yes," I said, "but it isn't in them, I suppose."

"No, b'gosh!" said he, lapsing suddenly from grace under the provocation, "them kids ain't got no sense, nohow!"

The Society maintains five of these boys' lodging-houses, and one for girls, in the city. The Duane Street Lodging House alone has sheltered since its foundation in 1855 nearly a quarter of a million different boys, at a total expense of a good deal less than half a million dollars. Of this amount, up to the beginning of the present year, the boys and the earnings of the house had contributed no less than $172,776.38. In all of the lodging-houses together, 12,153 boys and girls were sheltered and taught last year. The boys saved up no inconsiderable amount of money in the savings banks provided for them in the houses, a simple system of lock-boxes that are emptied for their benefit once a month. Besides these, the Society has established and operates in the tenement districts twenty-one industrial schools, co-ordinate with the public schools in authority, for the children of the poor who cannot find room in the city's school-houses, or are too ragged to go there; two free reading-rooms, a dress-making and typewriting school and a laundry for the instruction of girls; a sick-children's mission in the city and two on the sea-shore, where poor mothers may take their babies; a cottage by the sea for crippled girls, and a brush factory for crippled boys in Forty-fourth Street. The Italian school in Leonard Street, alone, had an average attendance of over six hundred pupils last year. The daily average attendance at all of them was 4,105, while 11,331 children were registered and taught. When the fact that there were among these 1,132 children of drunken parents, and 416 that had been found begging in the street, is contrasted with the showing of $1,337.21 deposited in the school savings banks by 1,745 pupils, something like an adequate idea is gained of the scope of the Society's work in the city.

A large share of it, in a sense the largest, certainly that productive of the happiest results, lies outside of the city, however. From the lodging-houses and the schools are drawn the battalions of young emigrants that go every year to homes in the Far West, to grow up self-supporting men and women safe from the temptations and the vice of the city. Their number runs far up in the thousands. The Society never loses sight of them. The records show that the great mass, with this start given them, become useful citizens, an honor to the communities in which their lot is cast. Not a few achieve place and prominence in their new surroundings. Rarely bad reports come of them. Occasionally one comes back, lured by homesickness even for the slums; but the briefest stay generally cures the disease for good. I helped once to see a party off for Michigan, the last sent out by that great friend of the homeless children, Mrs. Astor,[122] before she died. In the party was a boy who had been an "Insider" at the Five Points House of Industry, and brought along as his only baggage a padlocked and iron-bound box that contained all his wealth, two little white mice of the friendliest disposition. They were going with him out to live on the fat of the land in the fertile West, where they would never be wanting for a crust. Alas! for the best-laid plans of mice and men. The Western diet did not agree with either. I saw their owner some months later in the old home at the Five Points. He had come back, walking part of the way, and was now pleading to be sent out once more. He had at last had enough of the city. His face fell when I asked him about the mice. It was a sad story, indeed. "They had so much corn to eat," he said, "and they couldn't stand it. They burned all up inside, and then they busted."

Mrs. Astor set an example during her noble and useful life in gathering every year a company of homeless boys from the streets and sending them to good homes, with decent clothes on their backs — she had sent out no less than thirteen hundred when she died, and left funds to carry on her work — that has been followed by many who, like her, had the means and the heart for such a labor of love. Most of the lodging-houses and school-buildings of the society were built by some one rich man or woman who paid all the bills, and often objected to have even the name of the giver made known to the world. It is one of the pleasant experiences of life that give one hope and courage in the midst of all this misery to find names, that stand to the unthinking mass only for money-getting and grasping, associated with such unheralded benefactions that carry their blessings down to generations yet unborn. It is not so long since I found the carriage of a woman, whose name is synonymous with millions, standing in front of the boys' lodging-house in Thirty-fifth Street. Its owner was at that moment busy with a surgeon making a census of the crippled lads in the brush-shop, the most miserable of all the Society's charges, as a preliminary to fitting them out with artificial limbs.

---

[122] Charlotte Astor (1825–1887). The wife of the wealthy financier John Jacob Astor and a generous supporter of the Children's Aid Society. — ED.

Farther uptown than any reared by the Children's Aid Society, in Sixty-seventh Street, stands a lodging-house intended for boys of a somewhat larger growth than most of those whom the Society shelters. Unlike the others, too, it was built by the actual labor of the young men it was designed to benefit. In the day when more of the boys from our streets shall find their way to it and to the New York Trade Schools, of which it is a kind of home annex, we shall be in a fair way of solving in the most natural of all ways the question what to do with this boy, in spite of the ignorant opposition of the men whose tyrannical policy is now to blame for the showing that, out of twenty-three millions of dollars paid annually to mechanics in the building trades in this city, less than six millions go to the workman born in New York, while his boy roams the streets with every chance of growing up a vagabond and next to none of becoming an honest artisan. Colonel Auchmuty[123] is a practical philanthropist to whom the growing youth of New York will one day owe a debt of gratitude not easily paid. The progress of the system of trade schools established by him, at which a young man may acquire the theory as well as the practice of a trade in a few months at a merely nominal outlay, has not been nearly as rapid as was to be desired, though the fact that other cities are copying the model, with their master mechanics as the prime movers in the enterprise, testifies to its excellence. But it has at last taken a real start, and with union men and even the officers of unions now sending their sons to the trade schools to be taught,[124] one may perhaps be permitted to hope that an era of better sense is dawning that shall witness a rescue work upon lines which, when the leaven has fairly had time to work, will put an end to the existence of the New York Street Arab, of the native breed at least.

---

[123] Richard Tylden Auchmuty (1831–1893). Architect who founded the New York Trade Schools in 1881. — ED.

[124] Colonel Auchmuty's own statement.

Chapter XVIII

The Reign of Rum

Where God builds a church the devil builds next door — a saloon, is an old saying that has lost its point in New York. Either the devil was on the ground first, or he has been doing a good deal more in the way of building. I tried once to find out how the account stood, and counted to 111 Protestant churches, chapels, and places of worship of every kind below Fourteenth Street, 4,065 saloons. The worst half of the tenement population lives down there, and it has to this day the worst half of the saloons. Uptown the account stands a little better, but there are easily ten saloons to every church to-day. I am afraid, too, that the congregations are larger by a good deal; certainly the attendance is steadier and the contributions more liberal the week round, Sunday included. Turn and twist it as we may, over against every bulwark for decency and morality which society erects, the saloon projects its colossal shadow, omen of evil wherever it falls into the lives of the poor.

Nowhere is its mark so broad or so black. To their misery it sticketh closer than a brother, persuading them that within its doors only is refuge, relief. It has the best of the argument, too, for it is true, worse pity, that in many a tenement-house block the saloon is the one bright and cheery and humanly decent spot to be found. It is a sorry admission to make, that to bring the rest of the neighborhood up to the level of the saloon would be one way of squelching it; but it is so. Wherever the tenements thicken, it multiplies. Upon the direst poverty of their crowds it grows fat and prosperous, levying upon it a tax heavier than all the rest of its grievous burdens combined. It is not yet two years since the Excise Board made the rule that no three corners of any street-crossing, not already so occupied, should thenceforward be licensed for rum-selling. And the tardy prohibition was intended for the tenement districts. Nowhere else is there need of it. One may walk many miles through the homes of the poor searching vainly for an open reading-room, a cheerful coffee-house, a decent club that is not a cloak for the traffic in rum. The dramshop[125] yawns at every step, the poor man's club, his forum and his haven of rest when weary and disgusted with the crowding, the quarrelling, and the wretchedness at home. With the poison dealt out there he takes his politics, in quality not far apart. As the source, so the stream. The rumshop

---

[125] Barroom. — Ed.

turns the political crank in New York. The natural yield is rum politics. Of what that means, successive Boards of Aldermen, composed in a measure, if not of a majority, of dive-keepers, have given New York a taste. The disgrace of the infamous "Boodle Board"[126] will be remembered until some corruption even fouler crops out and throws it into the shade.

What relation the saloon bears to the crowds, let me illustrate by a comparison. Below Fourteenth Street were, when the Health Department took its first accurate census of the tenements a year and a half ago, 13,220 of the 32,390 buildings classed as such in the whole city. Of the eleven hundred thousand tenants, not quite half a million, embracing a host of more than sixty-three thousand children under five years of age, lived below that line. Below it, also, were 234 of the cheap lodging-houses accounted for by the police last year, with a total of four millions and a half of lodgers for the twelvemonth, 59 of the city's 110 pawnshops, and 4,065 of its 7,884 saloons. The four most densely peopled precincts, the Fourth, Sixth, Tenth, and Eleventh, supported together in round numbers twelve hundred saloons, and their returns showed twenty-seven per cent. of the whole number of arrests for the year. The Eleventh Precinct, that has the greatest and the poorest crowds of all — it is the Tenth Ward — and harbored one-third of the army of homeless lodgers and fourteen per cent. of all the prisoners of the year, kept 485 saloons going in 1889. It is not on record that one of them all failed for want of support. A number of them, on the contrary, had brought their owners wealth and prominence. From their bars these eminent citizens stepped proudly into the councils of the city and the State. The very floor of one of the bar-rooms, in a neighborhood that lately resounded with the cry for bread of starving workmen, is paved with silver dollars!

East Side poverty is not alone in thus rewarding the tyrants that sweeten its cup of bitterness with their treacherous poison. The Fourth Ward points with pride to the honorable record of the conductors of its "Tub of Blood," and a dozen bar-rooms with less startling titles; the West Side to the wealth and "social" standing of the owners of such resorts as the "Witches' Broth" and the "Plug Hat" in the region of Hell's Kitchen three-cent whiskey, names ominous of the concoctions brewed there and of their fatally generous measure. Another ward, that boasts some of the best residences and the bluest blood on Manhattan Island, honors with political leadership in the ruling party the proprietor of one of the most disreputable Black-and-Tan dives and

---

[126] Boodle is a slang term for counterfeit money. Riis is referring to a group of corrupt New York City politicians who held office during the years of Boss Tweed's Ring (1866–1871). — ED.

dancing-hells to be found anywhere. Criminals and policemen alike do him homage. The list might be strung out to make texts for sermons with a stronger home flavor than many that are preached in our pulpits on Sunday. But I have not set out to write the political history of New York. Besides, the list would not be complete. Secret dives are skulking in the slums and out of them, that are not labelled respectable by a Board of Excise and support no "family entrance." Their business, like that of the stale-beer dives, is done through a side-door the week through. No one knows the number of unlicensed saloons in the city. Those who have made the matter a study estimate it at a thousand, more or less. The police make occasional schedules of a few and report them to headquarters. Perhaps there is a farce in the police court, and there the matter ends. Rum and "influence" are synonymous terms. The interests of the one rarely suffer for the want of attention from the other.

With the exception of these free lances that treat the law openly with contempt, the saloons all hang out a sign announcing in fat type that no beer or liquor is sold to children. In the down-town "morgues" that make the lowest degradation of tramp-humanity pan out a paying interest, as in the "reputable resorts" uptown where Inspector Byrnes's men spot their worthier quarry elbowing citizens whom the idea of associating with a burglar would give a shock they would not get over for a week, this sign is seen conspicuously displayed. Though apparently it means submission to a beneficent law, in reality the sign is a heartless, cruel joke. I doubt if one child in a thousand, who brings his growler to be filled at the average New York bar, is sent away empty-handed, if able to pay for what he wants. I once followed a little boy, who shivered in bare feet on a cold November night so that he seemed in danger of smashing his pitcher on the icy pavement, into a Mulberry Street saloon where just such a sign hung on the wall, and forbade the barkeeper to serve the boy. The man was as astonished at my interference as if I had told him to shut up his shop and go home, which in fact I might have done with as good a right, for it was after 1 A.M., the legal closing hour. He was mighty indignant too, and told me roughly to go away and mind my business, while he filled the pitcher. The law prohibiting the selling of beer to minors is about as much respected in the tenement-house districts as the ordinance against swearing. Newspaper readers will recall the story, told little more than a year ago, of a boy who after carrying beer a whole day for a shopful of men over on the East Side, where his father worked, crept into the cellar to sleep off the effects of his own share in the rioting. It was Saturday evening. Sunday his parents sought him high and low; but it was not until

A Downtown "Morgue."

Monday morning, when the shop was opened, that he was found, killed and half-eaten by the rats that overran the place.

All the evil the saloon does in breeding poverty and in corrupting politics; all the suffering it brings into the lives of its thousands of innocent victims, the wives and children of drunkards it sends forth to curse the community; its fostering of crime and its shielding of criminals — it is all as nothing to this, its worst offence. In its affinity for the thief there is at least this compensation that, as it makes, it also unmakes him. It starts him on his career only to trip him up and betray him into the hands of the law, when the rum he exchanged for his honesty has stolen his brains as well. For the corruption of the child there is no restitution. None is possible. It saps the very vitals of society; undermines its strongest defences, and delivers them over to the enemy. Fostered and filled by the saloon, the "growler" looms up in the New York street boy's life, baffling the most persistent efforts to reclaim him. There is no escape from it; no hope for the boy, once its blighting grip is upon him. Thenceforward the logic of the slums, that the world which gave him poverty and ignorance for his portion "owes him a living," is his creed, and the career of the "tough" lies open before him, a beaten track to be blindly followed to a bad end in the wake of the growler.

Chapter XIX

The Harvest of Tares[127]

The "growler" stood at the cradle of the tough. It bosses him through his boyhood apprenticeship in the "gang," and leaves him, for a time only, at the door of the jail that receives him to finish his training and turn him loose upon the world a thief, to collect by stealth or by force the living his philosophy tells him that it owes him, and will not voluntarily surrender without an equivalent in the work which he hates. From the moment he, almost a baby, for the first time carries the growler for beer, he is never out of its reach, and the two soon form a partnership that lasts through life. It has at least the merit, such as it is, of being loyal. The saloon is the only thing that takes kindly to the lad. Honest play is interdicted in the streets. The policeman arrests the ball-tossers, and there is no room in the back-yard. In one of these, between two enormous tenements that swarmed with children, I read this ominous notice: *"All boys caught in this yard will be delt with accorden to law."*

Along the water-fronts, in the holes of the dock-rats, and on the avenues, the young tough finds plenty of kindred spirits. Every corner has its gang, not always on the best of terms with the rivals in the next block, but all with a common programme: defiance of law and order, and with a common ambition: to get "pinched," *i.e.,* arrested, so as to pose as heroes before their fellows. A successful raid on the grocer's till is a good mark, "doing up" a policeman cause for promotion. The gang is an institution in New York. The police deny its existence while nursing the bruises received in nightly battles with it that tax their utmost resources. The newspapers chronicle its doings daily, with a sensational minuteness

---

[127] Tares are noxious weeds. — ED.

of detail that does its share toward keeping up its evil traditions and inflaming the ambition of its members to be as bad as the worst. The gang is the ripe fruit of tenement-house growth. It was born there, endowed with a heritage of instinctive hostility to restraint by a generation that sacrificed home to freedom, or left its country for its country's good. The tenement received and nursed the seed. The intensity of the American temper stood sponsor to the murderer in what would have been the common "bruiser" of a more phlegmatic clime. New York's tough represents the essence of reaction against the old and the new oppression, nursed in the rank soil of its slums. Its gangs are made up of the American-born sons of English, Irish, and German parents. They reflect exactly the conditions of the tenements from which they sprang. Murder is as congenial to Cherry Street or to Battle Row, as quiet and order to Murray Hill. The "assimilation" of Europe's oppressed hordes, upon which our Fourth of July orators are fond of dwelling, is perfect. The product is our own.

Such is the genesis of New York's gangs. Their history is not so easily written. It would embrace the largest share of our city's criminal history for two generations back, every page of it dyed red with blood. The guillotine Paris set up a century ago to avenge its wrongs was not more relentless, or less discriminating, than this Nemesis of New York. The difference is of intent. Murder with that was the serious purpose; with ours it is the careless incident, the wanton brutality of the moment. Bravado and robbery are the real purposes of the gangs; the former prompts the attack upon the policeman, the latter that upon the citizen. Within a single week last spring, the newspapers recorded six murderous assaults on unoffending people, committed by young highwaymen in the public streets. How many more were suppressed by the police, who always do their utmost to hush up such outrages "in the interests of justice," I shall not say. There has been no lack of such occurrences since, as the records of the criminal courts show. In fact, the past summer has seen, after a period of comparative quiescence of the gangs, a reawakening to renewed turbulence of the East Side tribes, and over and over again the reserve forces of a precinct have been called out to club them into submission. It is a peculiarity of the gangs that they usually break out in spots, as it were. When the West Side is in a state of eruption, the East Side gangs "lie low," and when the toughs along the North River are nursing broken heads at home, or their revenge in Sing Sing, fresh trouble breaks out in the tenements east of Third Avenue. This result is brought about by the very efforts made by the police to put down the gangs. In spite of local feuds, there is between them a species of ruffianly

Freemasonry that readily admits to full fellowship a hunted rival in the face of the common enemy. The gangs belt the city like a huge chain from the Battery to Harlem — the collective name of the "chain gang" has been given to their scattered groups in the belief that a much closer connection exists between them than commonly supposed — and the ruffian for whom the East Side has become too hot, has only to step across town and change his name, a matter usually much easier for him than to change his shirt, to find a sanctuary in which to plot fresh outrages. The more notorious he is, the warmer the welcome, and if he has "done" his man he is by common consent accorded the leadership in his new field.

From all this it might be inferred that the New York tough is a very fierce individual, of indomitable courage and naturally as blood-thirsty as a tiger. On the contrary he is an arrant coward. His instincts of ferocity are those of the wolf rather than the tiger. It is only when he hunts with the pack that he is dangerous. Then his inordinate vanity makes him forget all fear or caution in the desire to distinguish himself before his fellows, a result of his swallowing all the flash literature and penny-dreadfuls he can beg, borrow, or steal — and there is never any lack of them — and of the strongly dramatic element in his nature that is nursed by such a diet into rank and morbid growth. He is a queer bundle of contradictions at all times. Drunk and foul-mouthed, ready to cut the throat of a defenceless stranger at the toss of a cent, fresh from beating his decent mother black and blue to get money for rum,[128] he will resent as an intolerable insult the imputation that he is "no gentleman." Fighting his battles with the coward's weapons, the brass-knuckles and the deadly sand-bag, or with brick-bats from the housetops, he is still in all seriousness a lover of fair play, and as likely as not, when his gang has downed a policeman in a battle that has cost a dozen broken heads, to be found next saving a drowning child or woman at the peril of his own life. It depends on the angle at which he is seen, whether he is a cowardly ruffian, or a possible hero with different training and under different social conditions. Ready wit he has at all times, and there is less meanness in his makeup than in that of the bully of the London slums; but an intense love of show and applause, that carries him to any length of bravado, which his twin-brother across the sea entirely lacks. I have a very vivid

---

[128] This very mother will implore the court with tears, the next morning, to let her renegade son off. A poor woman, who claimed to be the widow of a soldier, applied to the Tenement-house Relief Committee of The King's Daughters last summer, to be sent to some home, as she had neither kith nor kin to care for her. Upon investigation it was found that she had four big sons, all toughs, who beat her regularly and took from her all the money she could earn or beg; she was "a respectable woman, of good habits," the inquiry developed, and lied only to shield her rascally sons.

recollection of seeing one of his tribe, a robber and murderer before he was nineteen, go to the gallows unmoved, all fear of the rope overcome, as it seemed, by the secret, exultant pride of being the centre of a first-class show, shortly to be followed by that acme of tenement-life bliss, a big funeral. He had his reward. His name is to this day a talisman among West Side ruffians, and is proudly borne by the gang of which, up till the night when he "knocked out his man," he was an obscure though aspiring member.

   The crime that made McGloin[129] famous was the cowardly murder of an unarmed saloonkeeper who came upon the gang while it was sacking his bar-room at the dead of night. McGloin might easily have fled, but disdained to "run for a Dutchman." His act was a fair measure of the standard of heroism set up by his class in its conflicts with society. The finish is worthy of the start. The first long step in crime taken by the half-grown boy, fired with ambition to earn a standing in his gang, is usually to rob a "lush," *i.e.,* a drunken man who has strayed his way, likely enough is lying asleep in a hallway. He has served an apprenticeship on copper-bottom wash-boilers and like articles found lying around loose, and capable of being converted into cash enough to give the growler a trip or two; but his first venture at robbery moves him up into full fellowship at once. He is no longer a "kid," though his years may be few, but a tough with the rest. He may even in time — he is reasonably certain of it — get his name in the papers as a murderous scoundrel, and have his cup of glory filled to the brim. I came once upon a gang of such young rascals passing the growler after a successful raid of some sort, down at the West Thirty-seventh Street dock and, having my camera along, offered to "take"[130] them. They were not old and wary enough to be shy of the photographer, whose acquaintance they usually first make in handcuffs and the grip of a policeman; or their vanity overcame their caution. It is entirely in keeping with the tough's character that he should love of all things to pose before a photographer, and the ambition is usually the stronger the more repulsive the tough. These were of that sort, and accepted the offer with great readiness, dragging into their group a disreputable-looking sheep that roamed about with them (the slaughter-houses were close at hand) as one of the band. The homeliest ruffian of the lot, who insisted on being taken with the growler to his "mug," took the opportunity to pour what was left in it down his throat and this caused a brief unpleasantness, but otherwise the performance

---

[129] Mike McGloin was hanged in 1883. — ED.
[130] To take one's picture. — ED.

A Growler Gang in Session.

was a success. While I was getting the camera ready, I threw out a vague suggestion of cigarette pictures, and it took root at once. Nothing would do then but that I must take the boldest spirits of the company "in character." One of them tumbled over against a shed, as if asleep, while two of the others bent over him, searching his pockets with a deftness that was highly suggestive. This, they explained for my benefit, was to show how they "did the trick." The rest of the band were so impressed with the importance of this exhibition that they insisted on crowding into the picture by climbing upon the shed, sitting on the roof with their feet dangling over the edge, and disposing themselves in every imaginable manner within view, as they thought. Lest any reader be led into the error of supposing them to have been harmless young fellows enjoying themselves in peace, let me say that within half an hour after our meeting, when I called at the police station three blocks away, I found there two of my friends of the "Montgomery Guards" under arrest for robbing a Jewish pedlar who had passed that way after I left them, and trying to saw his head off, as they put it, "just for fun. The sheeny cum along an' the saw was there, an' we socked it to him." The prisoners were described to me by the police as Dennis, "the Bum," and "Mud" Foley.

It is not always that their little diversions end as harmlessly as did this, even from the standpoint of the Jew, who was pretty badly hurt. Not far from the preserves of the Montgomery Guards, in Poverty Gap, directly opposite the scene of the murder to which I have referred in a note explaining the picture of the Cunningham family (p. 170), a young lad, who was the only support of his aged parents, was beaten to death within a few months by the "Alley Gang," for the same offence that drew down the displeasure of its neighbors upon the pedlar: that of being at work trying to earn an honest living. I found a part of the gang asleep the next morning, before young Healey's death was known, in a heap of straw on the floor of an unoccupied room in the same row of rear tenements in which the murdered boy's home was. One of the tenants, who secretly directed me to their lair, assuring me that no worse scoundrels went unhung, ten minutes later gave the gang, to its face, an official character for sobriety and inoffensiveness that very nearly startled me into an unguarded rebuke of his duplicity. I caught his eye in time and held my peace. The man was simply trying to protect his own home, while giving such aid as he safely could toward bringing the murderous ruffians to justice. The incident shows to what extent a neighborhood may be terrorized by a determined gang of these reckless toughs.

In Poverty Gap there were still a few decent people left. When it comes to Hell's Kitchen, or to its compeers at the other end of Thirty-ninth Street over by the East River, and further down First Avenue in "the Village," the Rag Gang and its allies have no need of fearing treachery in their periodical battles with the police. The entire neighborhood takes a hand on these occasions, the women in the front rank, partly from sheer love of the "fun," but chiefly because husbands, brothers, and sweethearts are in the fight to a man and need their help. Chimney-tops form the staple of ammunition then, and stacks of loose brick and paving-stones, carefully hoarded in upper rooms as a prudent provision against emergencies. Regular patrol posts are established by the police on the housetops in times of trouble in these localities, but even then they do not escape whole-skinned, if, indeed, with their lives; neither does the gang. The policeman knows of but one cure for the tough, the club, and he lays it on without stint whenever and wherever he has the chance, knowing right well that, if caught at a disadvantage, he will get his outlay back with interest. Words are worse than wasted in the gang-districts. It is a blow at sight, and the tough thus accosted never stops to ask questions. Unless he is "wanted" for some signal outrage, the policeman rarely bothers with arresting him. He can point out half a dozen at sight against whom indictments are pending by the basketful, but whom no jail ever held many hours. They only serve to make him more reckless, for he knows that the political backing that has saved him in the past can do it again. It is a commodity that is only exchangeable "for value received," and it is not hard to imagine what sort of value is in demand. The saloon, in ninety-nine cases out of a hundred, stands behind the bargain.

For these reasons, as well as because he knows from frequent experience his own way to be the best, the policeman lets the gangs alone except when they come within reach of his long night-stick. They have their "clubrooms" where they meet, generally in a tenement, sometimes under a pier or a dump, to carouse, play cards, and plan their raids; their "fences," who dispose of the stolen property. When the necessity presents itself for a descent upon the gang after some particularly flagrant outrage, the police have a task on hand that is not of the easiest. The gangs, like foxes, have more than one hole to their dens. In some localities, where the interior of a block is filled with rear tenements, often set at all sorts of odd angles, surprise alone is practicable. Pursuit through the winding ways and passages is impossible. The young thieves know them all by heart. They have their runways over roofs and fences which no one else could find. Their lair is generally selected with special reference to its possibilities of escape. Once pitched upon, its occupation by the gang, with its ear-mark of nightly symposiums, "can-rackets" in the slang of the street, is the signal for a rapid deterioration of the tenement, if that is possible. Relief is only to be had by ousting the intruders. An instance came under my notice in which valuable property had been well-nigh ruined by being made the thoroughfare of thieves by night and by day. They had chosen it because of a passage that led through the block by way of several connecting halls and yards. The place came soon to be known as "Murderers Alley." Complaint was made to the Board of Health, as a last resort, of the condition of the property. The practical inspector who was sent to report upon it suggested to the owner that he build a brick-wall in a place where it would shut off communication between the streets, and he took the advice. Within the brief space of a few months the house changed character entirely, and became as decent as it had been before the convenient runway was discoverd.

This was in the Sixth Ward, where the infamous Whyo Gang until a few years ago absorbed the worst depravity of the Bend and what is left of the Five Points. The gang was finally broken up when its leader was hanged for murder after a life of uninterrupted and unavenged crimes, the recital of which made his father confessor turn pale, listening in the shadow of the scaffold, though many years of labor as chaplain of the Tombs had hardened him to such rehearsals. The great Whyo had been a "power in the ward," handy at carrying elections for the party or faction that happened to stand in need of his services and was willing to pay for them in money or in kind. Other gangs have sprung up since with as high ambition and a fair prospect of outdoing their predecessor. The conditions that bred it still exist, practically unchanged. Inspector Byrnes is authority for the statement that throughout the city the young tough has more "ability" and "nerve" than the thief whose example he successfully emulates. He begins earlier, too. Speaking of the increase of the native element among criminal prisoners exhibited in the census returns of the last thirty years,[131] the Rev. Fred. H. Wines says, "their youth is a very striking fact." Had he confined his observations to the police courts of New York, he might have emphasized that remark and found an explanation of the discovery that "the ratio of prisoners in cities is two and one-quarter times as great as in the country at large," a computation that takes no account of the reformatories for juvenile delinquents, or the exhibit would have been still more striking. Of the 82,200 persons arrested by the police in 1889, 10,505 were under twenty years old. The last report of the Society for the Prevention of Cruelty to Children enumerates, as "a few typical cases," eighteen "professional cracksmen,"[132] between nine and fifteen years old, who had been caught with burglars' tools, or in the act of robbery. Four of them, hardly yet in long trousers, had "held up" a wayfarer in the public street and robbed him of $73. One, aged sixteen, "was the leader of a noted gang of young robbers in Forty-ninth Street. He committed murder, for which he is now serving a term of nineteen years in State's Prison." Four of the eighteen were girls

---

[131] "The percentage of foreign-born prisoners in 1850, as compared with that of natives, was more than five times that of native prisoners, now (1880) it is less than double." — American Prisons in the Tenth Census.

[132] A safe-breaker. — ED.

Typical Toughs (from the Rogues' Gallery).

and quite as bad as the worst. In a few years they would have been living with the toughs of their choice without the ceremony of a marriage, egging them on by their pride in their lawless achievements, and fighting side by side with them in their encounters with the "cops."

The exploits of the Paradise Park Gang in the way of highway robbery showed last summer that the embers of the scattered Whyo Gang, upon the wreck of which it grew, were smouldering still. The hanging of Driscoll broke up the Whyos because they were a comparatively small band, and, with the incomparable master-spirit gone, were unable to resist the angry rush of public indignation that followed the crowning outrage. This is the history of the passing away of famous gangs from time to time. The passing is more apparent than real, however. Some other daring leader gathers the scattered elements about him soon, and the war on society is resumed. A bare enumeration of the names of the best-known gangs would occupy pages of this book. The Rock Gang, the Rag Gang, the Stable Gang, and the Short Tail Gang down about the "Hook" have all achieved bad eminence, along with scores of others that have not paraded so frequently in the newspapers. By day they loaf in the

Hunting River Thieves.

corner-groggeries on their beat, at night they plunder the stores along the avenues, or lie in wait at the river for unsteady feet straying their way. The man who is sober and minds his own business they seldom molest, unless he be a stranger inquiring his way, or a policeman and the gang twenty against the one. The tipsy wayfarer is their chosen victim, and they seldom have to look for him long. One has not far to go to the river from any point in New York. The man who does not know where he is going is sure to reach it sooner or later. Should he foolishly resist or make an outcry — dead men tell no tales. "Floaters"[133] come ashore every now and then with pockets turned inside out, not always evidence of a post-mortem inspection by dock-rats. Police patrol the rivers as well as the shore on constant look-out for these, but seldom catch up with them. If overtaken after a race during which shots are often exchanged from the boats, the thieves have an easy way of escaping and at the same time destroying the evidence against them; they simply upset the boat. They swim, one and all, like real rats; the lost plunder can be recovered at leisure the next day by diving or grappling. The loss of the boat counts for little. Another is stolen, and the gang is ready for business again.

The fiction of a social "club," which most of the gangs keep up, helps them to a pretext for blackmailing the politicians and the storekeepers in their bailiwick at the annual seasons of their picnic, or ball. The "thieves' ball" is as well known and recognized an institution on the East Side as the Charity Ball in a different social stratum, although it does not go by that name, in print at least. Indeed, the last thing a New York tough will admit is that he is a thief. He dignifies his calling with the pretence of gambling. He does not steal: he "wins" your money or your watch, and on the police returns he is a "speculator." If, when he passes around the hat for "voluntary" contributions, any storekeeper should have the temerity to refuse to chip in, he may look for a visit from the gang on the first dark night, and account himself lucky if his place escapes being alto-gether wrecked. The Hell's Kitchen Gang and the Rag Gang have both distinguished themselves within recent times by blowing up objection-able stores with stolen gunpowder. But if no such episode mar the celebration, the excursion comes off and is the occasion for a series of drunken fights that as likely as not end in murder. No season has passed within my memory that has not seen the police reserves called out to receive some howling pandemonium returning from a picnic grove on the Hudson or on the Sound. At least one peaceful community up the river, that had borne with this nuisance until patience had ceased to be a virtue, received a boat-load of such picnickers in a style befitting the occasion and the cargo. The outraged citizens planted a howitzer on the dock, and bade the party land at their peril. With the loaded gun pointed dead at them, the furious toughs gave up and the peace was not broken on the Hudson that day, at least not ashore. It is good cause for congrat-ulation that the worst of all forms of recreation popular among the city's

[133] The bodies of those who have been dumped in the river. — ED.

toughs, the moonlight picnic, has been effectually discouraged. Its opportunities for disgraceful revelry and immorality were unrivalled anywhere.

In spite of influence and protection, the tough reaches eventually the end of his rope. Occasionally — not too often — there is a noose on it. If not, the world that owes him a living, according to his creed, will insist on his earning it on the safe side of a prison wall. A few, a very few, have been clubbed into an approach to righteousness from the police standpoint. The condemned tough goes up to serve his "bit" or couple of "stretches," followed by the applause of his gang. In the prison he meets older thieves than himself, and sits at their feet listening with respectful admiration to their accounts of the great doings that sent them before. He returns with the brand of the jail upon him, to encounter the hero-worship of his old associates as an offset to the cold shoulder given him by all the rest of the world. Even if he is willing to work, disgusted with the restraint and hard labor of prison life, and in a majority of cases that thought is probably uppermost in his mind, no one will have him around. If, with the assistance of Inspector Byrnes, who is a philanthropist in his own practical way, he secures a job, he is discharged on the slightest provocation, and for the most trifling fault. Very soon he sinks back into his old surroundings, to rise no more until he is lost to view in the queer, mysterious way in which thieves and fallen women disappear. No one can tell how. In the ranks of criminals he never rises above that of the "laborer," the small thief or burglar, or general crook, who blindly does the work planned for him by others, and runs the biggest risk for the poorest pay. It cannot be said that the "growler" brought him luck, or its friendship fortune. And yet, if his misdeeds have helped to make manifest that all effort to reclaim his kind must begin with the conditions of life against which his very existence is a protest, even the tough has not lived in vain. This measure of credit at least should be accorded him, that, with or without his good-will, he has been a factor in urging on the battle against the slums that bred him. It is a fight in which eternal vigilance is truly the price of liberty and the preservation of society.

Chapter XX

The Working Girls of New York

Of the harvest of tares, sown in iniquity and reaped in wrath, the police returns tell the story. The pen that wrote the "Song of the Shirt"[134] is needed to tell of the sad and toil-worn lives of New York's working-women. The cry echoes by night and by day through its tenements:

Oh, God! that bread should be so dear,
And flesh and blood so cheap!

Six months have not passed since at a great public meeting in this city, the Working Women's Society reported: "It is a known fact that men's wages cannot fall below a limit upon which they can exist, but woman's wages have no limit, since the paths of shame are always open to her. It is simply impossible for any woman to live without assistance on the low salary a saleswoman earns, without depriving herself of real necessities. ... It is inevitable that they must in many instances resort to evil." It was only a few brief weeks before that verdict was uttered, that the community was shocked by the story of a gentle and refined woman who, left in direst poverty to earn her own living alone among strangers, threw herself from her attic window, preferring death to dishonor. "I would have done any honest work, even to scrubbing," she wrote, drenched and starving, after a vain search for work in a driving storm. She had tramped the streets for weeks on her weary errand, and the only living wages that were offered her were the wages of sin. The ink was not dry upon her letter before a woman in an East Side tenement wrote down her reason for self-murder: "Weakness, sleeplessness, and yet obliged to work. My strength fails me. Sing at my coffin: 'Where does the soul find a home and rest?'" Her story may be found as one of two typical "cases of despair" in one little church community, in the *City Mission Society's Monthly* for last February. It is a story that has many parallels in the experience of every missionary, every police reporter and every family doctor whose practice is among the poor.

It is estimated that at least one hundred and fifty thousand women and girls earn their own living in New York; but there is reason to believe that this estimate falls far short of the truth when sufficient account is taken of the large number who are not wholly dependent upon their own labor, while contributing by it to the family's earnings. These alone constitute a

[134] Written by the poet Thomas Hood (1799–1845) in 1843. — Ed.

214

large class of the women wage-earners, and it is characteristic of the situation that the very fact that some need not starve on their wages condemns the rest to that fate. The pay they are willing to accept all have to take. What the "everlasting law of supply and demand," that serves as such a convenient gag for public indignation, has to do with it, one learns from observation all along the road of inquiry into these real woman's wrongs. To take the case of the saleswomen for illustration: The investigation of the Working Women's Society[135] disclosed the fact that wages averaging from $2 to $4.50 a week were reduced by excessive fines, "the employers placing a value upon time lost that is not given to services rendered." A little girl, who received two dollars a week, made cash-sales amounting to $167 in a single day, while the receipts of a fifteen-dollar male clerk in the same department footed up only $125; yet for some trivial mistake the girl was fined sixty cents out of her two dollars. The practice prevailed in some stores of dividing the fines between the superintendent and the time-keeper at the end of the year. In one instance they amounted to $3,000, and "the superintendent was heard to charge the time-keeper with not being strict enough in his duties." One of the causes for fine in a certain large store was sitting down. The law requiring seats for saleswomen, generally ignored, was obeyed faithfully in this establishment. The seats were there, but the girls were fined when found using them.

Cash-girls receiving $1.75 a week for work that at certain seasons lengthened their day to sixteen hours were sometimes required to pay for their aprons. A common cause for discharge from stores in which, on account of the oppressive heat and lack of ventilation, "girls fainted day after day and came out looking like corpses," was too long service. No other fault was found with the discharged saleswomen than that they had been long enough in the employ of the firm to justly expect an increase of salary. The reason was even given with brutal frankness, in some instances.

These facts give a slight idea of the hardships and the poor pay of a business that notoriously absorbs child-labor. The girls are sent to the store before they have fairly entered their teens, because the money they can earn there is needed for the support of the family. If the boys will not work, if the street tempts them from home, among the girls at least there must be no drones. To keep their places they are told to lie about their age and to say that they are over fourteen. The precaution is usually superfluous. The Women's Investigating Committee[136] found the major-

---

[135] Society established in 1888 to protect the interests of working women. — ED.

[136] Committee created to look into illegal labor practices, especially the use of underage children. — ED.

ity of the children employed in the stores to be under age, but heard only in a single instance of the truant officers calling. In that case they came once a year and sent the youngest children home; but in a month's time they were all back in their places, and were not again disturbed. When it comes to the factories, where hard bodily labor is added to long hours, stifling rooms, and starvation wages, matters are even worse. The Legislature has passed laws to prevent the employment of children, as it has forbidden saloon-keepers to sell them beer, and it has provided means of enforcing its mandate, so efficient, that the very number of factories in New York is *guessed* at as in the neighborhood of twelve thousand. Up till this summer, a single inspector was charged with the duty of keeping the run of them all, and of seeing to it that the law was respected by the owners.

Sixty cents is put as the average day's earnings of the 150,000, but into this computation enters the stylish "cashier's" two dollars a day, as well as the thirty cents of the poor little girl who pulls threads in an East Side factory, and, if anything, the average is probably too high. Such as it is, however, it represents board, rent, clothing, and "pleasure" to this army of workers. Here is the case of a woman employed in the manufacturing department of a Broadway house. It stands for a hundred like her own. She averages three dollars a week. Pays $1.50 for her room; for breakfast she has a cup of coffee; lunch she cannot afford. One meal a day is her allowance. This woman is young, she is pretty. She has "the world before her." Is it anything less than a miracle if she is guilty of nothing worse than the "early and improvident marriage," against which moralists exclaim as one of the prolific causes of the distress of the poor? Almost any door might seem to offer welcome escape from such slavery as this. "I feel so much healthier since I got three square meals a day," said a lodger in one of the Girls' Homes.[137] Two young sewing-girls came in seeking domestic service, so that they might get enough to eat. They had been only half-fed for some time, and starvation had driven them to the one door at which the pride of the American-born girl will not permit her to knock, though poverty be the price of her independence.

The tenement and the competition of public institutions and farmers' wives and daughters, have done the tyrant shirt to death, but they have not bettered the lot of the needle-women. The sweater of the East Side has appropriated the flannel shirt. He turns them out to-day at forty-five cents a dozen, paying his Jewish workers from twenty to thirty-five cents. One of these testified before the State Board of Arbitration, during the

[137] Institution designed to house and feed homeless girls. — ED.

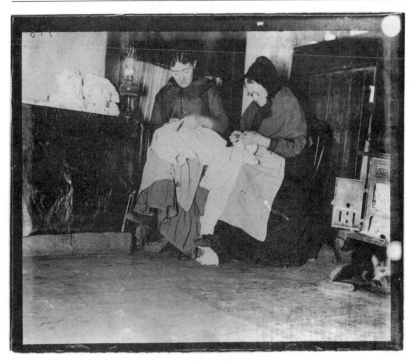

Sewing and Starving in an Elizabeth Street Attic.

shirtmakers' strike,[138] that she worked eleven hours in the shop and four at home, and had never in the best of times made over six dollars a week. Another stated that she worked from 4 o'clock in the morning to 11 at night. These girls had to find their own thread and pay for their own machines out of their wages. The white shirt has gone to the public and private institutions that shelter large numbers of young girls, and to the country. There are not half as many shirtmakers in New York to-day as only a few years ago, and some of the largest firms have closed their city shops. The same is true of the manufacturers of underwear. One large Broadway firm has nearly all its work done by farmers' girls in Maine, who think themselves well off if they can earn two or three dollars a week to pay for a Sunday silk, or the wedding outfit, little dreaming of the part they are playing in starving their city sisters. Literally, they sew "with double thread, a shroud as well as a shirt." Their pin-money sets the rate

[138] In March 1890 unionized and unorganized shirtmakers struck for a ten-hour day and weekly wages. — ED.

of wages for thousands of poor sewing-girls in New York. The average earnings of the worker on underwear to-day do not exceed the three dollars which her competitor among the Eastern hills is willing to accept as the price of her play. The shirtmaker's pay is better only because the very finest custom work is all there is left for her to do.

Calico wrappers at a dollar and a half a dozen — the very expert sewers able to make from eight to ten, the common run five or six — neckties at from 25 to 75 cents a dozen, with a dozen as a good day's work, are specimens of women's wages. And yet people persist in wondering at the poor quality of work done in the tenements! Italian cheap labor has come of late also to possess this poor field, with the sweater in its train. There is scarce a branch of woman's work outside of the home in which wages, long since at low-water mark, have not fallen to the point of actual starvation. A case was brought to my notice recently by a woman doctor, whose heart as well as her life-work is with the poor, of a widow with two little children she found at work in an East Side attic, making paper-bags. Her father, she told the doctor, had made good wages at it; but she received only five cents for six hundred of the little three-cornered bags, and her fingers had to be very swift and handle the paste-brush very deftly to bring her earnings up to twenty-five and thirty cents a day. She paid four dollars a month for her room. The rest went to buy food for herself and the children. The physician's purse, rather than her skill, had healing for their complaint.

I have aimed to set down a few dry facts merely. They carry their own comment. Back of the shop with its weary, grinding toil — the home in the tenement, of which it was said in a report of the State Labor Bureau: "Decency and womanly reserve cannot be maintained there — what wonder so many fall away from virtue?" Of the outlook, what? Last Christmas Eve my business took me to an obscure street among the West Side tenements. An old woman had just fallen on the doorstep, stricken with paralysis. The doctor said she would never again move her right hand or foot. The whole side was dead. By her bedside, in their cheerless room, sat the patient's aged sister, a hopeless cripple, in dumb despair. Forty years ago the sisters had come, five in number then, with their mother, from the North of Ireland to make their home and earn a living among strangers. They were lace embroiderers and found work easily at good wages. All the rest had died as the years went by. The two remained and, firmly resolved to lead an honest life, worked on though wages fell and fell as age and toil stiffened their once nimble fingers and dimmed their sight. Then one of them dropped out, her hands palsied and her courage gone. Still the other toiled on, resting neither by night nor by day, that the sister might not want. Now that she too had been stricken, as she was going to the store for the work that was to keep them through the holidays, the battle was over at last. There was before them starvation, or the poor-house. And the proud spirits of the sisters, helpless now, quailed at the outlook.

These were old, with life behind them. For them nothing was left but to sit in the shadow and wait. But of the thousands, who are travelling the road they trod to the end, with the hot blood of youth in their veins, with the love of life and of the beautiful world to which not even sixty cents a day can shut their eyes — who is to blame if their feet find the paths of shame that are "always open to them?" The very paths that have effaced the saving "limit," and to which it is declared to be "inevitable that they must in many instances resort." Let the moralist answer. Let the wise economist apply his rule of supply and demand, and let the answer be heard in this city of a thousand charities where justice goes begging.

To the everlasting credit of New York's working-girl let it be said that, rough though her road be, all but hopeless her battle with life, only in the rarest instances does she go astray. As a class she is brave, virtuous, and true. New York's army of profligate women is not, as in some foreign cities, recruited from her ranks. She is as plucky as she is proud. That "American girls never whimper" became a proverb long ago, and she accepts her lot uncomplainingly, doing the best she can and holding her cherished independence cheap at the cost of a meal, or of half her daily ration, if need be. The home in the tenement and the traditions of her childhood have neither trained her to luxury nor predisposed her in favor of domestic labor in preference to the shop. So, to the world she presents a cheerful, uncomplaining front that sometimes deceives it. Her courage will not be without its reward. Slowly, as the conviction is thrust upon society that woman's work must enter more and more into its planning, a better day is dawning. The organization of working girls' clubs, unions, and societies with a community of interests, despite the obstacles to such a movement, bears testimony to it, as to the devotion of the unselfish women who have made their poorer sister's cause their own, and will yet wring from an unfair world the justice too long denied her.

Chapter XXI

Pauperism in the Tenements

The reader who has followed with me the fate of the Other Half thus far, may not experience much of a shock at being told that in eight years 135,595 families in New York were registered as asking or receiving charity. Perhaps, however, the intelligence will rouse him that for five years past one person in every ten who died in this city was buried in the Potter's Field. These facts tell a terrible story. The first means that in a population of a million and a half, very nearly, if not quite, half a million persons were driven, or chose, to beg for food, or to accept it in charity at some period of the eight years, if not during the whole of it. There is no mistake about these figures. They are drawn from the records of the Charity Organization Society,[139] and represent the time during which it has been in existence. It is not even pretended that the record is complete. To be well within the limits, the Society's statisticians allow only three and a half to the family, instead of the four and a half that are accepted as the standard of calculations which deal with New York's population as a whole. They estimate upon the basis of their every-day experience that, allowing for those who have died, moved away, or become for the time being at least self-supporting, eighty-five per cent. of the registry are still within, or lingering upon, the borders of dependence. Precisely how the case stands with this great horde of the indigent is shown by a classification of 5,169 cases that were investigated by the Society in one year. This was the way it turned out: 327 worthy of continuous relief, or 6.4 per cent.; 1,269 worthy of temporary relief, or 24.4 per cent.; 2,698 in need of work, rather than relief, or 52.2 per cent.; 875 unworthy of relief, or 17 per cent.

That is, nearly six and a half per cent. of all were utterly helpless — orphans, cripples, or the very aged; nearly one-fourth needed just a lift to start them on the road to independence, or to permanent pauperism, according to the wisdom with which the lever was applied. More than half were destitute because they had no work and were unable to find any, and one-sixth were frauds, professional beggars, training their children to follow in their footsteps — a veritable "tribe of Ishmael," tightening its

---

[139] One of the many nationwide Societies or Charities set up to administer and organize the activities of those engaged in private philanthropic and charity work. The New York Charity Organization Society was led by Josephine Shaw Lowell. — ED.

A Flat in the Pauper Barracks, West Thirty-Eighth Street, with All Its Furniture.

grip on society as the years pass, until society shall summon up pluck to say with Paul,[140] "if any man will not work neither shall he eat," and stick to it. It is worthy of note that almost precisely the same results followed a similar investigation in Boston. There were a few more helpless cases of the sort true charity accounts it a gain to care for, but the proportion

---

[140] Riis is referring to the Apostle Paul. — ED.

of a given lot that was crippled for want of work, or unworthy, was exactly the same as in this city. The bankrupt in hope, in courage, in purse, and in purpose, are not peculiar to New York. They are found the world over, but we have our full share. If further proof were wanted, it is found in the prevalence of pauper burials. The Potter's Field stands ever for utter, hopeless surrender. The last the poor will let go, however miserable their lot in life, is the hope of a decent burial. But for the five years ending with 1888 the average of burials in the Potter's Field has been 10.03 per cent. of all. In 1889 it was 9.64. In that year the proportion to the total mortality of those who died in hospitals, institutions, and in the Almshouse was as 1 in 5.

The 135,595 families inhabited no fewer than 31,000 different tenements. I say tenements advisedly, though the society calls them buildings, because at least ninety-nine per cent. were found in the big barracks, the rest in shanties scattered here and there, and now and then a fraud or an exceptional case of distress in a dwelling-house of better class. Here, undoubtedly, allowance must be made for the constant moving about of those who live on charity, which enables one active beggar to blacklist a dozen houses in the year. Still the great mass of the tenements are shown to be harboring alms-seekers. They might almost as safely harbor the small-pox. That scourge is not more contagious than the alms-seeker's complaint. There are houses that have been corrupted through and through by this pestilence, until their very atmosphere breathes beggary. More than a hundred and twenty pauper families have been reported from time to time as living in one such tenement.

The truth is that pauperism grows in the tenements as naturally as weeds in a garden lot. A moral distemper, like crime, it finds there its most fertile soil. All the surroundings of tenement-house life favor its growth, and where once it has taken root it is harder to dislodge than the most virulent of physical diseases. The thief is infinitely easier to deal with than the pauper, because the very fact of his being a thief presupposes some bottom to the man. Granted that it is bad, there is still something, a possible handle by which to catch him. To the pauper there is none. He is as hopeless as his own poverty. I speak of the *pauper,* not of the honestly poor. There is a sharp line between the two; but athwart it stands the tenement, all the time blurring and blotting it out. "It all comes down to character in the end," was the verdict of a philanthropist whose life has been spent wrestling with this weary problem. And so it comes down to the tenement, the destroyer of individuality and character everywhere. "In nine years," said a wise and charitable physician, sadly, to me, "I have known of but a single case of permanent improvement in a poor tenement family." I have known of some, whose experience, extending over an even longer stretch, was little better.

The beggar follows the "tough's" rule of life that the world owes him a living, but his scheme of collecting it stops short of violence. He has not the pluck to rob even a drunken man. His highest flights take in at most an unguarded clothes-line, or a little child sent to buy bread or beer with the pennies he clutches tightly as he skips along. Even then he prefers to attain his end by stratagem rather than by force, though occasionally, when the coast is clear, he rises to the height of the bully. The ways he finds of "collecting" under the cloak of undeserved poverty are number-less, and often reflect credit on the man's ingenuity, if not on the man himself. I remember the shock with which my first experience with his kind — her kind, rather, in this case: the beggar was a woman — came home to me. On my way to and from the office I had been giving charity regularly, as I fondly believed, to an old woman who sat in Chatham Square with a baby done up in a bundle of rags, moaning piteously in sunshine and rain, "Please, help the poor." It was the baby I pitied and thought I was doing my little to help, until one night I was just in time to rescue it from rolling out of her lap, and found the bundle I had been wasting my pennies upon just rags and nothing more, and the old hag dead drunk. Since then I have encountered bogus babies, borrowed babies, and drugged babies in the streets, and fought shy of them all. Most of them, I am glad to say, have been banished from the street since; but they are still occasionally to be found. It was only last winter that the officers of the Society for the Prevention of Cruelty to Children arrested an Italian woman who was begging along Madison Avenue with a poor little wreck of a girl, whose rags and pinched face were calculated to tug hard at the purse-strings of a miser. Over five dollars in nickles and pennies were taken from the woman's pockets, and when her story of poverty and hunger was investigated at the family's home in a Baxter Street tenement, bank-books turned up that showed the Masonis to be regular pauper capitalists, able to draw their check for three thousand dollars, had they been so disposed. The woman was fined $250, a worse punishment undoubtedly than to have sent her to prison for the rest of her natural life. Her class has, unhappily, representatives in New York that have not yet been brought to grief.

Nothing short of making street begging a crime has availed to clear our city of this pest to an appreciable extent. By how much of an effort this result has been accomplished may be gleaned from the fact that the Charity Organization Society alone, in five years, caused the taking up of 2,594 street beggars, and the arrest and conviction of 1,474 persistent offenders. Last year it dealt with 612 perambulating mendicants. The police report only 19 arrests for begging during the year 1889, but the real facts of the case are found under the heading "vagrancy." In all, 2,633 persons were charged with this offence, 947 of them women. A goodly proportion of these latter came from the low groggeries[141] of the Tenth Ward, where a peculiar variety of the female tramp-beggar is at home, the "scrub." The scrub is one degree perhaps above the average pauper in this, that she is willing to work at least one day in the week, generally the Jewish Sabbath. The orthodox Jew can do no work of any sort from Friday evening till sunset on Saturday, and this interim the scrub fills out in Ludlow Street. The pittance she receives for this vicarious sacrifice of herself upon the altar of the ancient faith buys her rum for at least two days of the week at one of the neighborhood "morgues."[142] She lives through the other four by begging. There are distilleries in Jewtown, or just across its borders, that depend almost wholly on her custom. Recently, when one in Hester Street was raided because the neighbors had complained of the boisterous hilarity of the hags over their beer, thirty-two aged "scrubs" were marched off to the station-house.

It is curious to find preconceived notions quite upset in a review of the nationalities that go to make up this squad of street beggars. The Irish head the list with fifteen per cent., and the native American is only a little way behind with twelve per cent., while the Italian, who in his own country turns beggary into a fine art, has less than two per cent. Eight per cent. were Germans. The relative prevalence of the races in our population does not account for this showing. Various causes operate, no doubt, to produce it. Chief among them is, I think, the tenement itself. It has no power to corrupt the Italian, who comes here in almost every instance to work — no beggar would ever emigrate from anywhere unless forced to do so. He is distinctly on its lowest level from the start. With the Irishman the case is different. The tenement, especially its lowest type, appears to possess a peculiar affinity for the worse nature of the Celt, to whose best and strongest instincts it does violence, and soonest and most thoroughly corrupts him. The "native" twelve per cent. represent the result of this process, the hereditary beggar of the second or third generation in the slums.

The blind beggar alone is winked at in New York's streets, because the authorities do not know what else to do with him. There is no provision for him anywhere after he is old enough to strike out for himself. The

---

[141] Barrooms. — ED.

[142] Bars along the Bowery that served especially potent, sometimes fatal, alcoholic concoctions. — ED.

annual pittance of thirty or forty dollars which he receives from the city serves to keep his landlord in good humor; for the rest his misfortune and his thin disguise of selling pencils on the street corners must provide. Until the city affords him some systematic way of earning his living by work (as Philadelphia has done, for instance) to banish him from the street would be tantamount to sentencing him to death by starvation. So he possesses it in peace, that is, if he is blind in good earnest, and begs without "encumbrance."[143] Professional mendicancy does not hesitate to make use of the greatest of human afflictions as a pretence for enlisting the sympathy upon which it thrives. Many New Yorkers will remember the French schoolmaster who was "blinded by a shell at the siege of Paris," but miraculously recovered his sight when arrested and deprived of his children by the officers of Mr. Gerry's society. When last heard of he kept a "museum" in Hartford, and acted the overseer with financial success. His sign with its pitiful tale, that was a familiar sight in our streets for years and earned for him the capital upon which he started his business, might have found a place among the curiosities exhibited there, had it not been kept in a different sort of museum here as a memento of his rascality. There was another of his tribe, a woman, who begged for years with a deformed child in her arms, which she was found to have hired at an almshouse in Genoa for fifteen francs a month. It was a good investment, for she proved to be possessed of a comfortable fortune. Some time before that, the Society for the Prevention of Cruelty to Children, that found her out, had broken up the dreadful padrone system,[144] a real slave trade in Italian children, who were bought of poor parents across the sea and made to beg their way on foot through France to the port whence they were shipped to this city, to be beaten and starved here by their cruel masters and sent out to beg, often after merciless mutilation to make them "take" better with a pitying public.

But, after all, the tenement offers a better chance of fraud on impulsive but thoughtless charity, than all the wretchedness of the street, and with fewer risks. To the tender-hearted and unwary it is, in itself, the strongest plea for help. When such a cry goes up as was heard recently from a Mott Street den, where the family of a "sick" husband, a despairing mother, and half a dozen children in rags and dirt were destitute of the "first necessities of life," it is not to be wondered at that a stream of gold comes pouring in to relieve. It happens too often, as in that case, that a little critical inquiry or reference to the "black list" of the Charity Organization

---

[143] Colloquial term used to describe children. — ED.

[144] Generally, a system in which a boss or patron secures work for unskilled and immigrant workers. — ED.

Coffee at One Cent.

Society, justly dreaded only by the frauds, discovers the "sickness" to stand for laziness, and the destitution to be the family's stock in trade; and the community receives a shock that for once is downright whole-some, if it imposes a check on an undiscriminating charity that is worse than none at all.

The case referred to furnished an apt illustration of how thoroughly corrupting pauperism is in such a setting. The tenement woke up early to the gold mine that was being worked under its roof, and before the day was three hours old the stream of callers who responded to the newspa-per appeal found the alley blocked by a couple of "toughs," who exacted toll of a silver quarter from each tearful sympathizer with the misery in the attic.

A volume might be written about the tricks of the professional beggar, and the uses to which he turns the tenement in his trade. The Boston "widow" whose husband turned up alive and well after she had buried him seventeen times with tears and lamentation, and made the public pay for the weekly funerals, is not without representatives in New York. The "gentleman tramp" is a familiar type from our streets, and the "once respectable Methodist" who patronized all the revivals in town with his profitable story of repentance, only to fall from grace into the saloon door nearest the church after the service was over, merely transferred the scene of his operations from the tenement to the church as the proper setting for his specialty. There is enough of real suffering in the homes of the poor to make one wish that there were some effective way of enforcing Paul's plan of starving the drones into the paths of self-support: no work, nothing to eat.

The message came from one of the Health Department's summer doctors, last July, to The King's Daughters' Tenement-house Committee, that a family with a sick child was absolutely famishing in an uptown tenement. The address was not given. The doctor had forgotten to write it down, and before he could be found and a visitor sent to the house the baby was dead, and the mother had gone mad. The nurse found the father, who was an honest laborer long out of work, packing the little corpse in an orange-box partly filled with straw, that he might take it to the Morgue for pauper burial. There was absolutely not a crust to eat in the house, and the other children were crying for food. The great immediate need in that case, as in more than half of all according to the record, was work and living wages. Alms do not meet the emergency at all. They frequently aggravate it, degrading and pauperizing where true help should aim at raising the sufferer to self-respect and self-dependence. The experience of the Charity Organization Society in raising, in eight years, 4,500 families out of the rut of pauperism into proud, if modest, independence, without alms, but by a system of "friendly visitation," and the work of the Society for Improving the Condition of the Poor and kindred organizations along the same line, shows what can be done by well-directed effort. It is estimated that New York spends in public and private charity every year a round $8,000,000. A small part of this sum intelligently invested in a great labor bureau, that would bring the seeker of work and the one with work to give together under auspices offering some degree of mutual security, would certainly repay the amount of the investment in the saving of much capital now worse than wasted, and would be prolific of the best results. The ultimate and greatest need, however, the real remedy, is to remove the cause — the tenement that was built for "a class of whom nothing was expected," and which has come fully up to the expectation. Tenement-house reform holds the key to the problem of pauperism in the city. We can never get rid of either the tenement or the pauper. The two will always exist together in New York. But by reforming the one, we can do more toward exterminating the other than can be done by all other means together that have yet been invented, or ever will be.

Chapter XXII

The Wrecks and the Waste

Pauperdom is to blame for the unjust yoking of poverty with punishment, "charities" with "correction," in our municipal ministering to the needs of the Nether Half. The shadow of the workhouse points like a scornful finger toward its neighbor, the almshouse, when the sun sets behind the teeming city across the East River, as if, could its stones speak, it would say before night drops its black curtain between them: "You and I are brothers. I am not more bankrupt in moral purpose than you. A common parent begat us. Twin breasts, the tenement and the saloon, nourished us. Vice and unthrift go hand in hand. Pauper, behold thy brother!" And the almshouse owns the bitter relationship in silence.

Over on the islands that lie strung along the river and far up the Sound[145] the Nether Half hides its deformity, except on show-days, when distinguished visitors have to be entertained and the sore is uncovered by the authorities with due municipal pride in the exhibit. I shall spare the reader the sight. The aim of these pages has been to lay bare its source. But a brief glance at our proscribed population is needed to give background and tone to the picture. The review begins with the Charity Hospital with its thousand helpless human wrecks; takes in the penitentiary, where the "tough" from Battle Row and Poverty Gap is made to earn behind stone walls the living the world owes him; a thoughtless, jolly convict-band with opportunity at last "to think" behind the iron bars, but little desire to improve it; governed like unruly boys, which in fact most of them are. Three of them were taken from the dinner-table while I was there one day, for sticking pins into each other, and were set with their faces to the wall in sight of six hundred of their comrades for punishment. Pleading incessantly for tobacco, when the keeper's back is turned, as the next best thing to the whiskey they cannot get, though they can plainly make out the saloon-signs across the stream where they robbed or "slugged" their way to prison. Every once in a while the longing gets the best of some prisoner from the penitentiary or the workhouse, and he risks his life in the swift currents to reach the goal that tantalizes him with the promise of "just one more drunk." The chances are at least even of his being run down by some passing steamer and drowned, even if he

---

[145] The Long Island Sound. — ED.

228

is not overtaken by the armed guards who patrol the shore in boats, or his strength does not give out.

This workhouse comes next, with the broken-down hordes from the dives, the lodging-houses, and the tramps' nests, the "hell-box"[146] rather than the repair-shop of the city. In 1889 the registry at the workhouse footed up 22,477, of whom some had been there as many as twenty times before. It is the popular summer resort of the slums, but business is brisk at this stand the year round. Not a few of its patrons drift back periodically without the formality of a commitment, to take their chances on the island when there is no escape from the alternative of work in the city. Work, but not too much work, is the motto of the establishment. The "workhouse step" is an institution that must be observed on the island, in order to draw any comparison between it and the snail's pace that shall do justice to the snail. Nature and man's art have made these islands beautiful; but weeds grow luxuriantly in their gardens, and spiders spin their cobwebs unmolested in the borders of sweet-smelling box. The work which two score of hired men could do well is too much for these thousands.

Rows of old women, some smoking stumpy, black clay-pipes, others knitting or idling, all grumbling, sit or stand under the trees that hedge in the almshouse, or limp about in the sunshine, leaning on crutches or bean-pole staffs. They are a "growler-gang" of another sort than may be seen in session on the rocks of the opposite shore at that very moment. They grumble and growl from sunrise to sunset, at the weather, the breakfast, the dinner, the supper; at pork and beans as at corned beef and cabbage; at their Thanksgiving dinner as at the half rations of the sick ward; at the past that had no joy, at the present whose comfort they deny, and at the future without promise. The crusty old men in the next building are not a circumstance to them. The warden, who was in charge of the almshouse for many years, had become so snappish and profane by constant association with a thousand cross old women that I approached him with some misgivings, to request his permission to "take" a group of a hundred or so who were within shot of my camera. He misunderstood me.

"Take them?" he yelled. "Take the thousand of them and be welcome. They will never be still, by ———, till they are sent up on Hart's Island in a box, and I'll be blamed if I don't think they will growl then at the style of the funeral."

And he threw his arms around me in an outburst of enthusiasm over the wondrous good luck that had sent a friend indeed to his door. I felt it

---

[146] In printing-offices the broken, worn-out, and useless type is thrown into the "hell-box," to be recast at the foundry.

to be a painful duty to undeceive him. When I told him that I simply wanted the old women's picture, he turned away in speechless disgust, and to his dying day, I have no doubt, remembered my call as the day of the champion fool's visit to the island.

When it is known that many of these old people have been sent to the almshouse to die by their heartless children, for whom they had worked faithfully as long as they were able, their growling and discontent is not hard to understand. Bitter poverty threw them all "on the county," often on the wrong county at that. Very many of them are old-country poor, sent, there is reason to believe, to America by the authorities to get rid of the obligation to support them. "The almshouse," wrote a good mission-ary, "affords a sad illustration of St. Paul's description of the 'last days.' The class from which comes our poorhouse population is to a large extent 'without natural affection.' " I was reminded by his words of what my friend, the doctor, had said to me a little while before: "Many a mother has told me at her child's death-bed, 'I cannot afford to lose it. It costs too much to bury it.' And when the little one did die there was no time for the mother's grief. The question crowded on at once, 'where shall the money come from?' Natural feelings and affections are smothered in the tene-ments." The doctor's experience furnished a sadly appropriate text for the priest's sermon.

Pitiful as these are, sights and sounds infinitely more saddening await us beyond the gate that shuts this world of woe off from one whence the light of hope and reason have gone out together. The shuffling of many feet on the macadamized roads heralds the approach of a host of women, hundreds upon hundreds — beyond the turn in the road they still keep coming, marching with the faltering step, the unseeing look and the incessant, senseless chatter that betrays the darkened mind. The lunatic women of the Blackwell's Island Asylum are taking their afternoon walk. Beyond, on the wide lawn, moves another still stranger procession, a file of women in the asylum dress of dull gray, hitched to a queer little wagon that, with its gaudy adornments, suggests a cross between a baby-car-riage and a circus-chariot. One crazy woman is strapped in the seat; forty tug at the rope to which they are securely bound. This is the "chain-gang," so called once in scoffing ignorance of the humane purpose the contriv-ance serves. These are the patients afflicted with suicidal mania, who cannot be trusted at large for a moment with the river in sight, yet must have their daily walk as a necessary part of their treatment. So this wagon was invented by a clever doctor to afford them at once exercise and amusement. A merry-go-round in the grounds suggests a variation of this scheme. Ghastly suggestion of mirth, with that stricken host advancing on its aimless journey! As we stop to see it pass, the plaintive strains of a familiar song float through a barred window in the gray stone building. The voice is sweet, but inexpressibly sad: "Oh, how my heart grows weary, far from ——— " The song breaks off suddenly in a low, troubled laugh. She has forgotten, forgotten ———. A woman in the ranks, whose head has been turned toward the window, throws up her hands with a scream. The rest stir uneasily. The nurse is by her side in an instant with words half soothing, half stern. A messenger comes in haste from the asylum to ask us not to stop. Strangers may not linger where the patients pass. It is apt to excite them. As we go in with him the human file is passing yet, quiet restored. The troubled voice of the unseen singer still gropes vainly among the lost memories of the past for the missing key: "Oh! how my heart grows weary, far from ——— "

"Who is she, doctor?"

"Hopeless case. She will never see home again."

An average of seventeen hundred women this asylum harbors; the asylum for men up on Ward's Island even more. Altogether 1,419 patients were admitted to the city asylums for the insane in 1889, and at the end of the year 4,913 remained in them. There is a constant ominous increase in this class of helpless unfortunates that are thrown on the city's charity. Quite two hundred are added year by year, and the asylums were long since so overcrowded that a great "farm" had to be established on Long Island to receive the surplus. The strain of our hurried, over-worked life has something to do with this. Poverty has more. For these are all of the poor. It is the harvest of sixty and a hundred-fold, the "fearful rolling up and rolling down from generation to generation, through all the ages, of the weakness, vice, and moral darkness of the past."[147] The curse of the island haunts all that come once within its reach. "No man or woman," says Dr. Louis L. Seaman, who speaks from many years' experience in a position that gave him full opportunity to observe the facts, "who is 'sent up' to these colonies ever returns to the city scot-free. There is a lien, visible or hidden, upon his or her present or future, which too often proves stronger than the best purposes and fairest opportunities of social rehabilitation. The under world holds in rigorous bondage every unfortunate or miscreant who has once 'served time.' There is often tragic interest in the struggles of the ensnared wretches to break away from the meshes spun about them. But the maelstrom has no bowels of mercy; and the would-be fugitives are flung back again and again into the devouring

---

[147] Dr. Louis L. Seaman, late chief of staff of the Blackwell's Island hospitals: "Social Waste of a Great City," read before the American Association for the Advancement of Science, 1886.

whirlpool of crime and poverty, until the end is reached on the dissecting-table, or in the Potter's Field. What can the moralist or scientist do by way of resuscitation? Very little at best. The flotsam and jetsam are mere shreds and fragments of wasted lives. Such a ministry must begin at the sources — is necessarily prophylactic, nutritive, educational. On these islands there are no flexible twigs, only gnarled, blasted, blighted trunks, insensible to moral or social influences."

Sad words, but true. The commonest keeper soon learns to pick out almost at sight the "cases" that will leave the penitentiary, the workhouse, the almshouse, only to return again and again, each time more hopeless, to spend their wasted lives in the bondage of the island.

The alcoholic cells in Bellevue Hospital are a way-station for a goodly share of them on their journeys back and forth across the East River. Last year they held altogether 3,694 prisoners, considerably more than one-fourth of the whole number of 13,813 patients that went in through the hospital gates. The daily average of "cases" in this, the hospital of the poor, is over six hundred. The average daily census of all the prisons, hospitals, workhouses, and asylums in the charge of the Department of Charities and Correction last year was about 14,000, and about one employee was required for every ten of this army to keep its machinery running smoothly. The total number admitted in 1889 to all the jails and institutions in the city and on the islands was 138,332. To the almshouse alone 38,600 were admitted; 9,765 were there to start the new year with, and 553 were born with the dark shadow of the poorhouse overhanging their lives, making a total of 48,918. In the care of all their wards the commissioners expended $2,343,372. The appropriation for the police force in 1889 was $4,409,550.94, and for the criminal courts and their machinery $403,190. Thus the first cost of maintaining our standing army of paupers, criminals, and sick poor, by direct taxation, was last year $7,156,112.94.

Chapter XXIII

The Man with the Knife

A man stood at the corner of Fifth Avenue and Fourteenth Street the other day, looking gloomily at the carriages that rolled by, carrying the wealth and fashion of the avenues to and from the big stores down town. He was poor, and hungry, and ragged. This thought was in his mind: "They behind their well-fed teams have no thought for the morrow; they know hunger only by name, and ride down to spend in an hour's shopping what would keep me and my little ones from want a whole year." There rose up before him the picture of those little ones crying for bread around the cold and cheerless hearth — then he sprang into the throng and slashed about him with a knife, blindly seeking to kill, to revenge.

The man was arrested, of course, and locked up. To-day he is probably in a mad-house, forgotten. And the carriages roll by to and from the big stores with their gay throng of shoppers. The world forgets easily, too easily, what it does not like to remember.

Nevertheless the man and his knife had a mission. They spoke in their ignorant, impatient way the warning one of the most conservative, dispassionate of public bodies had sounded only a little while before: "Our only fear is that reform may come in a burst of public indignation destructive to property and to good morals."[148] They represented one solution of the problem of ignorant poverty *versus* ignorant wealth that has come down to us unsolved, the danger-cry of which we have lately heard in the shout that never should have been raised on American soil — the shout of "the masses against the classes" — the solution of violence.

There is another solution, that of justice. The choice is between the two. Which shall it be?

"Well!" say some well-meaning people; "we don't see the need of putting it in that way. We have been down among the tenements, looked them over. There are a good many people there; they are not comfortable, perhaps. What would you have? They are poor. And their houses are not such hovels as we have seen and read of in the slums of the Old World. They are decent in comparison. Why, some of them have brown-stone fronts. You will own at least that they make a decent show."

Yes! that is true. The worst tenements in New York do not, as a rule, *look bad.* Neither Hell's Kitchen, nor Murderers' Row bears its

---

[148] Forty-fourth Annual Report of the Association for Improving the Condition of the Poor. 1887.

true character stamped on the front. They are not quite old enough, perhaps. The same is true of their tenants. The New York tough may be ready to kill where his London brother would do little more than scowl; yet, as a general thing he is less repulsively brutal in looks. Here again the reason may be the same: the breed is not so old. A few generations more in the slums, and all that will be changed. To get at the pregnant facts of tenement-house life one must look beneath the surface. Many an apple has a fair skin and a rotten core. There is a much better argument for the tenements in the assurance of the Registrar of Vital Statistics that the death-rate of these houses has of late been brought below the general death-rate of the city, and that it is lowest in the biggest houses. This means two things: one, that the almost exclusive attention given to the tenements by the sanitary authorities in twenty years has borne some fruit, and that the newer tenements are better than the old — there is some hope in that; the other, that the whole strain of tenement-house dwellers has been bred down to the conditions under which it exists, that the struggle with corruption has begotten the power to resist it. This is a familiar law of nature, necessary to its first and strongest impulse of self-preservation. To a certain extent, we are all creatures of the conditions that surround us, physically and morally. But is the knowledge reassuring? In the light of what we have seen, does not the question arise: what sort of creature, then, this of the tenement? I tried to draw his likeness from observation in telling the story of the "tough." Has it nothing to suggest the man with the knife?

I will go further. I am not willing even to admit it to be an unqualified advantage that our New York tenements have less of the slum look than those of older cities. It helps to delay the recognition of their true character on the part of the well-meaning, but uninstructed, who are always in the majority.

The "dangerous classes"[149] of New York long ago compelled recognition. They are dangerous less because of their own crimes than because of the criminal ignorance of those who are not of their kind. The danger to society comes not from the poverty of the tenements, but from the ill-spent wealth that reared them, that it might earn a usurious interest from a class from which "nothing else was expected." That was the broad foundation laid down, and the edifice built upon it corresponds to the groundwork. That this is well understood on the "unsafe" side of the line

[149] Riis uses the phrase made popular by Charles Loring Brace's book *The Dangerous Classes of New York and Twenty Years' Work Among Them* (1872). — ED.

that separates the rich from the poor, much better than by those who have all the advantages of discriminating education, is good cause for disquietude. In it a keen foresight may again dimly discern the shadow of the man with the knife.

Two years ago a great meeting was held at Chickering Hall — I have spoken of it before — a meeting that discussed for days and nights the question how to banish this spectre; how to lay hold with good influences of this enormous mass of more than a million people, who were drifting away faster and faster from the safe moorings of the old faith. Clergymen and laymen from all the Protestant denominations took part in the discussion; nor was a good word forgotten for the brethren of the other great Christian fold who labor among the poor. Much was said that was good and true, and ways were found of reaching the spiritual needs of the tenement population that promise success. But at no time throughout the conference was the real key-note of the situation so boldly struck as has been done by a few far-seeing business men, who had listened to the cry of that Christian builder: "How shall the love of God be understood by those who have been nurtured in sight only of the greed of man?" Their practical programme of "Philanthropy and five per cent."[150] has set examples in tenement building that show, though they are yet few and scattered, what may in time be accomplished even with such poor opportunities as New York offers to-day of undoing the old wrong. This is the gospel of justice, the solution that must be sought as the one alternative to the man with the knife.

"Are you not looking too much to the material condition of these people," said a good minister to me after a lecture in a Harlem church last winter, "and forgetting the inner man?" I told him, "No! for you cannot expect to find an inner man to appeal to in the worst tenement-house surroundings. You must first put the man where he can respect himself. To reverse the argument of the apple: you cannot expect to find a sound core in a rotten fruit."

---

[150] The slogan of a reform program that sought to convince builders and landlords to give five percent of their profits for the construction of model tenements. — ED.

Chapter XXIV

What Has Been Done

In twenty years what has been done in New York to solve the tenement-house problem?

The law has done what it could. That was not always a great deal, seldom more than barely sufficient for the moment. An aroused municipal conscience endowed the Health Department with almost autocratic powers in dealing with this subject, but the desire to educate rather than force the community into a better way dictated their exercise with a slow conservatism that did not always seem wise to the impatient reformer. New York has its St. Antoine, and it has often sadly missed a Napoleon III.[151] to clean up and make light in the dark corners. The obstacles, too, have been many and great. Nevertheless the authorities have not been idle, though it is a grave question whether all the improvements made under the sanitary regulations of recent years deserve the name. Tenements quite as bad as the worst are too numerous yet; but one tremendous factor for evil in the lives of the poor has been taken by the throat, and something has unquestionably been done, where that was possible, to lift those lives out of the rut where they were equally beyond the reach of hope and of ambition. It is no longer lawful to construct barracks to cover the whole of a lot. Air and sunlight have a legal claim, and the day of rear tenements is past. Two years ago a hundred thousand people burrowed in these inhuman dens; but some have been torn down since. Their number will decrease steadily until they shall have become a bad tradition of a heedless past. The dark, unventilated bedroom is going with them, and the open sewer. The day is at hand when the greatest of all evils that now curse life in the tenements — the dearth of water in the hot summer days — will also have been remedied, and a long step taken toward the moral and physical redemption of their tenants.

Public sentiment has done something also, but very far from enough. As a rule, it has slumbered peacefully until some flagrant outrage on decency and the health of the community aroused it to noisy but ephemeral indignation, or until a dreaded epidemic knocked at our door. It is this unsteadiness of purpose that has been to a large extent responsible for the apparent lagging of the authorities in cases not involving immedi-

---

[151] Louis Napoleon Bonaparte (1808–1873). Nephew of Napoleon and emperor of France between 1852 and 1870. — Ed.

Evolution of the Tenement in
Twenty Years.

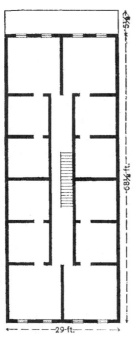

Old Style Tenement.

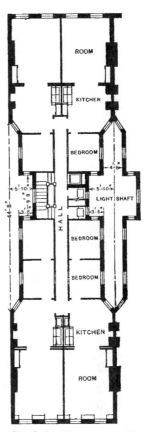

Single Lot Tenement of To-day.

ate danger to the general health. The law needs a much stronger and readier backing of a thoroughly enlightened public sentiment to make it as effective as it might be made. It is to be remembered that the health officers, in dealing with this subject of dangerous houses, are constantly trenching upon what each landlord considers his private rights, for which he is ready and bound to fight to the last. Nothing short of the strongest pressure will avail to convince him that these individual rights are to be surrendered for the clear benefit of the whole. It is easy enough to convince a man that he ought not to harbor the thief who steals people's property; but to make him see that he has no right to slowly kill his neighbors, or his tenants, by making a death-trap of his house, seems to be the hardest of all tasks. It is apparently the slowness of the process that obscures his mental sight. The man who will fight an order to repair the plumbing in his house through every court he can reach, would suffer tortures rather than shed the blood of a fellow-man by actual violence. Clearly, it is a matter of education on the part of the landlord no less than the tenant.

In spite of this, the landlord has done his share; chiefly perhaps by yielding — not always gracefully — when it was no longer of any use to fight. There have been exceptions, however: men and women who have mended and built with an eye to the real welfare of their tenants as well as to their own pockets. Let it be well understood that the two are inseparable, if any good is to come of it. The business of housing the poor, if it is to amount to anything, must be business, as it was business with our fathers to put them where they are. As charity, pastime, or fad, it will miserably fail, always and everywhere. This is an inexorable rule, now thoroughly well understood in England and continental Europe, and by all who have given the matter serious thought here. Call it poetic justice, or divine justice, or anything else, it is a hard fact, not to be gotten over. Upon any other plan than the assumption that the workman has a just claim to a decent home, and the right to demand it, any scheme for his relief fails. It must be a fair exchange of the man's money for what he can afford to buy at a reasonable price. Any charity scheme merely turns him into a pauper, however it may be disguised, and drowns him hopelessly in the mire out of which it proposed to pull him. And this principle must pervade the whole plan. Expert management of model tenements succeeds where amateur management, with the best intentions, gives up the task, discouraged, as a flat failure. Some of the best-conceived enterprises, backed by abundant capital and goodwill, have been wrecked on this rock. Sentiment, having prompted the effort, forgot to stand aside and let business make it.

Business, in a wider sense, has done more than all other agencies together to wipe out the worst tenements. It has been New York's real Napoleon III., from whose decree there was no appeal. In ten years I have seen plague-spots disappear before its onward march, with which health officers, police, and sanitary science had struggled vainly since such struggling began as a serious business. And the process goes on still. Unfortunately, the crowding in some of the most densely packed quarters down town has made the property there so valuable, that relief from this source is less confidently to be expected, at all events in the near future. Still, their time may come also. It comes so quickly sometimes as to fairly take one's breath away. More than once I have returned, after a few brief weeks, to some specimen rookery in which I was interested, to find it gone and an army of workmen delving twenty feet underground to lay the foundation of a mighty warehouse. That was the case with the "Big Flat" in Mott Street. I had not had occasion to visit it for several months last winter, and when I went there, entirely unprepared for a change, I could not find it. It had always been conspicuous enough in the landscape before, and I marvelled much at my own stupidity until, by examining the number of the house, I found out that I had gone right. It was the "flat" that had disappeared. In its place towered a six-story carriage factory with business going on on every floor, as if it had been there for years and years.

This same "Big Flat" furnished a good illustration of why some well-meant efforts in tenement building have failed. Like Gotham Court, it was originally built as a model tenement, but speedily came to rival the Court in foulness. It became a regular hot-bed of thieves and peace-breakers, and made no end of trouble for the police. The immediate reason, outside of the lack of proper supervision, was that it had open access to two streets in a neighborhood where thieves and "toughs" abounded. These took advantage of an arrangement that had been supposed by the builders to be a real advantage as a means of ventilation, and their occupancy drove honest folk away. Murderers' Alley, of which I have spoken elsewhere, and the sanitary inspector's experiment with building a brick wall athwart it to shut off travel through the block, is a parallel case.

The causes that operate to obstruct efforts to better the lot of the tenement population are, in our day, largely found among the tenants themselves. This is true particularly of the poorest. They are shiftless, destructive, and stupid; in a word, they are what the tenements have made them. It is a dreary old truth that those who would fight for the poor must fight the poor to do it. It must be confessed that there is little enough in their past experience to inspire confidence in the sincerity of the effort to help them. I recall the discomfiture of a certain well-known philanthropist, since deceased, whose heart beat responsive to other suffering than that of human kind. He was a large owner of tenement property, and once undertook to fit out his houses with stationary tubs, sanitary plumbing, wood-closets, and all the latest improvements. He introduced his rough tenants to all this magnificence without taking the precaution of providing a competent housekeeper, to see that the new acquaintances got on together. He felt that his tenants ought to be grateful for the interest he took in them. They were. They found the boards in the wood-closets fine kindling wood, while the pipes and faucets were as good as cash at the junk shop. In three months the owner had to remove what was left of his improvements. The pipes were cut and the houses running full of water, the stationary tubs were put to all sorts of uses except washing, and of the wood-closets not a trace was left. The philanthropist was ever after a firm believer in the total depravity of tenement-house people. Others have been led to like reasoning by as plausible arguments, without discovering that the shiftlessness and ignorance that offended them were the consistent crop of the tenement they were trying to reform, and had to be included in the effort. The owners of a block of model tenements uptown had got their tenants comfortably settled, and were indulging in high hopes of their redemption under proper management, when a contractor ran up a row of "skin" tenements,[152] shaky but fair to look at, with brown-stone trimmings and gewgaws.[153] The result was to tempt a lot of the well-housed tenants away. It was a very astonishing instance of perversity to the planners of the benevolent scheme; but, after all, there was nothing strange in it. It is all a matter of education, as I said about the landlord.

That the education comes slowly need excite no surprise. The forces on the other side are ever active. The faculty of the tenement for appropriating to itself every foul thing that comes within its reach, and piling up and intensifying its corruption until out of all proportion to the beginning, is something marvellous. Drop a case of scarlet fever, of measles, or of diphtheria into one of these barracks, and, unless it is caught at the very start and stamped out, the contagion of the one case will sweep block after block, and half people a graveyard. Let the police break up a vile dive, goaded by the angry protests of the neighborhood — forthwith the outcasts set in circulation by the raid betake themselves to the tenements, where in their hired rooms, safe from interference, they set up as many independent centres of contagion, infinitely more destructive, each and every one, than was the known dive before. I am not willing to affirm that this is the police reason for letting so many of the dives alone; but it might well be. They are perfectly familiar with the process, and quite powerless to prevent it.

This faculty, as inherent in the problem itself — the prodigious increase of the tenement-house population that goes on without cessation, and its consequent greater crowding — is the chief obstacle to its solution. In 1869 there were 14,872 tenements in New York, with a population of 468,492 persons. In 1879 the number of the tenements was estimated at 21,000, and their tenants had passed the half-million mark. At the end of the year 1888, when a regular census was made for the first time since 1869, the showing was: 32,390 tenements, with a population of 1,093,701

---

[152] Poor-quality tenements built with impressive facades. — Ed.
[153] Bauble or trinket. — Ed.

souls. To-day we have 37,316 tenements, including 2,630 rear houses, and their population is over 1,250,000. A large share of this added population, especially of that which came to us from abroad, crowds in below Fourteenth Street, where the population is already packed beyond reason, and confounds all attempts to make matters better there. At the same time new slums are constantly growing up uptown, and have to be kept down with a firm hand. This drift of the population to the great cities has to be taken into account as a steady factor. It will probably increase rather than decrease for many years to come. At the beginning of the century the percentage of our population that lived in cities was as one in twenty-five. In 1880 it was one in four and one-half, and in 1890 the census will in all probability show it to be one in four. Against such tendencies, in the absence of surburban outlets for the crowding masses, all remedial measures must prove more or less ineffective. The "confident belief" expressed by the Board of Health in 1874, that rapid transit would solve the problem, is now known to have been a vain hope.

Workingmen, in New York at all events, will live near their work, no matter at what sacrifice of comfort — one might almost say at whatever cost, and the city will never be less crowded than it is. To distribute the crowds as evenly as possible is the effort of the authorities, where nothing better can be done. In the first six months of the present year 1,068 persons were turned out of not quite two hundred tenements below Houston Street by the sanitary police on their midnight inspections, and this covered only a very small part of that field. The uptown tenements were practically left to take care of themselves in this respect.

The quick change of economic conditions in the city that often outpaces all plans of relief, rendering useless to-day what met the demands of the situation well enough yesterday, is another cause of perplexity. A common obstacle also — I am inclined to think quite as common as in Ireland, though we hear less of it in the newspapers — is the absentee landlord. The home article, who fights for his rights, as he chooses to consider them, is bad enough; but the absentee landlord is responsible for no end of trouble. He was one of the first obstructions the sanitary reformers stumbled over, when the Health Department took hold. It reported in 1869 that many of the tenants were entirely uncared for, and that the only answer to their requests to have the houses put in order was an invitation to pay their rent or get out. "Inquiry often disclosed the fact that the owner of the property was a wealthy gentleman or lady, either living in an aristocratic part of the city, or in a neighboring city, or, as was occasionally found to be the case, in Europe. The property is usually managed entirely by an agent, whose instructions are simple but emphatic: Collect the rent in advance, or, failing, eject the occupants." The Committee having the matter in charge proposed to compel owners of tenements with ten families or more to put a housekeeper in the house, who should be held responsible to the Health Department. Unluckily the powers of the Board gave out at that point, and the proposition was not acted upon then. Could it have been, much trouble would have been spared the Health Board, and untold suffering the tenants in many houses. The tribe of absentee landlords is by no means extinct in New York. Not a few who fled from across the sea to avoid being crushed by his heel there have groaned under it here, scarcely profiting by the exchange. Sometimes — it can hardly be said in extenuation — the heel that crunches is applied in saddening ignorance. I recall the angry indignation of one of these absentee landlords, a worthy man who, living far away in the country, had inherited city property, when he saw the condition of his slum tenements. The man was shocked beyond expression, all the more because he did not know whom to blame except himself for the state of things that had aroused his wrath, and yet, conscious of the integrity of his intentions, felt that he should not justly be held responsible.

The experience of this landlord points directly to the remedy which the law failed to supply to the early reformers. It has since been fully demonstrated that a competent agent on the premises, a man of the best and the highest stamp, who knows how to instruct and guide with a firm hand, is a prerequisite to the success of any reform tenement scheme. This is a plain business proposition, that has been proved entirely sound in some notable instances of tenement building, of which more hereafter. Even among the poorer tenements, those are always the best in which the owner himself lives. It is a hopeful sign in any case. The difficulty of procuring such assistance without having to pay a ruinous price, is one of the obstructions that have vexed in this city efforts to solve the problem of housing the poor properly, because it presupposes that the effort must be made on a larger scale than has often been attempted.

The readiness with which the tenants respond to intelligent efforts in their behalf, when made under fair conditions, is as surprising as it is gratifying, and fully proves the claim that tenants are only satisfied in filthy and unwholesome surroundings because nothing better is offered. The moral effect is as great as the improvement of their physical health. It is clearly discernible in the better class of tenement dwellers to-day. The change in the character of the colored population in the few years since it began to move out of the wicked rookeries of the old "Africa" to the decent tenements in Yorkville, furnishes a notable illustration, and a still better one is found in the contrast between the model tenement in the Mulberry Street Bend and the barracks across the way, of which I spoke in the chapter devoted to the Italian. The Italian himself is the strongest argument of all. With his fatal contentment in the filthiest surroundings, he gives undoubted evidence of having in him the instinct of cleanliness that, properly cultivated, would work his rescue in a very little while. It is a queer contradiction, but the fact is patent to anyone who has observed the man in his home-life. And he is not alone in this. I came across an instance, this past summer, of how a refined, benevolent personality works like a leaven in even the roughest tenement-house crowd. This was no model tenement; far from it. It was a towering barrack in the Tenth Ward, sheltering more than twenty families. All the light and air that entered its interior came through an air-shaft two feet square, upon which two bedrooms and the hall gave in every story. In three years I had known of two domestic tragedies, prompted by poverty and justifiable disgust with life, occurring in the house, and had come to look upon it as a typically bad tenement, quite beyond the pale of possible improvement. What was my surprise, when chance led me to it once more after a while, to find the character of the occupants entirely changed. Some of the old ones were there still, but they did not seem to be the same people. I discovered the secret to be the new housekeeper, a tidy, mild-mannered, but exceedingly strict little body, who had a natural faculty of drawing her depraved surroundings within the beneficent sphere of her strong sympathy, and withal of exacting respect for her orders. The worst elements had been banished from the house in short order under her management, and for the rest a new era of self-respect had dawned. They were, as a body, as vastly superior to the general run of their class as they had before seemed below it. And this had been effected in the short space of a single year.

My observations on this point are more than confirmed by those of nearly all the practical tenement reformers I have known, who have patiently held to the course they had laid down. One of these, whose experience exceeds that of all of the rest together, and whose influence for good has been very great, said to me recently: "I hold that not ten per cent. of the people now living in tenements would refuse to avail themselves of the best improved conditions offered, and come fully up to the use of them, properly instructed; but they cannot get them. They are up to them now, fully, if the chances were only offered. They don't have to come up. It is all a gigantic mistake on the part of the public, of which these poor people are the victims. I have built homes for more than five hundred families in fourteen years, and I have been getting daily more faith in human nature from my work among the poor tenants, though approaching that nature on a plane and under conditions that could scarcely promise better for disappointment." It is true that my friend has built his houses in Brooklyn; but human nature does not differ greatly on the two shores of the East River. For those who think it does, it may be well to remember that only five years ago the Tenement House Commission summed up the situation in this city in the declaration that, "the condition of the tenants is in advance of the houses which they occupy," quite the severest arraignment of the tenement that had yet been uttered.

The many philanthropic efforts that have been made in the last few years to render less intolerable the lot of the tenants in the homes where many of them must continue to live, have undoubtedly had their effect in creating a disposition to accept better things, that will make plainer sailing for future builders of model tenements. In many ways, as in the "College Settlement" of courageous girls, the Neighborhood Guilds, through the efforts of The King's Daughters, and numerous other schemes of practical mission work, the poor and the well-to-do have been brought closer together, in an every-day companionship that cannot but be productive of the best results, to the one who gives no less than to the one who receives. And thus, as a good lady wrote to me once, though the problem stands yet unsolved, more perplexing than ever; though the bright spots in the dreary picture be too often bright only by comparison, and many of the expedients hit upon for relief sad makeshifts, we can dimly discern behind it all that good is somehow working out of even this slough of despond the while it is deepening and widening in our sight, and in His own good season, if we labor on with courage and patience, will bear fruit sixty and a hundred fold.

Chapter XXV

How the Case Stands

What, then, are the bald facts with which we have to deal in New York?

I. That we have a tremendous, ever swelling crowd of wage-earners which it is our business to house decently.

II. That it is not housed decently.

III. That it must be so housed *here* for the present, and for a long time to come, all schemes of suburban relief being as yet utopian, impracticable.

IV.   That it pays high enough rents to entitle it to be so housed, as a right.

V.   That nothing but our own slothfulness is in the way of so housing it, since "the condition of the tenants is in advance of the condition of the houses which they occupy" (Report of Tenement-house Commission).

VI.   That the security of the one no less than of the other half demands, on sanitary, moral, and economic grounds, that it be decently housed.

VII. That it will pay to do it. As an investment, I mean, and in hard cash. This I shall immediately proceed to prove.

VIII. That the tenement has come to stay, and must itself be the solution of the problem with which it confronts us.

This is the fact from which we cannot get away, however we may deplore it. Doubtless the best would be to get rid of it altogether; but as we cannot, all argument on that score may at this time be dismissed as idle. The practical question is what to do with the tenement. I watched a Mott Street landlord, the owner of a row of barracks that have made no end of trouble for the health authorities for twenty years, solve that question for himself the other day. His way was to give the wretched pile a coat of paint, and put a gorgeous tin cornice on with the year 1890 in letters a yard long. From where I stood watching the operation, I looked down upon the same dirty crowds camping on the roof, foremost among them an Italian mother with two stark-naked children who had apparently never made the acquaintance of a wash-tub. That was a landlord's way, and will not get us out of the mire.

The "flat" is another way that does not solve the problem. Rather, it extends it. The flat is not a model, though it is a modern, tenement. It gets rid of some of the nuisances of the low tenement, and of the worst of them, the overcrowding — if it gets rid of them at all — at a cost that takes it at once out of the catalogue of "homes for the poor," while imposing some of the evils from which they suffer upon those who ought to escape from them.

There are three effective ways of dealing with the tenements in New York:

I.   By law.

II.   By remodelling and making the most out of the old houses.

III. By building new, model tenements.

Private enterprise — conscience, to put it in the category of duties, where it belongs — must do the lion's share under these last two heads. Of what the law has effected I have spoken already. The drastic measures adopted in Paris, in Glasgow, and in London are not practicable here on anything like as large a scale.[154] Still it can, under strong pressure of public opinion, rid us of the worst plague-spots. The Mulberry Street Bend will go the way of the Five Points when all the red tape that binds the hands of municipal effort has been unwound. Prizes were offered in public competition, some years ago, for the best plans of modern tenement-houses. It may be that we shall see the day when the building of model tenements will be encouraged by subsidies in the way of a rebate of taxes. Meanwhile the arrest and summary punishment of landlords, or their agents, who persistently violate law and decency, will have a salutary effect. If a few of the wealthy absentee landlords, who are the worst offenders, could be got within the jurisdiction of the city, and by arrest be compelled to employ proper overseers, it would be a proud day for New York. To remedy the overcrowding, with which the night inspections of the sanitary police cannot keep step, tenements may eventually have to be licensed, as now the lodging-houses, to hold so many tenants, and no more; or the State may have to bring down the rents that cause the crowding, by assuming the right to regulate them as it regulates the fares on the elevated roads. I throw out the suggestion, knowing quite well that it is open to attack. It emanated originally from one of the brightest minds that have had to struggle officially with this tenement-house question in the last ten years. In any event, to succeed, reform by law must aim at making it unprofitable to own a bad tenement. At best, it is apt to travel at a snail's pace, while the enemy it pursues is putting the best foot foremost.

In this matter of profit the law ought to have its strongest ally in the landlord himself, though the reverse is the case. This condition of things I believe to rest on a monstrous error. It cannot be that tenement property that is worth preserving at all can continue to yield larger returns, if allowed to run down, than if properly cared for and kept in good repair. The point must be reached, and soon, where the cost of repairs, necessary with a house full of the lowest, most ignorant tenants, must overbalance the saving of the first few years of neglect; for this class is everywhere the most destructive, as well as the poorest paying. I have the experience of owners, who have found this out to their cost, to back me up in the

---

[154] Riis is referring to the programs of massive urban renovation undertaken by these cities. — ED.

assertion, even if it were not the statement of a plain business fact that proves itself. I do not include tenement property that is deliberately allowed to fall into decay because at some future time the ground will be valuable for business or other purposes. There is unfortunately enough of that kind in New York, often leasehold property owned by wealthy estates or soulless corporations that oppose all their great influence to the efforts of the law in behalf of their tenants.

There is abundant evidence, on the other hand, that it can be made to pay to improve and make the most of the worst tenement property, even in the most wretched locality. The example set by Miss Ellen Collins in her Water Street houses will always stand as a decisive answer to all doubts on this point. It is quite ten years since she bought three old tenements at the corner of Water and Roosevelt Streets, then as now one of the lowest localities in the city. Since then she has leased three more adjoining her purchase, and so much of Water Street has at all events been purified. Her first effort was to let in the light in the hallways, and with the darkness disappeared, as if by magic, the heaps of refuse that used to be piled up beside the sinks. A few of the most refractory tenants disappeared with them, but a very considerable proportion stayed, conforming readily to the new rules, and are there yet. It should here be stated that Miss Collins's tenants are distinctly of the poorest. Her purpose was to experiment with this class, and her experiment has been more than satisfactory. Her plan was, as she puts it herself, fair play between tenant and landlord. To this end the rents were put as low as consistent with the idea of a business investment that must return a reasonable interest to be successful. The houses were thoroughly refitted with proper plumbing. A competent janitor was put in charge to see that the rules were observed by the tenants, when Miss Collins herself was not there. Of late years she has had to give very little time to personal superintendence, and the care-taker told me only the other day that very little was needed. The houses seemed to run themselves in the groove once laid down. Once the reputed haunt of thieves, they have become the most orderly in the neighborhood. Clothes are left hanging on the lines all night with impunity, and the pretty flower-beds in the yard where the children not only from the six houses, but of the whole block, play, skip, and swing, are undisturbed. The tenants, by the way, provide the flowers themselves in the spring, and take all the more pride in them because they are their own. The six houses contain forty-five families, and there "has never been any need of putting up a bill." As to the income from the property, Miss Collins said to me last August: "I have had six and even six and three-quarters per cent. on the capital invested; on the whole, you may safely say five and a half per cent. This I regard as entirely satisfactory." It should be added that she has persistently refused to let the corner-store, now occupied by a butcher, as a saloon; or her income from it might have been considerably increased.

Miss Collins's experience is of value chiefly as showing what can be accomplished with the worst possible material, by the sort of personal interest in the poor that alone will meet their real needs. All the charity in the world, scattered with the most lavish hand, will not take its place. "Fair play" between landlord and tenant is the key, too long mislaid, that unlocks the door to success everywhere as it did for Miss Collins. She has not lacked imitators whose experience has been akin to her own. The case of Gotham Court has been already cited. On the other hand, instances are not wanting of landlords who have undertaken the task, but have tired of it or sold their property before it had been fully redeemed, with the result that it relapsed into its former bad condition faster than it had improved, and the tenants with it. I am inclined to think that such houses are liable to fall even below the average level. Backsliding in brick and mortar does not greatly differ from similar performances in flesh and blood.

Backed by a strong and steady sentiment, such as these pioneers have evinced, that would make it the personal business of wealthy owners with time to spare to look after their tenants, the law would be able in a very short time to work a salutary transformation in the worst quarters, to the lasting advantage, I am well persuaded, of the landlord no less than the tenant. Unfortunately, it is in this quality of personal effort that the sentiment of interest in the poor, upon which we have to depend, is too often lacking. People who are willing to give money feel that that ought to be enough. It is not. The money thus given is too apt to be wasted along with the sentiment that prompted the gift.

Even when it comes to the third of the ways I spoke of as effective in dealing with the tenement-house problem, the building of model structures, the personal interest in the matter must form a large share of the capital invested, if it is to yield full returns. Where that is the case, there is even less doubt about its paying, with ordinary business management, than in the case of reclaiming an old building, which is, like putting life into a defunct newspaper, pretty apt to be up-hill work. Model tenement building has not been attempted in New York on anything like as large a scale as in many other great cities, and it is perhaps owing to this, in a measure, that a belief prevails that it cannot succeed here. This is a wrong notion entirely. The various undertakings of that sort that have been made here under intelligent management have, as far as I know, all been successful.

From the managers of the two best-known experiments in model tenement building in the city, the Improved Dwellings Association and the Tenement-house Building Company, I have letters dated last August, declaring their enterprises eminently successful. There is no reason why their experience should not be conclusive. That the Philadelphia plan is not practicable in New York is not a good reason why our own plan, which is precisely the reverse of our neighbor's, should not be. In fact it is an argument for its success. The very reason why we cannot house our working masses in cottages, as has been done in Philadelphia — viz., that they must live on Manhattan Island, where the land is too costly for small houses — is the best guarantee of the success of the model tenement house, properly located and managed. The drift in tenement building, as in everything else, is toward concentration, and helps smooth the way. Four families on the floor, twenty in the house, is the rule of to-day. As the crowds increase, the need of guiding this drift into safe channels becomes more urgent. The larger the scale upon which the model tenement is planned, the more certain the promise of success. The utmost ingenuity cannot build a house for sixteen or twenty families on a lot 25 × 100 feet in the middle of a block like it, that shall give them the amount of air and sunlight to be had by the erection of a dozen or twenty houses on a common plan around a central yard. This was the view of the committee that awarded the prizes for the best plan for the conventional tenement, ten years ago. It coupled its verdict with the emphatic declaration that, in its view, it was "impossible to secure the requirements of physical and moral health within these narrow and arbitrary limits." Houses have been built since on better plans than any the committee saw, but its judgment stands unimpaired. A point, too, that is not to be overlooked, is the reduced cost of expert superintendence — the first condition of successful management — in the larger buildings.

The Improved Dwellings Association put up its block of thirteen houses in East Seventy-second Street nine years ago. Their cost, estimated at about $240,000 with the land, was increased to $285,000 by troubles with the contractor engaged to build them. Thus the Association's task did not begin under the happiest auspices. Unexpected expenses came to deplete its treasury. The neighborhood was new and not crowded at the start. No expense was spared, and the benefit of all the best and most recent experience in tenement building was given to the tenants. The families were provided with from two to four rooms, all "outer" rooms, of course, at rents ranging from $14 per month for the four on the ground floor, to $6.25 for two rooms on the top floor. Coal lifts, ash-chutes, common laundries in the basement, and free baths, are features of these buildings that were then new enough to be looked upon with suspicion by the doubting Thomases who predicted disaster. There are rooms in the block for 218 families, and when I looked in recently all but nine of the apartments were let. One of the nine was rented while I was in the building. The superintendent told me that he had little trouble with disorderly tenants, though the buildings shelter all sorts of people. Mr. W. Bayard Cutting, the President of the Association, writes to me:

> By the terms of subscription to the stock before incorporation, dividends were limited to five per cent. on the stock of the Improved Dwellings Association. These dividends have been paid (two per cent. each six months) ever since the expiration of the first six months of the buildings operation. All surplus has been expended upon the buildings. New and expensive roofs have been put on for the comfort of such tenants as might choose to use them. The buildings have been completely painted inside and out in a manner not contemplated at the outset. An expensive set of fire-escapes has been put on at the command of the Fire Department, and a considerable number of other improvements made. *I regard the experiment as eminently successful and satisfactory,* particularly when it is considered that the buildings were the first erected in this city upon anything like a large scale, where it was proposed to meet the architectural difficulties that present themselves in the tenement-house problem. I have no doubt that the experiment could be tried to-day with the improved knowledge which has come with time, and a much larger return be shown upon the investment. The results referred to have been attained in spite of the provision which prevents the selling of liquor upon the Association's premises. You are aware, of course, how much larger rent can be obtained for a liquor saloon than for an ordinary store. An investment at five per cent. net upon real estate security worth more than the principal sum, ought to be considered desirable.

The Tenement House Building Company made its "experiment" in a much more difficult neighborhood, Cherry Street, some six years later. Its houses shelter many Russian Jews, and the difficulty of keeping them in order is correspondingly increased, particularly as there are no ash-chutes in the houses. It has been necessary even to shut the children out of the yards upon which the kitchen windows give, lest they be struck by something thrown out by the tenants, and killed. It is the Cherry Street style, not easily got rid of. Nevertheless, the houses are well kept. Of the one hundred and six "apartments," only four were vacant in August. Professor Edwin R. A. Seligman, the secretary of the company, writes to me: "The Tenements are now a decided success." In the three years since they were built, they have returned an interest of from five to five and a half per cent. on the capital invested. The original intention of making the tenants profit-sharers on a plan of rent insurance, under which all earnings above four per cent. would be put to the credit of the tenants, has not yet been carried out.

A scheme of dividends to tenants on a somewhat similar plan has been carried out by a Brooklyn builder, Mr. A. T. White, who has devoted a life of beneficent activity to tenement building, and whose experience, though it has been altogether across the East River, I regard as justly applying to New York as well. He so regards it himself. Discussing the cost of building, he says: "There is not the slightest reason to doubt that the financial result of a similar undertaking in any tenement-house district of New York City would be equally good. . . . High cost of land is no detriment, provided the value is made by the pressure of people seeking residence there. Rents in New York City bear a higher ratio to Brooklyn rents than would the cost of land and building in the one city to that in the other." The assertion that Brooklyn furnishes a better class of tenants than the tenement districts in New York would not be worth discussing seriously, even if Mr. White did not meet it himself with the statement that the proportion of day-laborers and sewing-women in his houses is greater than in any of the London model tenements, showing that they reach the humblest classes.

Mr. White has built homes for five hundred poor families since he began his work, and has made it pay well enough to allow good tenants a share in the profits, averaging nearly one month's rent out of the twelve, as a premium upon promptness and order. The plan of his last tenements, reproduced on p. 252, may be justly regarded as the *beau ideal* of the model tenement for a great city like New York. It embodies all the good features of Sir Sydney Waterlow's London plan, with improvements suggested by the builder's own experience. Its chief merit is that it gathers three hundred real homes, not simply three hundred families, under one roof. Three tenants, it will be seen, use each entrance hall. Of the rest of the three hundred they may never know, rarely see, one. Each has his private front-door. The common hall, with all that it stands for, has disappeared. The fire-proof stairs are outside the house, a perfect fire-escape. Each tenant has his own scullery and ash-flue. There are no air-shafts, for they are not needed. Every room, under the admirable arrangement of the plan, looks out either upon the street or the yard, that is nothing less than a great park with a play-ground set apart for the children, where they may dig in the sand to their heart's content. Weekly concerts are given in the park by a brass band. The drying of clothes is

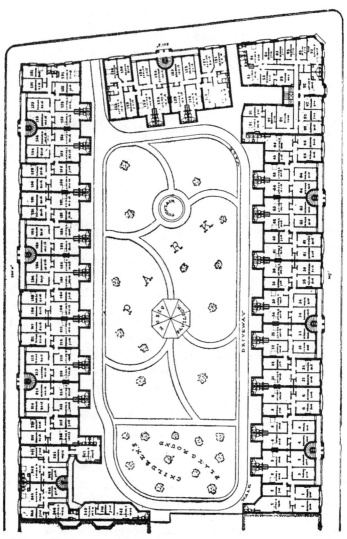

General Plan of the Riverside Buildings (A. T. White's) in Brooklyn.

done on the roof, where racks are fitted up for the purpose. The outside stairways end in turrets that give the buildings a very smart appearance. Mr. White never has any trouble with his tenants, though he gathers in the poorest; nor do his tenements have anything of the "institution character" that occasionally attaches to ventures of this sort, to their damage. They are like a big village of contented people, who live in peace with one another because they have elbow-room even under one big roof.

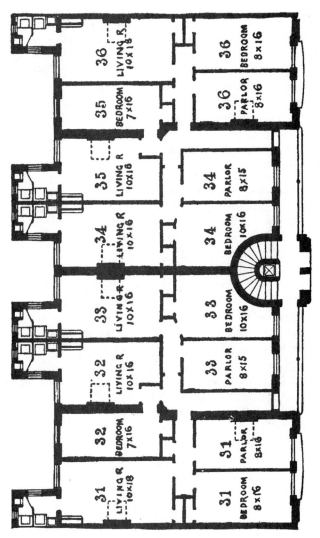

Floor Plan of One Division in the Riverside Buildings, Showing Six "Apartments."

Enough has been said to show that model tenements can be built successfully and made to pay in New York, if the owner will be content with the five or six per cent. he does not even dream of when investing his funds in "governments" at three or four. It is true that in the latter case he has only to cut off his coupons and cash them. But the extra trouble of looking after his tenement property, that is the condition of his highest and lasting success, is the penalty exacted for the sins of our fathers that "shall be visited upon the children, unto the third and fourth generation." We shall indeed be well off, if it stop there. I fear there is too much reason to believe that our own iniquities must be added to transmit the curse still further. And yet, such is the leavening influence of a good deed in that dreary desert of sin and suffering, that the erection of a single good tenement has the power to change, gradually but surely, the character of a whole bad block. It sets up a standard to which the neighborhood must rise, if it cannot succeed in dragging it down to its own low level.

And so this task, too, has come to an end. Whatsoever a man soweth, that shall he also reap. I have aimed to tell the truth as I saw it. If this book shall have borne ever so feeble a hand in garnering a harvest of justice, it has served its purpose. While I was writing these lines I went down to the sea, where thousands from the city were enjoying their summer rest. The ocean slumbered under a cloudless sky. Gentle waves washed lazily over the white sand, where children fled before them with screams of laughter. Standing there and watching their play, I was told that during the fierce storms of winter it happened that this sea, now so calm, rose in rage and beat down, broke over the bluff, sweeping all before it. No barrier built by human hands had power to stay it then. The sea of a mighty population, held in galling fetters, heaves uneasily in the tenements. Once already our city, to which have come the duties and responsibilities of metropolitan greatness before it was able to fairly measure its task, has felt the swell of its resistless flood. If it rise once more, no human power may avail to check it. The gap between the classes in which it surges, unseen, unsuspected by the thoughtless, is widening day by day. No tardy enactment of law, no political expedient, can close it. Against all other dangers our system of government may offer defence and shelter; against this not. I know of but one bridge that will carry us over safe, a bridge founded upon justice and built of human hearts. I believe that the danger of such conditions as are fast growing up around us is greater for the very freedom which they mock. The words of the poet, with whose lines I prefaced this book, are truer to-day, have far deeper meaning to us, than when they were penned forty years ago:

> " — Think ye that building shall endure
> Which shelters the noble and crushes the poor?"

Appendix

STATISTICS BEARING ON THE TENEMENT PROBLEM

Statistics of population were left out of the text in the hope that the results of this year's census would be available as a basis for calculation before the book went to press. They are now at hand, but their correctness is disputed. The statisticians of the Health Department claim that New York's population has been underestimated a hundred thousand at least, and they appear to have the best of the argument. A re-count is called for, and the printer will not wait. Such statistics as follow have been based on the Health Department estimates, except where the census source is given. The extent of the quarrel of official figures may be judged from this one fact, that the ordinarily conservative and careful calculations of the Sanitary Bureau make the death-rate of New York, in 1889, 25.19 for the thousand of a population of 1,575,073, while the census would make it 26.76 in a population of 1,482,273.

Population of New York, 1880 (census)	1,206,299
London, 1881 (census)	3,816,483
Philadelphia, 1880 (census)	846,980
Brooklyn, 1880 (census)	566,689
Boston, 1880 (census)	362,535
New York, 1889 (estimated)	1,575,073
London, 1889 (estimated)	4,351,738
Philadelphia, 1889 (estimated)	1,040,245
Brooklyn, 1889 (estimated)	814,505
Boston, 1889 (estimated)	420,000
New York under five years of age, in 1880	140,327
1889	–
(estimated)	182,770

Population of tenements in New York in 1869* (census)	468,492
1888† (census)	1,093,701
1888 under five years of age	143,243
Population of New York in 1880 (census)	1,206,299
Manhattan Island in 1880 (census)	1,164,673
Tenth Ward in 1880 (census)	47,554
Eleventh Ward in 1880 (census)	68,778
Thirteenth Ward in 1880 (census)	37,797
New York in 1890 (census)	1,513,501
Manhattan Island in 1890 (census)	1,440,101
Tenth Ward in 1890 (census)	57,514
Eleventh Ward in 1890 (census)	75,708
Thirteenth Ward in 1890 (census)	45,882
Number of acres in New York City	24,890
Manhattan Island	12,673
Tenth Ward	110
Eleventh Ward	196
Thirteenth Ward	107
Density of population per acre in 1880, New York City	48.4
Density of population per acre in 1880, Manhattan Island	92.6
Density of population per acre in 1880, Tenth Ward	432.3
Density of population per acre in 1880, Eleventh Ward	350.9
Density of population per acre in 1880, Thirteenth Ward	353.2
Density of population per acre in 1890, New York City (census)	60.08
Density of population per acre in 1890, Manhattan Island (census)	114.53
Density of population per acre in 1890, Tenth Ward (census)	522.00
Density of population per acre in 1890, Eleventh Ward (census)	386.00
Density of population per acre in 1890, Thirteenth Ward (census)	428.8
Density of population to the square mile in 1880, New York City (census)	30,976
Density of population to the square mile in 1880, Manhattan Island (census)	41,264

---

* In 1869 a tenement was a house occupied by four families or more.
† In 1888, a tenement was a house occupied by three families or more.

Density of population to the square mile in 1880, Tenth Ward (census)	276,672
Density of population to the square mile in 1880, Eleventh Ward (census)	224,576
Density of population to the square mile in 1880, Thirteenth Ward (census)	226,048
Density of population to the square mile in 1890, New York City (census)	38,451
Density of population to the square mile in 1890, Manhattan Island (census)	73,299
Density of population to the square mile in 1890, Tenth Ward (census)	334,080
Density of population to the square mile in 1890, Eleventh Ward (census)	246,040
Density of population to the square mile in 1890, Thirteenth Ward (census)	274,432
Number of persons to a dwelling in New York, 1880 (census)	16.37
Number of persons to a dwelling in London, 1881 (census)	7.9
Number of persons to a dwelling in Philadelphia, 1880 (census)	5.79
Number of persons to a dwelling in Brooklyn, 1880 (census)	9.11
Number of persons to a dwelling in Boston, 1880 (census)	8.26
Number of deaths in New York, 1880	31,937
London, 1881	81,431
Philadelphia, 1880	17,711
Brooklyn, 1880	13,222
Boston, 1880	8,612
Death-rate of New York, 1880	26.47
London, 1881	21.3
Philadelphia, 1880	20.91
Brooklyn, 1880	23.33
Boston, 1880	23.75
Number of deaths in New York, 1889	39,679
London, 1889	75,683
Philadelphia, 1889	20,536
Brooklyn, 1889	18,288
Boston, 1889	10,259
Death-rate of New York, 1889	25.19
London, 1889	17.4

Death-rate of Philadelphia, 1889	19.7
Brooklyn, 1889	22.5
Boston, 1889	24.42

For every person who dies there are always two disabled by illness, so that there was a regular average of 79,358 New Yorkers on the sick-list at any moment last year. It is usual to count 28 cases of sickness the year round for every death, and this would give a total for the year 1889 of 1,111,082 of illness of all sorts.

Number of deaths in tenements in New York, 1869	13,285
1888	24,842
Death-rate in tenements in New York, 1869	28.35
1888	22.71

This is exclusive of deaths in institutions, properly referable to the tenements in most cases. The adult death-rate is found to decrease in the larger tenements of newer construction. The child mortality increases, reaching 114.04 per cent. of 1,000 living in houses containing between 60 and 80 tenants. From this point it decreases with the adult death-rate.

Number of deaths in prisons, New York, 1889	85
hospitals, New York, 1889	6,102
lunatic asylums, New York, 1889	448
institutions for children, New York, 1889	522
homes for aged, New York, 1889	238
almshouse, New York, 1889	424
other institutions, New York, 1889	162
Number of burials in city cemetery (paupers), New York, 1889	3,815
Percentage of such burials on total	9.64
Number of tenants weeded out of overcrowded tenements, New York, 1889	1,246
Number of tenants weeded out of overcrowded tenements, in first half of 1890*	1,068
Number of sick poor visited by summer corps of doctors, New York, 1890	16,501

---

* These figures represent less than two hundred of the worst tenements below Houston Street.

Police Statistics

	Males	Females
Arrests made by the police in 1889	62,274	19,926
Number of arrests for drunkenness and disorderly conduct	20,253	8,981
Number of arrests for disorderly conduct	10,953	7,477
assault and battery	4,534	497
theft	4,399	721
robbery	247	10
vagrancy	1,686	947
Prisoners unable to read or write	2,399	1,281

Number of lost children found in the streets, 1889	2,968
sick and destitute cared for, 1889	2,753
Found sick in the streets	1,211
Number of pawnshops in city, 1889	110
cheap lodging-houses, 1889	270
saloons, 1889	7,884

Immigration

Immigrants landed at Castle Garden in 20 years, ending with 1889	5,335,396
Immigrants landed at Castle Garden in 1889	349,233
Immigrants from England landed at Castle Garden in 1889	46,214
Immigrants from Scotland landed at Castle Garden in 1889	11,415
Immigrants from Ireland landed at Castle Garden in 1889	43,090
Immigrants from Germany landed at Castle Garden in 1889	75,458

	1883	1884	1885	1886	1887	1888	1889
Italy	25,485	14,076	16,033	29,312	44,274	43,927	28,810
Russia Poland	7,577	12,432	16,578	23,987	33,203	33,052	31,329
Hungary	13,160	15,797	11,129	18,135	17,719	12,905	15,678
Bohemia	4,877	7,093	6,697	4,222	6,449	3,982	5,412

Tenements

Number of tenements in New York, December 1, 1888	32,390
Number built from June 1, 1888, to August 1, 1890	3,733
Rear tenements in existence, August 1, 1890	2,630
Total number of tenements, August 1, 1890	37,316
Estimated population of tenements, August 1, 1890	1,250,000
Estimated number of children under five years in tenements, 1890	163,712

Corner tenements may cover all of the lot, except 4 feet at the rear. Tenements in the block may only cover seventy-eight per cent. of the lot. They must have a rear yard 10 feet wide, and air-shafts or open courts equal to twelve per cent. of the lot.

Tenements or apartment houses must not be built over 70 feet high in streets 60 feet wide.

Tenements or apartment houses must not be built over 80 feet high in streets wider than 60 feet.

A Riis Chronology
(1849–1914)

1849

May 3: Jacob Augustus Riis, the third of Carolina and Niels Riis's 14 children, is born in Ribe, Denmark.

1865

Riis is employed as a carpenter's apprentice.

1868

Becomes a member of the carpenter's guild.

1870

June 5: Arrives at Castle Garden, New York, on the steamship *Iowa*.

1870–73

Travels throughout the northeast struggling to earn a living during a period of "working and wandering."
Fall of 1873: Lands a job as the city editor of *The Review*, a Long Island weekly. Quits after going unpaid for two weeks.

1874

May 20: Gets job as a reporter for the *South Brooklyn News*.
December: Purchases the *South Brooklyn News*, putting down $75 toward the $650 asking price.

1875

June 5: Pays off debt owed on *South Brooklyn News*.
Winter: Sells the *South Brooklyn News* for five times more than it cost him.
December: Returns to Denmark to marry his childhood sweetheart, Elisabeth.

1876

March 5: Riis and Elisabeth are married in Denmark.
Summer: The newlyweds return to Brooklyn. Riis works as editor of *South Brooklyn News.*

1877

Leaves the *South Brooklyn News.*
Goes into the advertising business, employing the stereopticon.
Gets a job as a reporter for the *New York Tribune.*

1879

Becomes interested in the "tenement-house question."

1884

Covers the proceedings of the Tenement-House Commission.

1885

Becomes an American citizen.

1886–87

Riis and family move from Brooklyn to the Long Island suburb of Richmond Hill.
Spring: Learns of flashlight powder.

1888

January: Teaches himself photography.
January 25: Delivers an illustrated lecture to the New York Society of Amateur Photographers titled "The Other Half: How It Lives and Dies in New York."
Begins lecture tours.
February 12: "Flashes from the Slums: Pictures Taken in Dark Places by the Lightning Process" appears in the *New York Sun.*
March 19: Secures copyright for the title "The Other Half: How It Lives and Dies in New York. With One Hundred Illustrations, Photographs from Real Life, of the Haunts of Poverty and Vice in the Great City."
May 9, 16: Publishes two-part essay in the *Christian Union* magazine titled "The Tenement House Question."

1889

December: "How the Other Half Lives" is published by *Scribner's* Magazine.

1890

November 15: *How the Other Half Lives* is published by Charles Scribner's Sons.
November: Leaves the *Tribune* and joins the *New York Evening Sun.*

1892

The Children of the Poor is published.

1893

Nisby's Christmas is published.

1895

June 6: Takes Theodore Roosevelt, a member of New York City's Board of Police Commissioners, on the first of what would become many tours of the Lower East Side.

1898

Out of Mulberry Street is published.
October: Helps Roosevelt campaign for Governor of New York.

1900

A Ten Years' War is published.

1901

Leaves the *Evening Sun* to pursue writing and lecturing full time. Riis's autobiography, *The Making of an American,* is published.

1902

The Battle with the Slum is published.

1903

Children of the Tenements and *The Peril and Preservation of the Home* are published.

1903–1904

Helps Roosevelt campaign for president.

1904

Theodore Roosevelt, The Citizen is published.
May: Riis's wife, Elisabeth, dies.
September: Takes Booker T. Washington and the Archbishop of Canterbury on a tour of the Lower East Side.

1907

July 29: Marries his secretary Mary Phillips.

1909

The Old Town is published.

1910

Hero Tales of the Far North is published.

1912

Helps Roosevelt campaign for president as the candidate for the Progressive, or Bull Moose, party.

1913

Riis and his wife move to a farm in Barre, Massachusetts.

1914

Neighbors is published.
May 26: Having battled heart trouble for several years, Riis dies of heart failure.

1923

Christmas Stories is published.

Questions for Consideration

1. What does *How the Other Half Lives* tell us about America at the turn of the nineteenth century?
2. How does Riis's view of poverty compare with those prevalent today?
3. How have our attitudes toward immigration and immigrants changed since Riis's time?
4. How does Riis's bigotry affect his work?
5. Does Riis sympathize with the plight of the "Other Half"? Explain.
6. What is the main argument presented in *How the Other Half Lives*? Is it convincing? Why or why not?
7. How is Riis's work an example of both progressive reform and conservative reaction?
8. In what ways does *How the Other Half Lives* anticipate the practice of photojournalism?
9. Does Riis effectively combine images and text? Explain.
10. What makes *How the Other Half Lives* as timely and provocative today as it was when it was first released more than one hundred years ago?

Selected Bibliography

Alland, Alexander, Sr. *Jacob A. Riis, Photographer & Citizen*. New York: Aperture, 1973.

Fried, Lewis and John Fierst. *Jacob A. Riis: A Reference Guide*. Boston: G. K. Hall, 1977.

Hales, Peter. *Silver Cities: The Photography of American Urbanization, 1839–1915*. Philadelphia: Temple University Press, 1984.

Lane, James. *Jacob A. Riis and the American City*. Port Washington: Kennikat Press, 1974.

Meyer, Edith. *"Not Charity but Justice": The Story of Jacob A. Riis*. New York: Vanguard, 1974.

Riis, Jacob. *The Making of an American*. New York: Macmillan, 1901, 1906.

Stange, Maren. *Symbols of Ideal Life: Social Documentary Photography in America, 1890–1950*. New York: Cambridge University Press, 1989.

Stein, Sally. "Making Connections with the Camera: Photography and Social Mobility in the Career of Jacob Riis." *Afterimage* 10, no. 10 (May 1983).

Ware, Louise. *Jacob A. Riis: Police Reporter, Reformer, Useful Citizen*. New York: Appleton-Century, 1938.

Yochelson, Bonnie. "What Are the Photographs of Jacob Riis?" *culturefront* (Fall 1994): 28–38.

Index